ACCLAIM FOR *House Built on Ashes*

"A beautiful portrayal of a world seldom seen in American letters, *House Built on Ashes* is needed, especially now."

SANDRA CISNEROS

author of *A House of My Own: Stories from My Life* and *The House on Mango Street*

"In *House Built on Ashes*, José Antonio Rodríguez has gifted us a luminous coming-of-age memoir, a tender, searching exploration of what it means to be a resident alien in more ways than one. Rodríguez is an intimate guide to the hoops of allegiance that a boy-becoming-man must leap."

ROB NIXON

author of *Slow Violence and the Environmentalism of the Poor* and *Dreambirds: The Strange History of the Ostrich in Fashion, Food, and Fortune*

"José Antonio Rodríguez has written a classic. Gently poetic, utterly authentic, packed with rich scenes, *House Built on Ashes* invites us into the author's worlds of growing up in a big family in the borderlands of Mexico and South Texas. Read this brilliant book by a true maestro—hold his many worlds with reverence and curiosity—you will never be the same."

NAOMI SHIHAB NYE

author of *Transfer* and *You and Yours*

W9-BWN-265

house built on ashes

CHICANA & CHICANO VISIONS OF THE AMÉRICAS

house built on ashes

A MEMOIR

JOSÉ ANTONIO RODRÍGUEZ

UNIVERSITY OF OKLAHOMA PRESS : NORMAN

Also by José Antonio Rodríguez:
The Shallow End of Sleep: Poems (2011)
Backlit Hour (2013)

An excerpt from . . . *And the Earth Did Not Devour Him*, by Tomás Rivera, is reprinted on page vii with permission from the publisher, © 2015 Arte Público Press–University of Houston.

LIBRARY OF CONGRESS CATALOGING-IN-PUBLICATION DATA

Name: Rodríguez, José Antonio, 1974– author.
Title: House built on ashes : a memoir / José Antonio Rodríguez.
Description: Norman, OK : University of Oklahoma Press, [2016] | Series:
    Chicana & chicano visions of the Américas series ; 20
Identifiers: LCCN 2016036139 | ISBN 978-0-8061-5501-2 (pbk. : alk. paper)
Subjects: LCSH: "Told through a series of vignettes, Rodríguez recalls his
    family's migration from La Sierrita, Mexico to McAllen, Texas, and his
    search for belonging, both as a resident alien and as a young man marked by
    childhood trauma and poverty struggling with the societal condemnation of
    his burgeoning homosexuality."—Provided by publisher. | Rodríguez, José
    Antonio, 1974– | Mexican Americans—Biography. | Rodríguez family. | Gay
    men—United States—Biography. | Immigrants—United States—Biography. |
    Mexicans—United States—Biography. | McAllen (Tex.)—Biography.
Classification: LCC E184.M5 R58718 2016 | DDC 973/.046872—dc23
LC record available at https://lccn.loc.gov/2016036139

House Built on Ashes: A Memoir is Volume 20 in the Chicana & Chicano Visions of the Américas series.

The paper in this book meets the guidelines for permanence and durability of the Committee on Production Guidelines for Book Longevity of the Council on Library Resources, Inc. ∞

1 2 3 4 5 6 7 8 9 10

FOR THE REFUGEE, THE UNHOMED, THE EXILE

FOR WILLIAM V. SPANOS

"The teacher was surprised when, hearing that they needed a button on the poster to represent the button industry, the child tore one off his shirt and offered it to her. She was surprised because she knew that this was probably the only shirt the child had. She didn't know whether he did this to be helpful, to feel like he belonged or out of love for her. She did feel the intensity of the child's desire and this was what surprised her most of all."

...And the Earth Did Not Devour Him, by Tomás Rivera,
translated by Evangelina Vigil-Piñón

contents

ACKNOWLEDGMENTS
xi

prologue: FALL 2009
3

part one: 1992
9

part two: 1978 TO 1979
17

part three: 1979 TO 1983
39

part four: 1984
79

part five: 1985 TO 1987
119

part six: 1988 TO 1991
157

part seven: 1992 TO 1993
175

AUTHOR'S NOTE
189

ACKNOWLEDGMENTS

Eterna gratitud a mi madre y a mi padre por su amor y fortaleza.

Special thank you to Sarah Jefferis and Kim Vose for being there from this project's start.

For community, support, and insight, thanks must go to Sandra Cisneros, Kristi Murray Costello, Liam Costello, Jeremiah Crotser, Heather Dorn, Augusto Luiz Facchini, Maria Mazziotti Gillan, Leslie Heywood, Geun-Sung Lee, Melinda Mejia, Naomi Shihab Nye, Emmy Pérez, Luis J. Rodríguez, Carmen Giménez Smith, CantoMundo, and Macondo Writers' Workshop.

To everyone at the University of Oklahoma Press, thank you for giving this work a home.

house built on ashes

prologue

The night wind sidles up against the window. I'm holed up in my college-town apartment in upstate New York packing for the trip down to Texas to visit family for the Thanksgiving break. The space is a bit of a dump, really, but it's cheap enough that it leaves me a little extra to fly back twice a year. A third-floor attic with a ceiling so low I can touch it without standing on tiptoe, even though I'm only five foot eight inches. Two tiny bedrooms for my roommate and me. Old peanut butter–colored carpet, stained and bulging on uneven floorboards. The rusty furnace at one end heats only a five-foot radius around it, not enough for upstate New York where it's already snowed several inches. Not good for someone from South Texas who's only been here two winters, whose blood hasn't thickened yet, as the locals say. The ceiling lights are dull yellow, like those of my childhood homes, meek lights that make you squint when you read. My room barely fits a twin bed and a two-by-four-foot foldout table from Staples that acts as a desk. But I relish every freezing second of it, every cold blast of air against my face, the ritual of layering, every shiver of my bony frame, because I'm here on a university fellowship to study, teach, and write. Amazing really—despite a Mexican culture that looks down on moving away from your parents, that judges you as selfish and uncaring unless your move is due to unavoidable circumstances, due to marriage or work—that I packed it all into my car and drove away, that I settled in this cold quiet town. That I came to find my stories, that the stories themselves brought me here, not simply their retelling but their rediscovery.

And when I think of those stories, I think of sweltering heat. The city of McAllen, where I grew up, sits right on the border with México, an hour inland from the Gulf Coast, close enough to breathe heavy with humidity but too far to get any significant rain. So distant from the arctic winds that you never feel even a hint of snow. The temperature rises to the nineties around April and hovers in that vicinity until October, except for the summer months when it boils past a hundred. Then the five o'clock news talks of eighty-some-year-old grandmas found alone in their tiny houses dead of heat exhaustion. The anchors sit behind desks in their tailored suits, ties tight against collars, as they recommend fans. And you sweat. Then you rush to the neighborhood grocery store to get garlic for the dinner's rice, smell the endless parade that is the bustling traffic, the concrete and rubber and exhaust from rickety pickup trucks, and you sweat some more. You rush back. You sweat as you eat. You sleep crammed in beds like suckling piglets, where the sheets stick to your slick body, where you sweat more than you thought was possible. In the morning you walk to the air-conditioned grade school, and you feel blessed because you don't sweat, because you can almost forget you have a body, almost for the entire day.

Then you come home to your Catholic mother, married at seventeen, with ten children by age thirty-four, her sunset-red hair and hazel eyes dimmed by that dazed look—motionless, sitting at the dining table in a nightgown, her arms plump, her hands on her lap swollen from scrubbing cloth against washboard. ¿Cómo te fue? she asks but doesn't wait for an answer. Your father comes home from a twelve-hour shift as a field hand for a citrus farm at the edge of town, his earning power limited by a third-grade education, a complete inability to pick up a word of English, a government-applied brand as cheap labor.

Only in his forties then, he moves like an old man, and his dark skin and black hair sigh gray with dust. He sits on the deflated couch, groans for help in removing his cowboy boots, and you kneel before him, pull them one at a time. First a quick jerk to lift the heel. Then gently. Then, in his socks, he shuffles out to the front porch.

In this part of town, the brownest part, all the mothers lean in kitchens thinking of new shapes in which to cut potatoes for dinner, all the fathers smoke in rusty lawn chairs in the front porches of withering frame houses. All of them slanted, weathered, the concrete piers under floorboards sinking in the sandy soil. Most of the city's white people are far away in the north part of town, the part of town with the nicest houses, ones with giant refrigerators, plump beds, climate control, manicured lawns. But you never see those houses.

4

For many years you don't even know those houses exist, because the only time you leave these streets is on weekends, when you pile into the cucaracha and drive south to México. Everyone fights for the window seat, a chance at a hot breeze lapping a face. An hour's drive over shimmering hot highways, past orange and grapefruit orchards and sugarcane fields, across a bridge straddling a slow mossy river, past dusty shops and people selling trinkets from pushcarts, puttering along a lonely bumpy road, trailing clouds of dust like curtains closing behind you, you finally reach La Sierrita, the Mexican village where you were born, where you breathed your first years. The one with a tiny Catholic church and no health clinic, the one with bleak houses as small as toolsheds leaning against meager crops of corn and sorghum, the one with roosters to call you back to life every morning. You're visiting your father's sister and her family for the day. Elders talk about the farmland, the tiny plot that used to be more but became only a few acres when a road and a ditch were carved from it many years ago, the plot your father passed over to his sister when all of your family left México because he couldn't keep it. The plot that your mother, when pressed, says just didn't yield enough anymore. She would like to mention corruption, fluctuating crop prices, a rigged system, but she'll just look away and nod her head in defeat, as if words have failed her.

You can't help notice the absence of 7-Elevens, concrete, traffic, toilets. Do you miss them already? A stone's throw away is the little shack with the corrugated tin roof that says Abandoned with its closed door and overgrown weeds jutting from it, the one where you were pushed out into a world far away from any doctor, any sterilized white linens, any weight scale, any clocks and their corrosive counting of time. The one where you and your family attempted sleep every night.

The evening's falling over every living thing, the dark descending like a great fog. Barely a drop of electric light hums through a neighbor's window in the late afternoon. Brush and mesquite move like they're dancing with shadows. A goat gnaws at something in the shade. The dirt road's pocked with animal droppings.

While you're saying your good-byes, getting ready to pile back into the car, the wind kicks up dirt that grinds in your teeth. Then all the lessons you've been taught about that golden land of promise called the United States sparkle before you like a glass of crystal cold water, and you marvel at your good fortune that you left, that every day you leave, move farther and farther away from this so-called dark corner, becoming something mighty and tall with all that no-one must ever doubt is right, becoming something you don't know yet you hope will render you almost unrecognizable to who you are now, becoming one of them, becoming American.

Done with packing, I call my father and let him know the scheduled time of my arrival in McAllen. Then I ask him if, while I'm down there, he'd like to go with me to La Sierrita. I'm still apprehensive about driving in México where traffic rules are practiced more as suggestions.

No, he mumbles.

Why not?

Drugs.

What?

Drug traffickers.

And I ask again and he tells me what few details he's gathered from visiting with relatives: traffickers now organized into paramilitary groups have infiltrated the village. Having fled the towns where they get into skirmishes with military forces, the traffickers have moved their operations to the rural areas. I imagine stealth. I imagine keeping a low profile, lying, if not completely successfully, to the few residents about their presence. I imagine them laboring in the dark hours. But it turns out they've established armed checkpoints at the two entrances to the village. So no, they're not hiding, not at all. Rather, they keep watch over the residents, intimidate them, subdue them. Yes, the village is less populated than it used to be; many have found it necessary to leave. Only a few families remain, but the grade school is still open, still calling children to it.

I've read about the "drug war" in American newspapers over and over—the ubiquity of high-caliber weapons, the brutal conflict, the innocent bystanders—violence relentless as a hurricane. Though this, of course, is different, isn't it? The violence I read about in the *New York Times* occurred in distant places I'd never been to and likely never would, places like Ciudad Juárez or México City, or the Guatemala-México border. The journalist's voice in my head as I read the article—clinical, detached, like the rendering of pure statistics. The violence I'd hear about in the local news, on the local American and Mexican channels, while visiting family in McAllen was shocking, yes, and painful but tempered somewhat by the sheen of the television screen—not quite present, whether articulated in English or Spanish. And it becomes expedient to change the channel before they go from talking about drug-related crime in the city of Reynosa to showing its plaza through which I've strolled, the architecture of the Catholic church with its bell tower, the market where Amá would buy tortillas and detergent. Change the channel before they go from talking about torture to showing the remains of the tortured, because they will show them. I've seen them—humans slaughtered like beasts, headless bodies sharing that elemental resemblance in death and dismemberment. The violence my parents' neighbors with family and friends south of the border spoke about, their assertion that the local news was not reporting everything, that what we heard was only a fraction of what was happening, was distressing but . . . It hadn't happened to people I knew. Not that I was aware of. Maybe I just didn't want to think about the vastness of that enterprise threatening so many so indiscriminately. Maybe I wanted to believe that at least my first home, even if only its remains surrounded by withering mesquites, was safe from much of this splintered world—tucked away from paved roads and duplicitous politicians, from garish store-window displays and middle-class tourist shoppers, from scrutinized drug markets and mass-produced weapons of warfare.

I think then of who we are before we are taught customs, flags, pledges of allegiance, names of nation-states, their margins on a map, and the armed men who guard them. I think of what we lose when we win.

I say goodbye to my father and sit on my bed, try to see through the window out into the night, but all I see is the outline of my image. And for one brief moment I am four years old again. There on the windowpane is the boy again. He is not here in the room with me but there in the village.

The boy and his mother sit on overturned buckets under the kitchen doorway that faces the sun slowly settling beyond the cornfield. In his mother's hands is a short cut of sugarcane, raw sugarcane like bamboo. He has never seen this before. Here, she says, and hands it to him so that he may suck the sweetness until it is nothing but flax. Then she shaves off the dry flax with a pocketknife before sucking the sweetness brought to the surface. This goes on back and forth, this sharing of sweetness at the threshold of a house overwhelmed by the early flitter of flies. The sugarcane has a brown spot farther down that looks like a bruise, and he fears this may mean that portion may be no good, may hold no sweetness. He fears it may be bitter. No, she says, this is the sweetest part. And when he takes it to his lips, he knows she is right.

Soon the small cut of sugarcane is reduced to nothing. And he doesn't know what is heavier: the memory of the sweetness on his tongue or the mourning of the emptiness in her hand. You're sleepy, she tells him, as she caresses his face, brushes the gnats and flies away, the ones frantic around his eyes like they want to touch what he sees, the ones around his mouth and chin where some of the sweetness may linger. With her apron she scrubs away the dirt and sweat—shapes like the winding borders of countries— from his face. Maps, she says softly, because his skin is grimy, marked by the debris that has settled on his body.

The boy stands and runs off through the cornfield stalks through the tilled earth, because it is all he can do with the memory of sweet on his tongue. He lets himself fall on all fours, clods of dirt crumbling under the weight of his hands, his hands and feet sinking into the cool like a blessed drowning of limbs, until the earth feels like the softest bed. Then falling is like sleeping. Everything is beautiful then. The warm-hued sky that trails a setting sun has come down to him, falls around him, making everything glow soft pink.

part one
1992

the three enemies

Those are the scholarship rules, the high school counselor said. I should have guessed that the scholarship would go only to U.S. citizens. A few years ago, when I was fourteen, I had to get a new Resident Alien card because I guess my photo as a five-year-old didn't portray my likeness accurately anymore. That would be the commonsense reason, but the truth is nobody says why. One day the man at the bridge, the one in the booth, the one with the gun, says I need a new passport and I'm glad he doesn't say I can't come back in until I get it. I went and had the photo taken again, the one with the right ear showing. I knew how to sit on the stool at the photo studio that time, no need for instruction, no need for a toy animal. This time, though, there was the fingerprint. I just don't like the messiness of the ink and it screams CRIMINAL, like I must be kept track of. Maybe I've watched too many cop shows. Maybe the Office of Immigration should warn immigrants not to watch too much TV or risk making all the unpleasant associations. Maybe without TV, the man grabbing your hand, soaking the thumb in a black ink pad, and pressing it against squares on a card might carry a different significance, something more innocuous—a grade school painting game perhaps. And it's also shitty to take off. It doesn't really come off completely until after a couple of days, so you end up eating and sleeping and wiping yourself with the mark of the prints.

It was all very strange, picking up the naturalization application at the Post Office, of all places, and then the questions in it got a little weird, questions whose answers I'd never thought of before: how many trips have you taken outside of the United States in the past five years? List the date you left, the date you returned . . . I didn't get it. The questions didn't really apply for people who live along the border. And wouldn't people like me form the majority of applicants? You'd think they'd have added a little note saying: If you visit another country regularly, provide an estimate. It's like the people who drafted the form didn't even consider the people living here.

Then there were the questions of affiliations: Have you ever been a member of the Communist party? Any other totalitarian party?

Totalitarian. The history teachers mentioned that term when talking about Russia. I was never exactly sure what the term meant, only that it was something very bad, something like a door you're never supposed to open, like that book of Karl Marx sitting on a table at the public library when I was in middle school, that book that I couldn't believe was actually there if Communism was so terrible, that book I was almost afraid to touch. Then there were the questions regarding good moral character: Have you ever consumed illegal drugs? Have you ever prostituted yourself? I half expected the application to ask if I'm a homosexual. I dreaded that question, but it wasn't there. No mention of that, and I felt fortunate.

Three months later I got the call for the interview, the one that is more like a test. I put on my dress pants, the ones I wore for graduation, a button-down shirt and my Payless dress shoes. I drove the fifty miles to the Office of Immigration and Naturalization, the place where Amá had to come regularly to bring all the requirements, the birth certificates, the cartas de registro, the this-and-that for her husband's and children's move here all those years ago. She never talks about it except to say Tío Pedro would take her because we didn't have a car then and all the gas money and it was so many different little things the office kept asking for it nearly drove her crazy. I would have thought the building would have been big and renovated now, with flags waving heavy on silver poles, but it isn't. It's a tiny little brick thing that looks like where you pay your light bill.

I review the special booklet for citizenship applicants—elementary history and government questions. You know, the colonies, the three branches of government, the names of Washington, Lincoln, and whoever the current president happens to be. I am ready and I try to remain focused, but it is hard to because there are a lot of people in the lobby wringing their hands and listening to large people behind counters, their heads leaning forward. And, I swear, the place looks like it used to be a grocery store, the same flickering fluorescent lights, the water-stained ceiling. Except here there are counters with glass windows and men in uniform.

So how many stars and stripes does the American flag have? asks the man with a big moustache and a short-sleeve shirt and tie. I wanted to roll my eyes at how easy this is. I thought it'd be a challenge.

Can you name the thirteen colonies?

I panic at the thought of the scholarship money vanishing into the bright, daylight sun.

Just tell me as many as you remember, he offers.

I recall the colonies with compass words—north, south—and colonies that started with New. Then I'm stumped and I feel like I've been a bad student, a bad son.

That's fine, he says. Now, who were the three enemies of the United States in World War II?

Well, this question was not in the booklet. I am certain of that, and also frustrated at the randomness of the process when so much depends on it. Why hand out an official question-and-answer booklet when the officer can ask this? Like he has a secret stash of questions hidden behind his desk. Hitler, I think. Germany, of course.

Germany, I say proudly. Then I think Mussolini and say Italy.

And I wrack my brain for a third name and come up empty. He isn't letting me off like he has with the names of the colonies. He just sits there in silence waiting for the third country, pen in hand, jotting notes. And I wonder if this question, the one not in the booklet, is the real question, the one that opens the gate or slams it shut. And it takes every reserve of will power to admit:

I'm sorry, but I don't know the third country, I say.

If this is how it's going to be, missing the third question already, this test/interview will not be pretty.

Japan, he says.

Then I remember Pearl Harbor and I want to apologize but not sure what for.

Right, of course, I mumble.

And just like that, it's over—three questions. He says I've passed and do I have my Resident Alien card with me, the one that has been my identification card for most of my life. Yes, I say, sure it is just for that, for identification purposes, because I can deduce I won't be getting my actual naturalization certificate for weeks, maybe months.

You'll have to surrender your card here, he says. My card already in his hands.

Like that—Surrender.

Now? I ask.

Yes, now.

Then he makes me sign the oath. Then all the questions on the application make sense, like puzzle pieces finally sliding unforced into their proper place, like that, like it was some inside-move I couldn't be privy to until this moment. I'd felt strange answering those questions in the application because they seemed like promises to make, something to be held to, something someone could come back with and say you checked this, look, here it is and it is forever. And they were, because this last one undergirds all the others. I must absolutely renounce all allegiance to any foreign prince or leader or state or sovereignty or . . . The list goes on and on to cover all forms of government outside the United States to make sure nothing can sneak through. Denounce all allegiance to México. The oddest thing is that I thought I'd been doing that all along, learning the un-trilled R, the difference between B and V, the diphthong-ed vowels of English, obeying all the laws, even the ones that weren't written—just in case—hearing the gunshot blast ricochet through my neighborhood at night, trying to gauge the distance from my room, and making a mental list of what else could account for the blast, shifting my stare away from the cop car parked across the street, closing the curtains and solving for x on the math homework on my lap. Honoring the classroom. Respecting my elders. Loving America. Knowing my place. But here in this room, before a man who holds out a pen for me, I sense that all that has not been enough, an ultimately unconvincing performance, a weak show of allegiance. He demands more.

There's the pen, the man almost says with his outstretched hand: You must say good-bye for good, you must say it out loud on this paper, and you can't be sorry about it. The thing is, I thought I was ready. I could have told any grown-up, any teacher, any counselor, any assistant principal, if they'd asked. Up until this moment, that village over there across the river with its border guards and police dogs seemed like nothing but outhouses, sweat, and dirt. Nothing to miss. Nothing at all.

part two
1978 *to* 1979

pigs know things

My father and my older brother Vicente are standing around the pigpen. They are talking. I walk over to where they're talking. There is one pig. When I climb the pen, my toes stick through the space between the boards. The pig rubs his nose against my toes. His nose is wet and cool. The pig used to be small like a baby but now he's bigger with hair that looks like wire. His tiny legs make his walk seem shy, but he's not if he doesn't mind living in a mud puddle. My sisters used to feed him milk, I hear. I don't remember. Now he eats whatever we don't. The pig is not very fat. Sometimes my sister Norma tries to place me on the pig for fun, but he won't let himself be ridden. He starts making noises and pushes off and maybe it's because I start wailing because I don't want to be dropped into the pen with a loud animal.

But today the pig starts making noises and running around like he's trying to get out. I'm not hanging over him, nobody is. I don't know why he's scared. My brother has a long steel rod in his hand. It is dark and straight and has a head like a giant nail. It glistens in the sun. My father and brother are big and strong, both with hair black like the bottom of a well. Vicente sometimes plays with me by letting me hang from his arms, his big arms. Vicente's strong arms lift the pole and I hope one day I can be as strong as he. Then Vicente brings the pole down hard on the back of the pig. Then I don't know what to hope for. The pig grunts and his legs bend a little, his body leaning against the walls just a little while, like resting. He slows down but continues circling the pen. And I feel bad for him because he will never get out.

I walk away because I think I know what is going to happen. My toes are not wet anymore because the sun takes away everything wet. My feet are splotchy and the dry pig's saliva adds another layer to the grime. I walk into the kitchen where Amá stands by the stove, but I don't say anything. And she doesn't ask.

dark loud

Amá was fanning me with my own shirt but she fell asleep. That's what happened, I remember now. So I nudge her awake. It's hard sometimes, waking her.

Amá Amá, I say.

Huh?

I can't sleep. The shirt.

What?

The shirt. With the shirt.

And she fans me with the shirt, the one that was on me today, all little black and gray squares and wrinkly fabric. Oh, the fanning is like a big bowl of beans just for me. She runs her hand through my hair that feels wet and slithery like earthworms matted against my forehead. She raises it and blows softly and this feels good, like it is the first time. I try to turn my body because it gets hot lying on one side. I want to cool my back but there's no room, shoulders and elbows and backs press against me like angry, pin me down. This is when I wish I didn't have so many brothers and sisters. And I'm smaller so I can't push them off. But at least there are no mosquitoes. It's not the season, says Amá. Because when they do come, they swarm all over you because they get in through the screens that are all torn. And during the day the doors are always open so really you just try to forget they're there.

The dark is loud with sounds like crickets singing, leaves swaying, trunks croaking. It is usually windy. The days are bright under the sun, which we're not supposed to stare at. I'm four. I'm still four. The bodies of my eight brothers and sisters are splayed over two beds, and under the light that comes from the moon that seeps in through the screen door and bounces up from the dirt floor, they don't look whole but like body parts, arms and legs that aren't anyone's. Everything damp, the sheets, the pillows, Amá.

I look at the roof, the ridges of the tin and the two-by-fours that criss-cross up in the air and it is like a maze. I want to look at all of it at the same time and my eyes cannot move fast enough from one corner of the roof to the other. But the angles that the beams make are straight and hard and pretty, different from everything outside—the trees with squiggly trunks and the pigs and chickens round and the dirt always shifting. Then I remember the beams look like the planks and tracks of the railroad, the one that carries that train that honks so loudly every morning I scream inside. Then I don't like the roof so much and I don't know where to look anymore, so I turn to Amá.

Can I lie on top of you? I ask her because I used to and it was then that I could sleep, lying on her belly. Yes, I used to sleep face down on her chest and soft belly. Then it was only air touching me, my back. No shoulders or elbows. Then her groan would wake me and she'd move me down beside her.

Close your eyes, she whispers, so I do and she sings with her quiet voice that sounds like one big yawn:

> Señora Santana, por qué llora el niño,
> Por una manzana que se le ha perdido.
> Iremos al huerto, cortaremos dos
> Una para el niño y otra para Dios.

milk

I was running around the house chasing lizards, which was good, until I started running through the kitchen, in one door and out the other. The lizard was gone but I kept running. I liked it—running. Just me, running around, not hearing her say Stop. Enough. I don't know why I didn't hear her, but I didn't. Then I got tired. I came in for a flour tortilla. I grabbed one from the stack, felt it warm in my hand, rolled it up, and starting chewing. And that's when she said it, turning a tortilla on the griddle, like she's always doing, her arm over the stove and her head over her shoulder, her chin up, like picking a fight: I don't love you anymore.

I walk back, away from her. She looks at me that way, like to look at me hurts her eyes.

I sit on the ground on the other side of the table, stare at the dirt, hard brown. This morning I was spooning milk from a cup so it would last longer than gulping it like water. That was happening, that was here. Amá loving me was always happening, like milk that never runs out, that was here, too. But now it is not happening. It has stopped. It is not here anymore. It is gone. I don't know what is here now in its place. Will she still feed me? Let me sleep by her? If she won't, who will? Where will I go? Where will I be?

The piece of tortilla in my mouth tastes like raw dough and it sticks in my throat. I want to spit it out, but I'm not supposed to waste food. Little ants with their little stings walk trails on the ground, move around my bare feet splotchy with sweat and dirt and the backsplash from peeing.

I didn't listen to her. I didn't behave. I didn't stop when she told me to stop. And now her love is not here. And it is forever. She didn't say: I love you less. She didn't say: I will love you less, or will not love you if. She said: Anymore. And the ants leave so very slowly, like they know and are careful to walk around me, to not touch me.

Then she's coming to me. Pats me on the head. I feel her like a giant, larger than anything I've ever seen, something without a name, like the night without stars, without wind in trees, without critters and their songs, without my siblings and their breathing, without her breath on my forehead, like a quiet quieter than sleep. I am scared.

C'mon, I do love you, she says. Then she smiles.

Her love is here again, happening. It has returned, is like it was before. She saw me sad and felt bad for me. That was it. She is not a giant anymore. Then I notice the sky behind her through the open door, the bright light of the day. Then she goes back to turning a tortilla on the griddle, a tortilla puffy and light like a cloud. She taps it and it deflates slowly, steam escaping through a little tear.

can of peas

I should have known. I should have known the way they were talking quietly to each other. You want to think it's not about you. No, it's about other things they're talking about that have nothing to do with you entering the store and buying something that is only an errand for Amá. They also run errands, I'm sure. No matter, I've been outrunning kids like these since I can remember. I am always careful of footsteps when I have to leave the house to run an errand. I can hear them no matter how far away they sound, no matter if the foot has shoes on or not. And the dirt is really ground down, the way it gets in the middle of a hot day, the sun having its way with everything, no clouds anywhere, not even at night.

It's always the names first, something about joto, vieja, marica. The only word I recognize is vieja, so I know it has something to do with being like an old woman. But is it about being old or being a woman? The boys look bigger than me, longer legs, so maybe it's about being like a woman, acting like one. But I don't know how. Then after the names come the stones, always the same color, the same size, the size of my palm. They are the stones from the railroad tracks, from between the wood planks. The railroad is on higher ground so some of them find their way down to the road, the one I have to take when I walk to the store. And they are sad, the stones, a gray blue color like an overcast sky. But I know better than to think about that right now. The dirt is hottest in the middle of the day, but if you walk arching your feet, so that only the toes and heel touch, it's not so bad. Except you can't do that if you have to run.

Still, I can't figure it out. Maybe I did something, said something, looked at them in an ugly, angry way. Maybe I was too happy with myself that I could do math with the lady behind the counter, the one I gave money to in exchange for a can of peas. Look at him, so little and can already count, she said. And she's right, I can. And I smiled, proud. Maybe I was being a show-off. Maybe that's why they yell those names that are angry, their faces tight like taut rubber bands, their eyes and lips becoming thin little slits, their hands tight around all of the stone, like hungry hands. Sometimes I can see the stone in the air flying faster than I can run. But they don't have very good aim. They keep yelling at me to leave, to get out of here and I keep thinking, I am leaving, can't you see I'm running as fast as I can? Are you angry that you're missing me with your stones? That you can't hit me? What if I let you hit me once?

Amá says I should always be nice and share, but I can't see where I could have. I wonder, but I know better than to stop and ask. By the little pathway that leads to my house are some bushes where turtles sometimes stop to rest. When I turn left onto the pathway they won't see me anymore and I hope this makes them stop. It usually does but I'm never sure if this will be the time they keep coming with their stones hitting the walls of my house, breaking the windows, finally coming to me in a corner. But then I don't know what would happen. I don't want to know.

I reach home. They are not there anymore. The dirt floor of the kitchen is cool and it is never dusty. The dirt is always hard like someone pressed down on it. Except when it rains and it gets a little muddy. I hand the can of peas and the change to Amá. I want to tell her the store owner didn't make a fool of me, didn't shortchange me. Yes, I am good with numbers. The store owner always says so, how peculiar that I can understand change and centavos, the parts of a peso that make up a peso, the coins that mean numbers, the bills that mean coins that mean numbers. It doesn't matter now, not until I have to go out again on some other errand. Next time I'll grab a stone or two before I leave the house. Two. Last time I went, I took an old piece of rusted metal with me and I threw it at them. But I didn't hit anyone and they kept coming.

I go sit at the lip of the door, the one that divides the kitchen from the other room where we sleep. The ground of the room that's not the kitchen is a little higher than the kitchen ground. I lie back, stare at the metal roof that roars like a train every time there is rain. Then I turn to the walls, flat wood painted pink, and I count the knots that are darker where the paint has collected in a swirl. Except now it's dry but still there. I like touching the knots, thinking of the tree they used to be. Amá says it is cheap wood so therefore all the knots. Nobody is here, all my siblings somewhere else. School I guess. I don't go to school yet. I want to tell Amá about the boys, how they chased after me, made me run away. But I don't. I'm here now and they are gone, leaving like running backwards until I don't hear them. If I just stay like this a little longer, the road I know will become empty of them. Quiet. Still.

call of the rooster

The rooster's call used to wake Apá. He'd leave to take care of the crop on the land. Amá would pray for rain or pray for the rain to stop. We don't have a lot of land and this means we can't get sick. This means we can't have candy, or those dark sodas the store owner calls Coca-Cola, or food between meals.

When I ask Amá why we can't have sodas, she says No hay dinero. No money, so we drink water and Apá drinks a cup of coffee in the morning and a cup of it at night when he eats when he comes home. When he used to come home. I can't have coffee because I'm little. I drink water from a bucket Amá dipped in a well across the railroad tracks.

Apá used to be here, until one day he wasn't. When I ask Amá where he is, she says he's on the other side, says it like she tells me this all the time.

Maybe I was busy peeing or shitting, because I don't remember saying Bye. Maybe I was climbing the mesquite and holding onto its thick limbs because the strong wind moves even the big mesquite. It sways and I sway with it. Yes, maybe I was in the mesquite tree with my eyes closed, waiting for sleep during the day, too anxious for the evening to come. One day the evening came, but he didn't. One morning the rooster called but didn't wake him.

burning garbage

Every fifteen days, says Amá when I ask her how often we burn our garbage. The cloud rises and covers the cacti in soot. But the cacti are very hardy, they never burn. They keep swaying slowly even through the smoke. Clorox bottles take the longest to burn and it's dangerous to get the burning plastic on your skin because it becomes gooey and it sticks and you won't be able to take it off and it'll burn like nothing you've ever felt before. But the leftovers of our burning aren't interesting. We already know what was in there.

The neighbor's, though, that's fun. They live in a pretty yellow house with potted plants out front, flowering plants at that, and toys in the front yard, like the kids don't even like them that much. Sometimes I wonder if they've completely forgotten them, if the toys have become unwanted, nobody's toys. But Amá says you can't just go around picking up someone else's things. The garbage they burn, though, that's clearly unwanted stuff. So when the fire is done, Yara and I go and run our hands through the ashes, hoping to touch something solid, hoping for things we can save. Yara's my sister, just a little taller than me with hair a little longer, so the curls bounce at the edges of her face like hiccups, and shimmer when she bends down to look for stuff. Sometimes there's nothing but the leftovers of Clorox bottles or half-burnt cardboard boxes. If the boxes were whole you could use them to fan yourself or to fold into something, but the fire eats them up before anything else. And we come and ask Amá to rinse our feet that are the color of a cloudy sky. And she gets angry sometimes, but just a little.

Today, though, Yara finds a coffee cup and I find a toy car wheel and a wooden block with a letter on it and those things we save, bring inside. Yara feels the smooth surface of painted clay, beige with little orange flowers that would form a circle if the cup was complete, and I spin the one tire from the wire axle like a top. Then I place the tire on the ground and see the rest of the car in my head. It would be a truck, actually, one of those yellow ones, and the truck would be so complete, so like the real thing, that I would never get bored running it along the ground or just holding it. I could place the wooden block with its sharp, straight sides in its bed. It could even hold Yara's cup.

When we're done, we place the things in a corner. Amá says we're just collecting junk, but she doesn't throw it away.

At the end of the day with the sky almost orange again, little black flakes start to fall from the sky, like singed leaves of grass, light as the paper frills of the big dolls hanging from shops in the city. The frills, in all sorts of bright colors, adorn the large dolls everywhere and they're beautiful because the paper is thin and the light shines through. Amá says the dolls are called piñatas but when I ask her what they are for, she keeps quiet. Yes, this is what they look like but black.

What is it? I ask.

Sugarcane, someone is burning sugarcane, says Amá.

Somewhere far away, someone is doing something, and something other than smoke has risen up to the sky. It has traveled from far away because fire leaves only the light part of things. The heavy part disappears. The little flakes are falling over me and it is like the evening is magic. Now I know why we can burn garbage in the back of our house, why the neighbors can do it, and never run out of space, because the wind takes away the ashes, carries them, and lets them fall far away.

beans

After a long time of running around outside chasing lizards, I get a headache and go sit by Amá who is kneeling in the shade by the house.

You're gonna get a nosebleed from running around all day in the sun, she says.

I stare at the pot of beans because it seems it should fall, tip over, as it sits all shaky on the grill that used to be bedspring coils. The coils are rusted. They sink into themselves under the weight of the pot. Amá keeps adding water to the pot. Next to the pot is a comal where she lays each tortilla that she makes into a perfect circle with the tortillera.

I'm hungry, I say, and she takes a tortilla, adds a pinch of salt, and rolls it up tight for me.

I smell the tortilla first. I love that smell, but I'm scared of the fire pit in the ground. The flames are always kicking up and the heat flashes out from the tips like fists of hot wind against your cheek. You have to stay away a little. Also, the burning wood smokes up and leaves a layer of soot on your face if you sit there long enough. Amá always looks a little gray, her eyes watery, unless the day is very windy. If it is very windy, having a fire outside is dangerous, and so she has to use the stove inside, and that uses up gas from the tank.

I run off to chase after lizards, the only animals out in the noonday sun. All the other animals stay under the shade in the hottest part of the day. We don't have any horses or cows but I see them sometimes by the side of the road when I have to go run an errand. And if it's very hot, they're always resting under a tree. I should learn from that but I don't.

Later I'm in bed with a nosebleed, pinching my nose to make it stop. Amá purses her lips, angry, because I didn't listen. I wonder if the neighbor kids I see running around their houses are also bleeding now inside them. She says sometimes talking to me is like talking to a dog, but who would talk to a dog? That's just silly.

I can feel the blood thick down my throat as I swallow, but I don't taste it. And I'm glad that I don't have to taste blood. Then I must have slept because when I get up, the house is noisy with the voices of my older brothers and sisters who are back from school or work. I go to the kitchen. Amá takes a wet rag and wipes my hands that are splotchy with dried blood and my face, which I figure must also be splotchy. I walk outside, play marbles with my brother Luis. Skinny-with-freckles Luis. It's not a lot of fun because we only have a few marbles and so the game is over right away. The best part is making the little hole in the ground for the marbles to land in because the dirt is cool just under the surface and it feels good on my fingertips. Lizards skitter by but I don't chase after them.

Come in for supper, we hear.

There are only three chairs in the kitchen so most everybody stands. Amá places a plate of refried beans before me, and the whiff of lard makes my mouth water. I take a piece of tortilla and scoop up a morsel of beans, always careful to stay on one end of the plate because the other end has a hole in it and we shouldn't be wasting food by letting it squish through the plate. This is why Amá lets the beans dry when she's mashing them, so they're not runny. When I am done, I have another glass of water, then I sit under the doorframe that faces the sun that is leaving. The sky is turning shades of orange and pink and blue. The weeds and the trees are already ringing with the songs of cicadas and the early chirping of crickets. A goat is bleating but the sound is soft, shy, hiding behind all the other sounds. It must be somewhere down the road in another house. Maybe it's tied to a tree or sitting inside a pen. I used to think goats bleated because they were tied up or trapped in a pen, but no, they're always bleating, even when they're out grazing on anything they can find. Still, it always sounds sad, like they're crying out for something they can't find.

I tell Amá I need to go to the bathroom. I'm scared of the dark so she tells my sister Alba to go with me. We go out behind the house, close to the ebony tree. I pull down my shorts and squat, resting my arms behind my knees so I can balance better. Alba stands next to me. We don't talk. When I'm done I grab a corncob within reach and wipe myself.

I go back to the doorframe. Just as everything is becoming black, somebody nudges my shoulder and leads me to bed.

potatoes

I hate it when a chicken comes around because it's hungry, too. The tank for the stove is out of gas and so my sister Norma, with her heavy-lidded eyes and yellow dress, cooks potatoes in a skillet on a dirt-filled barrel outside. It's different to eat outside, exciting, eating where there is light. The kindling is mostly little sticks and torn pages from my older brother's comic books, pages with so many big-chested women and angry-looking men lying in bed together and kissing but not how relatives kiss us when they come visit. Amá is not here, she's on the other side, visiting Apá, who's working hard. The potatoes are half raw because we've run out of kindling or because my sister has gotten tired of turning them. I don't know, but I don't say anything. I just keep eating. The chicken's run out of worms, I guess, and comes around wanting food, sneaking out from under the cactus. Its white feathers look so pretty against the pale gray green of the cactus. They ask with their beady yellow eye. I know the look. It stays just a little longer than usual on the thing it wants. Then it moves on to other things, the look, but the chicken sticks around, walking in circles, pretending, like we're not going to figure it out. It moves but never leaves, hoping for something to fall from our hands, slip out of our potato tacos. I don't think they like potatoes, but they're hoping they might. The chicken zigzags. My brother Luis hits it with a stick, too hard. The chicken wobbles.

Luis, what did you do? Norma shrieks.

Nothing. I just wanted to scare it away.

And it's true, that is all he wanted. I can tell he feels bad because his head hangs down a little and he eats more slowly. We'll have to nurse the chicken back to health or kill it. And we don't want to kill it, it's too young, mostly bones, not enough meat. That afternoon the chicken is still kind of wobbly, slow. Norma crushes a pill in a spoon and dilutes it in a cup of water. I wish the pill was for me because when Amá gives us one when something hurts, she crushes it with a little bit of sugar. It tastes a little medicine-y but still kind of like candy.

Norma scoops the chicken from the ground and it doesn't even startle. Norma dips its beak in the water. I hold the cup but it's not really drinking. It doesn't know the water has medicine that will make it better. I wonder if the pill would help it anyway. It helps me when my head aches, like something is pressing against the inside of it. Amá says it's because I'm out in the sun too much, like a lizard. And I try to remember this but I always forget. I think the chicken's going to die because it hasn't clucked very much today and it's got sleepy eyes. I think we're gonna have soup, but not a lot.

A whistle blares outside. It means the train that rides the tracks a few feet from the house is making a stop. The whistle always hurts my ears, but it means Amá may be coming back so I run to the side of the road to wait for her. As the train makes that sound that means it's starting up again, it's leaving, Amá walks up the pathway with several fat bags pulling her arms down. She stops and hands me a little wind-up monkey playing a drum. It's ugly. And it doesn't matter that this is the first new toy I've ever gotten. It's still ugly. She can tell I don't like it. She's upset like, Ahh, forget it, walks past me, goes inside, lays the packages on the table in the kitchen, and slumps down on a chair.

She says we'll be leaving soon, far away to the other side, to a place called the United States. I don't know why it is called "the other side." Maybe it's somewhere on the other side of the canal that runs close to the houses around here. But I've seen the other side of that canal and it looks the same as this side, with little houses and little potted plants and swings made out of car tires.

She says Apá is on the other side of a bridge, but I've never seen any bridge other than the one that crosses over the canal. But that is not the bridge. Apá is across another bridge, one that is far away. Far away.

When you stand on the railroad tracks and look down at the wooden plank and then the next one and the next one, it gets so that you can't count anymore and the planks keep going away from you in a straight line. Then you just end up looking at the sky, because far away it looks like it touches the tracks, the clouds not above anymore but down there with the tracks. I wonder if where Apá is he can see the clouds around him, walk through them, touch them.

skunk

I look at the sheets, see the splotches of dried urine, the water I make, the edges always reaching farther out until they cover the entire surface of the bed, making it look brownish yellow, making it look old. Skunk, Amá calls me, like joking but also a little angry. Or tired. It's hard to tell. She says the sheets are covered in maps. This means she has to wash the sheets more often, which is more work and she's always cooking or washing, cooking or washing, cooking or washing.

I run outside because I don't want to look at the maps anymore. I'm not sure what they are, but they smell like a rotting cactus. I run to the tall mesquite and climb it. Then when I get bored of that, I go stare at the flowers of the cactus that isn't rotting, one layer of yellow petals, simple flower, like the simple cactus that looks like fat heavy leaves growing out of each other. No trunk, no limbs, but still somehow working their way off of the ground. Sometimes my sisters take the inside beads of the flowers and press them to their ears like earrings, but if I do that they get angry. After that I go to the pigpen where a pig rolls in the mud. I wish I could roll in the mud, but Amá would get very angry because I'd have dirtied my shorts.

After a while I get tired and go sit indoors. Sometimes Amá bathes me—I stand on a rock outside under the sun and she pours water over me and it feels cool—but not always. Sometimes she just looks at me, my ankles moist from the sweat that trickles down my legs making odd shapes as it works itself over and around the layer of dirt that coats everything, everything that moves and everything that doesn't.

More maps, says Amá, and she means my legs and arms and everything else that is me. But she says it soft this time, like she's used to it, like these things really are old, these things that I make, these things that make themselves on me because I can't help it.

flicker

Amá's love is not here again. It is gone. I ran it off and that means I am bad.

In the corner of the room a little snake pokes its head through a hole in the ground. It looks at me, sticks its tongue out, then dips below and disappears. C'mon, I do love you, she comes to me in a soft voice. The love is back. For now.

The chicken walking around stares at me too long, one leg up off the ground. It should be looking at the ground for kernels of corn or rice. But it keeps looking at me.

Amá is like the flicker of a lightning bug, her face turning hard then soft again. I run out. I stop. On a grassless patch is a lizard the color of dust. His neck gets big and small like a balloon filling with air, then letting it out, like sighing over and over. I can see his breathing and his glossy eyes see me. But he doesn't know because he can't, because lizards are like that too, like dogs and goats. He only licks his eyes and runs and hides from me, not bothering to look back to make sure I haven't come after him, stubborn to hurt him, to stomp on him, mash him open like a purple bruise. I climb the large mesquite tree behind the outhouse, wrap myself around a limb, and close my eyes. The tough bark scratches my thighs, raws my palms, but right now I am still like a lizard, a lizard who doesn't know words, who wouldn't know what it meant when a person cried out, even if he might wonder. Sunlight flickers through the leaves and dances on my eyelids. Amá calls out to me, but I can't hear her.

rocking horse

Over there by the neighbors' house, across the pine trees, sits a small plastic horse. He is one horse, split from nose to tail with a seat in the middle, a seat like a bridge keeping the two halves from falling, a seat like a little rocking chair, a chair I could pull up to the kitchen table to eat my bean taco. I've seen the wind rock him. He has feet stuck to a curved bottom and soft colors all over like pink, blue, yellow almost white with sun, the colors of the sky when the day is ending. On his face is a smile that never turns into a frown. He is like the baby kind of the real ones by the side of the road. Sometimes I see him standing in the same place out in front of their house. Sometimes I don't see him. Sometimes I see him in a different place. This is how I know he is somebody's, belongs to that somebody.

Sometimes I want to run over there and sit in him for a second and run back. Sometimes I think of running and it is like I am running. I think I could run fast enough and nobody would see, nobody would notice. But I don't because what if somebody does.

One day the people in that house won't want that horse, he'll be brittle or broken, and they'll put him in the garbage dump and then he'll be mine, mine to carry into the kitchen.

Fire sometimes makes things ugly, twists them, breaks them, turns them into something you don't want, even if you know it was something you wanted before the burn. Because even though you can't un-burn something, you can see from what's left that it was once pretty. One day that horse will be set on fire, but I think he is too big to be all turned into ash, he must be. This is why I know something of him will stay. And even if this of him is twisted and broken, gray, eyeless, no bridge to hold the halves together, smile burned away, he will never be ugly. I will want him when nobody else wants him. I will hold him when nobody else will.

This is why today, when I don't see him outside, I run to the garbage dump, get down on all fours, sift through the ashes, deep in the ashes. They aren't warm so they don't feel new, but maybe it was a small fire with only a few things, maybe it was just him they were burning and what stayed is waiting there for me.

part three

1979 *to* **1983**

rooms and rooms

One moment I was in my house in bed, trying to keep warm now that it's cold outside, and now I'm here, in this house that is so big, so incredible, I don't know what to call it. The walls look smooth and white like the side of a stove. No wood, no boards, no knots, no maze on the ceiling, no pink, no dirt, no flies. Everything is sharp corners and lit bright like a pharmacy. A crisp clean smell like laundry soap—a smell different from the smell of tortillas on the griddle, different from the smell of dirt, different from the smell of wind rushing through doors—floats all around me so that I don't know how to stand still in it, how not to touch it.

Then Amá is here, saying some compadres crossed us over in the night—me, Yara, Luis, and Alba—that we were sleeping and so don't remember. When I ask her how, she doesn't say. I hear Myrna will be coming soon. Apá is here already. He carries me with his hairy arms, strong like tree limbs, and kisses me, and it is like he never left. It is okay that I never got to see the bridge, the one Apá crossed, the one he never crossed back.

I'd never seen Tía Lydia before, but Amá says she is her sister and so I have to be respectful. She is tall and has curly hair like my mother's, but hers is dark and my mother's is red. She's also rich, must be, with a house that has too many rooms to count. We slept in what Tía Lydia calls the garage, which is supposed to be a room for cars. Why would cars need a room? Why would they even need a roof? The only concrete floor I'd seen up until now was in the pharmacy in the city of Río Bravo. But here this house has concrete everywhere. We slept on the floor—on sheets of foam, like really thin mattresses, with blankets—but it was still hard. It was like sleeping right on the concrete, which is way harder than sleeping on dirt. But it doesn't matter because the sleeping was only at night, and the house is warmer than our house on the other side.

The house has three rooms with beds in them and little rooms in them called closets with doors and everything. A separate room for clothes!

Again, why would clothes need a room to themselves? My tíos' bedroom has the largest bed I've ever seen. It's gigantic, so big their bodies could move around all night and never touch. My boy cousin has his own room, too, and my two girl cousins share another room. They each have a whole bed to themselves. There's a large space at the center called a living room and I think it's bigger than our entire house on the other side. Next to it is the largest table I've ever seen, with eight chairs around it. And I count only five people in Tía Lydia's family, so I don't know why they have so many extra chairs. And there are big glass doors that slide open, leading into what Tía calls the backyard. The sliding doors, though, I've never seen, not even in Río Bravo.

The strangest and best thing is that I'm not cold when I'm inside the house. This is where we're staying now, until we find a place to live here on the other side. That's what Amá said before she gave me the big speech about not being a pest, not hanging around the kitchen, saying No thank you if I am offered food, not playing with anything that is not mine, not touching anything, not asking for anything.

Why can't I be in the kitchen? I asked.

Because it isn't ours, she said.

But nothing here is.

And we need to be nice and behave.

I asked her if I could ask for water. And she said Yes, you can ask for water, and I felt better.

toilet

I was about to go outside, but Amá noticed me squirming and brought me here. It is another room, a small one with a strange chair with a big hole and a pool of water in the middle. Amá says I can go to the bathroom here. Tía Lydia calls it a toilet.

I say Okay, like nothing, but the truth is I'm afraid to fall through just like in the outhouse that smells mean like a rotting possum with its teeth out.

You close the door and when you're done and you wipe yourself, you press this lever. Understand?

Yes.

I close the door like Amá tells me to, and it is like all the other doors in the house, like the door in the doctor's office, thick and complete—no light shines through, no air whispers in or out. But this time I notice a little thing that moves right in the center of the knob. And when you place it just so, the knob won't turn and the door won't open. The doors of our house on the other side had a latch. There was no secret there. The door in the kitchen had a round hook like a skinny moon or a claw that caught itself into a metal loop. That was pretty, watching it fall in, hearing the clink like a bell. But I can't tell how this knob manages to keep the door closed, and I'm not sure if I'm supposed to turn that little knob in the middle of the big knob or not. I decide to ask Amá later. The room also has a faucet like the one in the kitchen, and I wonder if they also wash dishes in here, but probably not.

The paper Amá says I can use to wipe myself is so soft, it feels a lot better than corncobs or little comic book pages I used back on the other side. The pages were the roughest, especially when they'd fold into sharp corners. When I'm zipped up, I press that lever that Amá told me to press, and that thing roars mean and loud, like I shouldn't have done it. I have to cover my ears but it just keeps going. Water falls into the hole from around the rim, and I crouch to try to see where the water is coming from but I can't.

Looks like it's coming out of the inside wall itself and drains away into the floor, just drains away. The shit's long gone and the water just keeps going, so much water that looks clean enough to drink. If we weren't supposed to waste water on the other side, then surely we're not supposed to waste water in somebody else's house. I figure maybe I've broken this special chair because the pool of water is gone, and I think for sure Amá's gonna be angry and maybe Tía Lydia. But soon the roaring stops and the pool comes back minus my shit and there is quiet again, except for that humming that comes through the walls, and I wonder where all that water went and if Tía Lydia has access to a large enough well to use up all that water in one go.

Soon after that, Amá tells me she's going to wash me and to follow her. I don't know why she has to wash me now because she washed me on the other side not too long ago, but I don't say anything. We end up in the same little room with the special chair, but behind some glass doors that you can't see through because the glass is foggy looking is another large faucet high on the wall. She helps me take off my clothes and lifts me into a large rectangular tub that's up against the wall. She turns some knobs and the water pours down like rain.

Sometimes it would rain on the other side, and if there wasn't too much lightning, Amá would let me play in it. I'd take my shorts off and run without clothes across the kitchen, past Amá, past Apá's brother Tío Baltazar, past Apá, and out the open door. I'd run around under the rain, feeling the cool mud squish between my toes. And when it was over, Amá would sit me on her lap and pat me dry with her apron and let me sit a little longer after she was done. All around, even between me and Amá, was the soft smell of wet dirt, like the song of leaves waking up. And for a little while I wasn't hot. I don't think I'll get to do that anymore, not in Tía Lydia's backyard, not if you can't pee outdoors or have Amá wash you outdoors, not if the door has a knob and a lock.

Water keeps falling over me and away beneath my feet, beneath the floor somewhere, just like the toilet. Amá turns the knobs again and the water stops. The last of it disappears into the floor through a little hole. It doesn't spill over a rock, like the rock I used to stand on while Ama poured water over me. It was the last of the water after washing and boiling beans and cooking and stuff so it was only a couple of cupfuls to soak me and rinse me. And so the water would run down me and soak itself into the dirt, then soon the dirt would be dry again. She'd put out a clean pair of shorts and soon I'd be running after lizards. Sometimes she'd get angry, You just can't wait to be dirty like a dog, but mostly she'd just look at me and sigh and keep on cooking or sweeping or ironing or sewing, or bathing somebody else. Here water doesn't dry. It just disappears underground and I wonder where it all goes, my pee, my shit, the soapy water.

After Amá dries me, she doesn't let me sit on her lap. She keeps saying we have to hurry because others might need to use the room. Anyway, there's no chair to sit on. She dresses me fast, opens the door, and when I step into the hallway, I see again the pretty flowers of floor called linoleum, but I can't stop thinking of what is beneath the floor. I want to know where the shit goes, where it sits, where the worms are.

refrigerator

All the things in Tía Lydia's house, the little things and the big things, the things they hold and the things that hold them, sparkle like they belong in a store. A hissing noise comes on and off during the day and I know not to ask what it is. The lamps sit on small tables next to a long chair for several people that has big soft cushions. It reminds me of the long chairs at the doctor's office. My cousins call it a sofa. They have a television set in every room. I don't know why that is, why they need more than one television set and if the same show can be seen in all televisions. The kitchen has running water. They don't need a well. The kitchen also has rows of little doors up high where I can't reach and down close to the floor where I can, but I don't know what's behind the doors or why they have so many of them. It's beautiful with all its moving doors framed with ridges and shiny handles, like a giant new toy that's never been in a fire, and I wish I could open all of them, crawl around them, find something new.

The refrigerator, with its doors side-by-side, sits big and heavy like a statue. I know what this is because I've seen something similar in the store on the other side, where they kept Cokes and chilled treats and cookies. It is beautiful, white and tall with smooth rounded corners. My blond cousin Clarisa opens the thinner door and it is filled with packets of frozen meat, tubs of ice cream, and boxes of treats, though I can't tell which ones exactly. They're practically falling out of little white wire baskets, even more treats than in the store on the other side. She opens a box and pulls out something wrapped in plastic. She asks me if I want one like she'd be happy to give me one, and I'm not sure what it is but I say No, thank you. Okay, she says, then she opens the package, an ice cream bar shaped like a round face with big dark brown round ears. The face is white and the eyes and smile are dark brown and the ears are covered in a hard film. She holds it from a smooth, even little stick. When she bites an ear I see the inside of the ears are dark brown too. The film crackles between her teeth. And she's licking and biting and the bar is really thick and it seems like it's too much ice cream for her. It begins to melt down her hand, around each knuckle. I think of telling her that it's dripping but I don't because I shouldn't be staring. That's another thing I'm not supposed to do.

When she's done, she licks the stick clean and the stick was smooth all the way up, rounded at the edges, no sharp corners. She throws it away in the waste basket and walks away down the hall. The refrigerator is silent. No, the refrigerator is humming. There is a motor of sorts, like the ones that make cars run, and it is keeping everything cold and everything else frozen. It does not move. I think of opening the thin door, taking an ice cream bar. But I can't, she offered and I said No and the offer is gone. She should have insisted. I've seen grownups insist to each other. Maybe if she would have insisted, I would have said Yes, not knowing what I was saying yes to and thrilled to discover the surprise. But Amá said nothing about people insisting and what to do in that case, how to keep saying no, when to finally say yes. And it doesn't matter anymore, except that the door is there and it is not locked and not heavy to open. I can reach the handle because it runs all the way down the edge of the door. And I am standing before it. And it hums and on the other side of the door is something soft and sweet and cold. And I start to pout and I don't know why I'm pouting because nobody is laughing at me, nobody is making fun of me, nobody is chasing me with stones in their hands. Still, my lips tighten and push out, and I'm glad nobody is watching. I walk outside, out back. Chain-link stands at the edge of the back yard and I know not to ask why the house has to be fenced.

sardines

Amá tells me to remember the address 2600 Houston Street in case I get lost walking home from the school. The town is called McAllen.

A chain-link fence stands tall all around three houses that are all owned by Tía Eugenia and Tío Pedro. Tía Eugenia has curly red hair and freckly arms just like my mother and her head is always a little tilted to the side like saying sorry. Tío Pedro has a lot of grey hair and teeth scrunched up as if they're stumbling over each other to get out and his head is never tilted, not even in the photo of him when he was young and in a uniform with shiny medals on his chest and a round hat. The nicest house is the one closest to the street; it has two rooms with beds, I think, and big windows and Tío Pedro's mother lives there. She is old. He and Tía Eugenia live in the house closest to the alley. That one has three rooms with beds and a glass box with water that stirs itself and has little fish swimming in it.

We rent the middle house from them. It's two rooms big, like the one on the other side, and also pink inside. But those are the only things that are the same. This house is smaller. You can barely walk inside. Can't take one step without bumping into someone. Like sardines, says Amá. And I laugh when I think of all of us squished together side by side, like copies of each other, sleeping inside a tin can, pressed against metal. The pink walls here have no knots. The outside is wood, but the inside is like a painted hard cardboard wall. And the floor is not dirt but linoleum with little pictures of flowers torn and peeling off everywhere. It looks similar to the the floor of Tía Lydia's house, but this doesn't shine anymore, and it sticks up and trips you, as if poking fun because the floor underneath is crooked like the wall of an outhouse. And the ceiling is not the roof but more of that hard cardboard. It's a perfect little box, all straight edges with one window like a mean joke. The house on the other side had three windows. I could hear the crickets then and other little animals talking to themselves in the night.

This is where we ended up, renting it from Amá's sister. It already had a lumpy cot with springs that whined every time you sat on it like it had a bad back. Amá and Apá bought a mattress at the flea market. The furniture to store clothes in called a chest of drawers and a dresser, they bought from Tía Eugenia who was going to throw it away anyway because she had a new set. Some handles are missing and it's rotting all over like a sick dog's hide. It's the humidity and they're not made of wood, Amá says. And she's right, you're always sweating a lot, and the furniture, when you look at it up close, is made of little chips of wood or cardboard squished together, tight together.

The kitchen only had a stinky gas stove, a little table for two people, and one cabinet with one little door that didn't shine. But we did get a refrigerator when my cousin Ruben, who works for a furniture store, delivered a refrigerator to customers who didn't want their old one. It has a freezer section and a regular cold section, but the doors are one on top and one on the bottom, not side-by-side like Tía Lydia's. Still, it's nice to open the door and feel the cold because it's getting really hot outside—the winter cold is gone. But we're not supposed to open the door too much because it wastes electricity. So we're only supposed to open it to grab something. But there isn't much to grab, and we're not supposed to eat between meals anyway. So mostly the refrigerator is off-limits to everyone except Amá. Well, sometimes we use the freezer to freeze coffee cups with milk and sugar at night so we don't get hungry before bedtime. Small cups and only a little bit of sugar because we're not made of money.

I miss Tía Lydia's house, mostly the humming behind the walls that kept the house warm when it was cold outside. And then cool when it got hot. And I miss the space to lift your arms out and spin, the quiet couches that didn't squeak, soft like beds to sleep in all day, and the big color television in the living room, even if we didn't see much television because we mostly just sat with each other, my brother and sisters and I, and if any of my cousins turned off the television, it stayed off. But I don't miss the having to not touch this, not say that, not go here, not sit there.

When Luis, Yara, and I go out to play, we always have to open and close a fence. Tía Lydia's house only had a fence in the back. But here there's a fence all around, like a corral. Everything is concrete. The sidewalks though are pretty, straight and long and with only a few cracks. I thought they were only around Tía Lydia's house but it's like this everywhere. I thought the dirt road on the other side was hot; that was nothing.

Now we must wear shoes all the time. And the fence keeps people from stopping by to talk to Amá, the way they did on the other side. Like Yola with her hands always folded in front of her like knitting an invisible doily, like Carmelita with her big yellow teeth and talk of train rides to the city, like Kika at a kitchen chair with her shiny black pony tail down to her waist, like Tío Baltazar chewing his words under his moustache, his bony hands dancing a riddle, doing the talking for him. Here people walk by but don't stop, look in, or say hi. They turn and turn away with the last flickers of the day, their eyes saying Nobody lives here.

there is my right ear

Amá says she'll keep it for me. When I ask her what it's for, she says it's for crossing to the other side. And I wonder if everybody needs one or if I am special, if we are special, because all of us have one. She shows it to me. There it is, a photo of me in a glossy little card with the letters R E S I D E N T A L I E N across the top. And there is my right ear, the one the photographer said I had to show. I know it's my right ear because it's opposite my left ear, which is on the side of the hand that I write with, which makes my tías say I write al revés. Backward. Amá just smiles. Yeah, she says, how strange. On the other side, my left hand would have been tied behind my back to make me learn to write with my right, but not here. Here it isn't a problem to fix. That's what Amá tells my tías.

Look at the teddy bear, the man behind the camera kept saying, but I didn't want to look. Its eyes two old marbles that shimmered under a light bulb tilted to shine right at it. A light above me and then dim space and then a light above the teddy bear. And the yellow glow around the furry toy reminded me of the Sagrado Corazón de Jesús, except instead of a heart with screaming flames in Jesús's chest, a nail pushed the teddy bear's chest into a wall. It looked like punishment.

With my thumbs I kept rubbing the last snap button of the shirt above the waist. Amá had picked this shirt for me and I loved it because it had snaps instead of buttons, how they clicked when fastened, a snap like an answer, how pebble smooth they were. And when I asked her where we were going, she said to take photos. And I didn't know why we needed photos. I didn't know, but I didn't ask because I liked that we were going somewhere, out and away from the tiny little hot rooms where we stay.

I kept wanting to turn to Amá because the room with the photo taking was dark and I didn't want to lose her.

Smile, said the man behind the camera. Look at the teddy bear. But I didn't know what there was to smile about, especially at the camera insisting, the camera aiming at me like a gun.

So I am not smiling in the photo. I look regular, maybe a little angry, sucking in my lower lip. The back of the little card has crooked lines like my dried pee patterns. Amá says it's a map of the United States, though I thought the United States was just another place, not a map on a card.

The surface of the entire card is patterned with squiggly lines and emblems. I've never seen anything like this, though I have seen the eagle before. The eagle on the emblem of the flag that is México's. But the flag that is México's is nowhere on the card, and there is no cactus and no snake, only arrows in the eagle's mean talons. And I don't know what the letters on top mean, only that they must mean something important because they are large and over my head, over everything, like a big announcement, like a billboard saying, Look at him.

crayons

I get to start kindergarten, real school like my siblings, because I am five years old now. We walk from our new house to the school. It's the first day. Amá walks with us, me and my sister Yara. The rest of my siblings walk off on their own. The streets that divide up the houses are straight like wide sidewalks. It's like the city on the other side, the one we visit when Amá takes us to the doctor. It has paved roads too, but it's all buses and stores and very dirty people who look sick wandering the street and so much dust that turns everything a little brown. Less dust blows here, and several houses have dogs that bark even if you don't look at them, like you want something they have. It's still kind of dark and I hold Amá's hand and Yara holds her other hand. We are the only ones in the street. After several left and right turns, we get to a bridge that is all white concrete and walls that go up to my shoulders, and then it is chain-link fence up high and across the top, like a chicken coop. I ask why the wire walls. Amá says So people don't fall off. The bridge crosses the busiest road I've ever seen. Four lines of cars, two one way and two the opposite way, are already moving under and away. On the other side the bridge begins to roll down in circles, not steps. It's funny, the way concrete can be bent. When we get off the bridge, we're at the school with the funny name: Guthrie. It trips my tongue when I say it, like I'm a baby again, how I must have been, just learning to say words.

Do you know English? asks the teacher with painted lips and a big wave of hair falling on her forehead. She sits behind a desk heavy with papers and pencils and a big plastic apple on a corner. The wall behind her is a maze of letters and numbers and pictures of animals in every color, bright like one big cheer.

Do you know English? the teacher asks, and she's impatient. I can tell impatient right away, the tight lips that clip the ends of words.

Sí, poquito, I answer. Because knowing how to say Bye and Hello counts as a little, doesn't it?

The teacher's eyes ask Amá if I know English, and Amá chuckles like embarrassed. Sorry sorry says her chuckle, and then No, nada. And why are you lying? she tells me without telling me. I'm not lying, but she doesn't hear me.

Behave and do as the teacher says. Do you hear me?

Yes.

Then Amá turns to leave and I scream at being left alone in a room of people I don't know, people with no names, people who never came to sit in the kitchen while Amá cooked, or walked by the house smiling good morning or good afternoon, or told me how much bigger I was getting and patted my head, or stopped to talk about too much rain or not enough.

I'll be back later, Amá says, but I don't know that I believe her because Apá left for a long time and he never came back, we had to come to him. But I can't talk, my throat feels like I have a big mouthful of potatoes stuck in it and no water to wash it down. The door closes behind her and it is heavy, shut with a thud like one big No. The door is heavier even than those in Tía Lydia's house, a bigger doorknob. I don't like doors. They hold me inside this room of so much color without her. Maybe this means she really doesn't love me after all.

The teacher takes my hand and walks me through the room, points to all it holds and slowly the choked up feeling falls away, not like feeling better, but like forgetting. And the room is so bright it shrinks my eyes, the so-white lights and a whole wall of windows, one right next to the other—so many windows—and the tables and chairs of different colors. Colors, like swimming in them. There are other kids in the room but I don't look at them. They are busy doing one thing or other, hunched over tables or kneeling on the floor. They are next to me but don't see me, maybe because they don't want to, maybe because the things they're doing keep them. I am alone.

The teacher tells me to take out my box of crayons and she offers me a piece of paper. I sit with color and draw. Now I know why Amá bought me this box of crayons. She said I couldn't use them until I went to school and wasn't even sure how. I see others drawing houses so I draw a picture of a house with two windows and a trail from the door to the edge of the paper. The crayons are smooth, waxy like candles. You can't color yourself with them, the color won't rub off. After a while the teacher pulls out mats, unfolds them, and we take naps. I nap and dream that I am on the other side, where there is no bridge to cross. When I wake I think it is another day and Amá comes back for me.

For a long time I think when I nap I sleep an entire night because I don't know about naps. But before I learn this, I learn to walk to and from school with Yara who spends her days in another classroom because she's in first grade, the two of us alone making our way through that bridge to a place that is not home.

cornflakes

Cornflakes are one of the best things I like about this new place, this new house where we live. Every morning, we pass the box around, reach in, and grab two fistfuls that we pour into a plastic cup. Add milk and breakfast is ready, plus a little bit of sugar because you don't want to be hungry again right away.

On the sides of cereal boxes are offers for toys, which I sometimes look at, though I never bother Amá with them because No money. I've heard that so many times, I hear it all the time everywhere, every time I walk the aisles of the supermarket with Amá while Apá smokes in the car, every time I see the doctor, and the pharmacy afterward with its tub of volleyballs bright as a belly laugh, every time I leave school and see the kids outside bunched against the candy vendor's pushcart.

But this picture on the side of a cereal box looks different. It's a canopy that looks like a little circus tent right there in the photo, the kid smiling out one of the window flaps. I go to my sister Myrna and she reads it and says if you cut out the offer, write down your name and address, and send five dollars, they will send you this. Only five dollars and actually more like a little house than a toy. A lot of money to ask for, but it isn't really just for me but for us—Luis and Yara. There's plenty of room in the backyard where Tío Pedro doesn't mind the grass so much, where I could set it up. Maybe even sleep in it. With its walls striped in bright colors, it would be like sleeping inside one of those pharmacy volleyballs. But when I ask Amá if she has five dollars to spare for this little house, she says No, and I think maybe she's too busy mashing beans for dinner so I go back to the room and watch a telenovela where women always move like curtains in the wind, always leaning on walls and thin with weeping, and men always cradle them like babies, coo at them like teaching them to speak.

After dinner, Amá sits alone at the table. She's always the last to eat, scraping what's left in the pan. Maybe now, I think.

Amá, just five dollars. Look. But she's not looking.

Amá, it's so pretty, I go on. Won't ask for anything ever again. Will do the cutting out and the mailing so you won't have to. Five dollars, that's all. Don't you have five? Just five?

She says nothing, which is good because she's not saying no.

Amá, it's so pretty and it wouldn't just be a toy. I could sleep in it, in the back where no one would have to look at it.

I don't know when she stopped looking at me but she's not. Her eyes are on something else just past me, like she's looking at the door behind me, the third door, the door that is always closed. She's looking at it, and she's not talking.

I keep asking but it is like I'm not asking, like I'm not talking. Maybe she's thinking of the others—Vicente, Lucía, Elsa, and Norma—my siblings who are so much older than me they look like grown-ups, my siblings who are still on the other side in the house with the dirt floor. Amá gets like this sometimes after coming back from there because she goes to see them because they can't come over here to McAllen yet. I don't know why, but they just can't. She's not touching her food, the tortilla in her hands, the pan with the beans, a little bit of mashed tomato and hot peppers over it to wake your tongue. She likes it like that sometimes. But she's not eating and I wonder if she'll forget that the pan is there, if she'll leave it out. I think of the mice that are always twitching their noses in corners, rushing scared, and how we're not supposed to leave food out because then mice will really be crawling all over the place. And then more traps that look like toys but are not toys will have to be put out, the kind that squish a mouse's head because he was reaching for the piece of dough in the middle of the night away from the traffic of dangerous feet. A piece of dough that he thought was cheese when it wasn't. Some mornings the mouse's guts will be spilling out from under him like he couldn't hold himself in anymore, spilling out of himself, and I think it's sad that being hungry can kill you that way. And sadder that you have to tell them no food for you, so they won't come back, so they won't come kiss the trap.

Her hands rest on her lap. The creases at the folds of her elbow form beads of damp dirt.

There are mothers who pick up their kids at the front of the school, pull up in cars with their long hair and makeup like my older sisters wear sometimes. But not Amá, her hair is crazy, curls sticking out all the time, and she never wears makeup. Her lips are pale with hardly any pink in them. Her lips are dry, brittle, like a mouth that is broken, a mouth that can't open. She's run out of words. Her eyes look at nothing, traces of red where only white should be. Eyebrows blond, almost invisible, lighter than her red hair, but drooping like wilted leaves. She looks sad, like those clown paintings for sale at the flea market. Like she's being punished in a corner. Like her mother told her she was bad.

And I keep asking the same question, keep pushing, when she's already let me know: no words means No.

I go back into the bedroom and ask my older sisters if they have the money for the tent on the box. Let me see, Myrna says and takes the box from me and looks at it a long time and I think maybe this time.

It's not true, they just want your money, she says softly, like she's sorry. And hands back the box.

Still, before I throw the box away, I cut the offer out, tuck it in a drawer, and hope the mice don't get to it.

dust swirls in the window

Here we go, here we go fast on the highway, last of the houses with cracked windows gone. Here I go, sitting on the armrest between the front seats facing the back of the long car, red car, rusty car Tío Pedro didn't want anymore and sold to Apá. Yara, Luis, Alba, and Myrna fitting in the backseat because they're all kinds of skinny, above them that big piece of glass where everything gets smaller and smaller until it disappears into a pinpoint, and behind me the radio with trumpets and violins and the big voice of Vicente Fernandez. Our hair fighting the wind roaring in through the open windows, as we fly back to where we used to live, back where Vicente, Lucía, Elsa, and Norma still live.

But first the bridge over a river, a booth where you pay a few coins to cross it and then enter the other side where men in brown uniforms, big moustaches, and guns ask Apá questions about what we're bringing in, what brings us to México. Nothing, visiting family, Apá always says. And always they look angry. Sometimes they make him open up the trunk to make sure. We stay quiet, stare at our hands like we didn't always have them.

After roaming down a busy street with lots of shops selling boots and brooms and so many pushcart vendors selling candies and rearview mirror ornaments and key chains and tiny Mexican flags, the stores become smaller, become less, until it's just the little wobbly shed like a loose tooth that fixes flat tires, then cornfields, cactus, huizache, and every once in a while, a doomed turtle trying to cross the road. Then we get to the canal where we have to turn left. Apá always stops a moment to pick the side of the canal to drive on, because if he picks the wrong side, it'll be a very slow ride with part of the road melted into the canal by recent rains or else hard and jagged with giant potholes that can swallow a whole tire. Sometimes we have to stop for sheep or cows to cross the road. They move slow like they just woke up and their large eyes stare as we crawl along, until we finally get there—first one little house, then two, then more, and from them people looking up at the car inching along, looking up to see if they know who has come back in a car, looking up from feeding their hens, from watering the potted hibiscus, from fanning themselves under a tree.

Always they turn their heads and look—the old man carrying a burlap sack on his back, the old woman leaning hard over a sudsy tin tub and washboard, the girl with a bottle of milk dangling from her hand.

We are here, all of us, again; Amá starts cooking, and I sit and wait. Sometimes my father's sister, Tía Jacinta, and her family come over and she always brings me a little plastic bag of gummy orange wedges because she likes me best. She says the bag is only for me. My cousin Jaimito asks for one wedge and I say Okay and offer him my bag so he may take it, the way Amá taught me, and he takes several and his amá scolds him for doing so. And I can tell by the way he looks at me that he doesn't like me very much after that.

Then Tía Jacinta leaves with her family. Night comes and it is like before, a dark without lampposts or screeching tires or police sirens. A dark with so many stars, I know not to count them. A dark that calls out the crickets and frogs to sing, now that we've climbed into bed, now that the rusty springs have stopped squeaking, now that night soaks everything.

When the morning comes, we say good-bye, a kiss from each one of us to each one of them who must stay because Amá says they don't have papers. It is a parade of hugs and "take care" and "see you soon." We pile back into the car, the same way we came, and in the big back window of it, they wave, getting smaller until we turn and they're gone. For a long time the dust swirls in the window, the wind wrestles again with our hair, and the radio doesn't sing.

nylon

My siblings from the other side are now here in McAllen. I don't know how, but one day they were able to cross the bridge. This means we sleep a little tighter. Still, Amá always makes sure there are no cockroaches on the bed when we get in, and she tells everybody to do the same, to keep an eye out. Luis sleeps on a cot. Yara, Alba, Myrna, Norma, Elsa, and Lucía sleep on blankets on the floor. They can crawl into your ear, Amá warns us, as if we're supposed to stay awake all night covering our ears. I tried to sleep with my brother in the cot, but he complained I wet the bed and so I sleep in my parents' bed.

I thought heat couldn't get worse than the other side but I was wrong, and there are no beams up top that look like mazes, only a blank wall that sometimes seems to sag in the dark.

Amá doesn't fan me anymore. I think she's just too sleepy. She even turns over and gives me her back, like she doesn't want to look at me. I used to nudge her not to turn away, and she'd lie on her back a little longer then turn when she thought I was sleeping. I don't say anything anymore, just hug her from behind and feel the soft nylon, trying not to wake her. In the middle of the night I get the urge to pee and I wake up because I try so hard to hold it in, but it's always too late, the warm pee soaking me, the wetness running down through the sheets. It feels like something else, something not me running fast and eager down my side. I don't know why it makes me sad. This makes sleeping almost impossible and I get angry but I don't know who with. I get up slowly, tiptoe through the bodies of my sisters. Amá does not move. The light of the moon sneaks in through the screen door and falls on my sisters not moving on the floor, all nylon nightgowns and skin and cockroaches crawling everywhere. There they are. But they make no sounds, their antennae swaying back and forth like two sharp strands of brown hair. I have heard they see with their antennae. I wish I had antennae. I step outside, sit on the one step.

Now that Tío Pedro is not looking, I place one foot on the grass and it tickles soft and cool. The crickets chirp, but that is all that reminds me of the other side, now empty—the bed springs quiet, the stove cold, the animals singing under the windows, and nobody there to hear them.

windowsill

The beans we planted in milk cartons and placed on the windowsills at school are finally coming out of the dirt. They look so pretty inside the little cartons of milk lined up along the wall, all the windows bringing light into the classroom, over the plants, over everything. I can see the sun but I don't have to feel its heat because the room is air-conditioned, like Tía Lydia's home.

I am happy that the teachers are helping me learn how to grow a bean plant because if you can grow your own beans, you don't have to buy them. Watering my plant is one of my favorite parts of the day, but today the leaves look smaller, withered. I think they are dying. And when the teacher sees them, she says nothing, like this is part of the lesson too, like there's no taking them out, no taking them home, no eating the beans. And I think of the other plants in the classroom and all the other plants in the windowsills of the other classrooms in the school, all the plants thinking they'll one day get to go outside and offer the food that was their whole point for being. And how it'll never happen.

dime

I am standing in front of the dresser in my girl cousin's room in Tía Lydia's house. Nobody knows I'm here because I've wandered off while the grown-ups visit—going on and on about other grownups I've never met. Their voices gone now, I am quiet in this room with two twin beds tall and full like cakes from a bakery, with high posts and lacy curtains and blankets that must be softer than clouds, I imagine because I won't touch them here in this room that smells sweet like pomegranate. They're so pink, so pretty. The mirror on the dresser shines clean, like brand new, but I don't bother seeing myself in it because every doll and toy on the dresser is also pink. It's like a fairy tale I never dreamt.

I open a smooth little box, cool on my fingers, and a tiny ballerina suddenly spins to music like magic, slow notes that remind me of the opening credits of a telenovela. She dances arms up, her little puffy skirt going round and round. It's as if the ballerina was always spinning, but it couldn't have been because the box was closed. I close the box again and open it slowly to figure out how the ballerina pops up. It's a spring, a spring that holds the ballerina, a spring that bends when the lid closes. Just a trick, not magic at all.

Inside the box are a loose white button, a little piece of wire, and a dime. They are all dusty, maybe the only dusty things in the whole house. It's like they've been there forever. I think of the ten-cent machines at the convenience store behind the house, the ones right by the cash register, and I take the dime. They won't miss it.

The store has a whole row of machines that eat coins—penny machines, nickel machines, dime machines, and quarter machines with all sorts of little toys pressed up against the plastic wall so you can almost touch them. The lever turns like that of a bank safe from the TV movies where somebody is always trying to steal money, and I try to look through the glass, to see what prize I've gotten for the dime I've fed it. It turns out to be a little rubber giraffe, mustard yellow, inside a clear plastic bubble with a green cap. I think I'll keep the container too, like a second toy. I'm walking back through the alley, back to my aunt's house, when I run into Norma, who is many years older than me.

Where did you get that?

At the store.

With what money?

A dime I found.

First I'm surprised how she could suspect anything wrong. Nobody saw me, I'm sure. But then I remember I'm not supposed to have money. She didn't have to see anything. I have a toy and that's enough.

She lets it go with a look, eyes becoming slits that say, Whatever you did to get that, don't do it again.

I hope my eyes say, I don't know what you're talking about.

She walks past me on the way to the store herself. I keep walking, bending the neck of the rubber giraffe with my index finger. Maybe I should find a way to return the ten cents, but where would I get them? I think I'll just have to hide the giraffe so nobody else asks, so I don't have to lie again and again.

In Tía Lydia's backyard is a papaya tree—taller than me and dark green—that tilts over their fence onto the alley. I stand under the shade of the papaya, look out at the backs of buildings, the space between them where I can see the street. Cars drive by so fast, all I see is color. All I hear is the hum. The alley is quiet, only a big truck comes by to pick up the garbage packed tight into large plastic bags because Tía Lydia does not burn it. It is unpaved, like the roads on the other side. Today the alley is dry, dusty under the noonday sun.

When I go inside, I walk quiet to my cousins' room. Nobody is there. I squish the giraffe soft between my fingers, look at it so tiny and so like the real thing I imagine. Nothing like that ugly monkey with a drum. But there's no point in having a little giraffe if you have to hide it. And I can't hide it. It's not just Amá making sure I don't touch or hold anything I shouldn't. It's also Norma, making it her job to make sure I behave. I can't return the ten cents anymore, so I put the giraffe in the box with the ballerina, place it in the corner where the dime was. I imagine one of my cousins opening the box one day, finding the giraffe coated in dust, and not being surprised, thinking it was theirs all along.

blink

We don't have to go to school for a long time because it's summer. When I ask Amá where we are going, she says Dimmit. When I ask her where that is, she says Al norte. When Apá opens up the map at the gas station, I peek at it. With his finger that points, I see Dimmit is in the top square part of the map of Texas, and we are way at the bottom. It is funny how things look near on paper, how towns are only a dot and the long roads are only squiggly lines like lizard tracks.

The highway is fast fun at first, and then it's not. The hair grows tired. The legs get antsy, bent like straw. The back windshield keeps playing the same image, and the radio goes dead. After something like a whole day, we arrive, unpack ourselves into one large room with one window high on the wall and a refrigerator, a stove, and table in one corner. No chairs. The bathroom is outside at the end of the barracks—four rooms with walls like weathered grave stones and strange kids crying inside.

At night the dark sits heavy over the floorboards, over the quilts laid out on the floor, over the bodies. There is a knock at the door and words I can't make out. A pair of arms nudges me, lifts me up and out. The grass is wet. We all climb into the car. When we arrive at the fields, I have to wake up again. The man in charge tells us what we're supposed to do. We have to pick onions from the ground, and fill large sacks with them, forty cents per filled sack. The onions, it turns out, are roots. At the grocery store, all clean and shiny, they don't look like roots. But here they are and they have to be pulled out, like pulling someone by their hair. Then you shake the dirt off, especially from its chin hair, its beard. Then you take large metal shears and cut off the chin hair, then cut off the top hair while holding it over the big plastic bucket so that it just drops. Two full buckets of onions make one sack that you have to leave standing up on the row, not laid out, as you move on to the next one. No one talks hardly, except for Amá who sometimes says, Study hard so you don't have to do this. I don't know how going to school is going to keep me from doing this, but I don't say anything because I'm not even sure she's talking to me, because she says it real low, like she's telling everyone, like she's telling no one.

Don't kneel, says the man in charge like a mean father, It wastes time. Stooping is faster. Other families know it, even the kids, and off they go. But we're slow. Apá says it's because we don't know this particular kind of work, this crop, that after a few days we'll be just as fast as them. My hands hurt from trying to work the large shears because they aren't like scissors, they are always open and you have to squeeze hard to close the blades. So I mostly pull onions from the ground and shake them clean for the others. Then I get tired or get in the way, and Amá sends me to sit in the car leaning at the edge of the field. The dirt is so cool though, so cool it feels wet. It's not hard dirt like road dirt. It's soft around your ankle when your heel sinks in. When I get a chance, I sink my hands in it too but not when Amá's looking, because we're not dogs. The peeing out by the road, though, she doesn't mind, because the tall boxes by the road that are bathrooms, hard like the plastic chairs in school, are dirty stinky from so many people, so going outside is better.

Then Amá sends me off to get the water thermos from the car. Then I take it back. Then the day is over and my right ear throbs like a lightning bug going on and off and the ache won't let me be still. Amá warms a clove of garlic on the stove and places it in my ear, but it does nothing. Amá and Apá keep wringing their hands because I don't think we can get to a doctor on the other side this time.

The clinic is so cool and clean, with little hard squares all across the floor, just like the office of Dr. Morton in the city of Río Bravo. Dr. Morton would always give me a lollipop after he was done with me. And Amá wouldn't have to pay him until the harvest was sold.

The doctor says something about an infection and tells me to lay back and his voice is like the sound of sheets drying on a line. The room all light, more light than in Dr. Morton's office, and white like the light of the sun, the sun throbbing from one side of the field to the other, and I close my eyes because I'm tired of squinting all day. I didn't wash myself today. I wanted to, but the last time I did, the water in the washroom at the end of the barracks was so cold it was like running into a wall. I couldn't breathe I was shaking so much. Luis kept rubbing my shoulders until we started laughing because our teeth were clacking loud like the cartoons. Then the laughing warmed us. Then it wasn't so bad because the washroom was dark, like being inside the shade, not just under it, with just enough light seeping in between the boards to see each other.

Now I only wash if Amá really gets after me. But she didn't even scrub my face with a washrag before we came. The corners of my mouth feel gummy, reminding me that I'm talking when I'm talking. It makes me not want to talk.

On top of this padded table that is softer than the floorboards in the barracks, I don't want to move, don't want to open my eyes. I want to see the back of my eyelids and feel the cool air fall on me. Sometimes at the end of the day's work Apá drives us all to the grocery store and buys avocados and a loaf of white bread and a six-pack of Pepsi while we wait in the car. And the avocado sandwiches taste like a long nap under a cool shade, and the Pepsi is like candy water, popping the top like a wish come true. It doesn't matter that the Pepsi is warm, because together the sandwich and the Pepsi taste like everything that I have ever been hungry for. But this right here, this table and this room is even better, because the sandwich only lasts a minute, and this here could last all night.

sometimes in the middle of the night

She's not speaking, though she moves her lips as if she's thinking and the thinking is spilling through her mouth. That's how she does it every time she gets up, as if she's thirsty. Her arms are around me and I think my moving has made her come back from sleep.

We're back in McAllen, back in the house with two windows, but one is in the kitchen and so it's no good at night when you're trying to make the breeze touch you. My two oldest brothers are all grown up and gone off and getting married soon, I think. I don't like sleeping between Amá and Apá. Smelling your own breath because even air has no room to move. The house is right between the two others. How would the breeze reach us? Amá says every morning, while making coffee, the smell of it pushing back the smell of old rags, something that's been in the dark way too long, something everyone has forgotten in that spiderweb corner under the bed. When we moved in, we thought it was the lack of people in it, that smell. We thought the opened doors would shoo the smell out.

Sometimes, in the middle of the night, I wake up and can't go back to sleep. Ama's back and Apa's shoulder, because he always sleeps on his back, are two walls rising high above me. Sometimes I'm awake so long, I can feel wet around my neck and under my arms and really the whole side of me that touches the bed, and I wish Amá would blow air through my hair, but I guess I'm too old for that. And I can't turn too much because I'll wake Amá and she'll get upset, tell me to stop squirming. So what I do then is crawl out of bed, make my way outside to the small space between our house and the front house where Doña María, Tío Pedro's really old mother with nothing but gray hair, lives. I used to sit on the steps outside the other door but this is much better because I can lie down all by myself. Lie down and think of the wrinkly paper bag of yummy crumbs old Doña María gives us sometimes, bits and pieces of sweet bread pastries, so many crumbs and sometimes even small pieces of cookies. How we take handfuls and stuff them into our mouths, how when they're gone, I tear the bag apart and lick the corners and the bottom where the paper folds over itself, where some crumbs and sugar hide underneath. The sweet is so much, I think of when Doña María might have another bag of crumbs for us, and curl up on the floorboards, and fall back to sleep.

When I wake, Amá is curled up behind me. Her belly feels soft on my back. We say nothing. I am glad she has come to hold me, though I'm not sure why, because I'm not scared of that last yawn of night, the one that is just this side of the morning sun. And by then all the dogs, even the ones that bark in the night, are sleeping. Everything is quiet and the sun is letting everything breathe an air that is moist but cool. The first time I did this, I thought Amá would scold me, that I shouldn't be sleeping outside like a dog, that Doña María would get angry that I'm dead weight right against her backdoor screen. But she said nothing.

When I sit up, I feel the nylon of her nightgown silky on my arm. I always wake before she does and get to see her waking up, raising her eyebrows that pull her lids open, folding in her lips as if trying to wet them. Cracked. I wait to see her open her eyes, to look at me. She smiles. Then nothing else matters, not even the ache on my side.

pumpkin

For lack of glue, I try my sisters' nail polish to stick the pumpkin I drew at school today to the wall at home, the drawing the teacher liked so much she smiled. The pumpkin sticks on the side of the doorway between the room and kitchen, flutters like a butterfly for a moment in a thin sleeve of a breeze. Amá sits on the bed staring at the screen door. She is not smiling and I remember the rule about the walls, about not drawing on them or marking them in any way because they are not our walls, they are rented walls. I say nothing, don't make any sudden moves, look long at her looking at the door, expecting her to turn and see what I've done to the wall and start in on me. She looks my way, smiles a thin smile, and I think maybe it's all okay.

The pumpkin is round and orange with black triangle eyes, big wide smile, and missing teeth. Kneeling before it, I think of the church on the other side, an altar with a large smooth cross and Jesus on it with a pumpkin head that smiles with missing teeth just the same, Jesus with a big orange face, Jesus like a monster, a good monster. I close my eyes and pray inside my head that Amá smiles a little more, that Tío Pedro won't get grouchy about us playing on his grass and send us out to the street, that Amá lets us eat from Tía Eugenia's peach tree in the backyard, that this Halloween we actually get to go ask for candy, that Amá won't keep us in because it isn't right, kids wandering alone at night.

fancy

This summer Apá got rid of the car and got a Suburban, the faded color of mustard and so big we could all fit for the trip back north to Dimmit—the trip with the same wide highways with their dull roar, the same sleepy hours when nobody says anything they want answered, the same warm bologna between two slices of white bread after the tacos Amá makes run out. All that doesn't matter, though, because this time we get the room next to the one we got last year, a bigger room which is really two rooms: a kitchen and a bedroom. The bedroom has no windows and also smells of old rags and has a big hole in one of the walls. Like somebody punched it, Luis says, but nobody's complaining, because the kitchen is larger than the one back home, the wall's all the way over there, with a real sink and many white cabinets that make it look fancy. And best of all, we have our own bathroom in the bedroom. A toilet all for ourselves that makes us feel like show-offs when we say, I'm going to the bathroom.

Luis, Yara, and I leave everybody to walk across an empty lot behind the barracks to a big place that looks like a warehouse. Almost every day we go and sweep the cement floor with big wide brooms around all the tables and chairs and drag out big plastic bags of trash that smell of smoke and other bitter things Luis also calls beer. The big lady in charge with the mean eyebrows says it's a dance hall and our parents should come some night and gives us each fifty cents when we're through. This money Amá says is only for us, that we can spend it on whatever we want, that she can also hold it for us if we want. So sometimes when Apá gets avocados and bread and Pepsi, we also get candy, that's right, 'cause we got money too.

blue

You can't go, it's too cold outside, says Amá in México in our old house where we sometimes come on weekends and where Tía Jacinta and my cousins have come to see us for Christmas. It's not Christmas yet, but the Baby Jesus is about to be born in a little cradle with hay and a blanket. My sisters and cousins—so many girls—are all getting ready, getting dressed and helping each other get their hair done in curls with rollers. Their makeup shimmers like fairy dust. All of them beautiful, decorated with colors that sparkle. Tonight is the last of the posada, of María and José's journey to Belén. Everything ends at the church, with a party and little paper bags of goodies for everyone, grown-ups and kids. I ask Alba to get me a bag. That's all I want. Filled with animal crackers and peanuts and candy and an orange. Amá doesn't go.

When they get back, I'm in bed, but I wake at the sound of the latch lifting. Here, Alba says, her sweater sweet with the scent of candle wax. I fall asleep with my paper bag.

Later I'm watching the telenovela *Los Ricos También Lloran* in Tía Eugenia's living room back in the United States. Veronica Castro, the main star is brown with green eyes. The opening credits are a close-up of her face. I don't know why I'm here, but she's beautiful, her eyes wide open, eyelashes curled big in surprise, her lips thin in a weak smile, like she's scared and happy at the same time. Yara and Luis are sitting next to me. It's dark out and the light of the television falls on Luis's freckly face and Yara's chubby cheeks, like sitting before a fire. Like we're waiting for something, but I'm not sure what.

Come, someone says through the screen door. So we get up and head back to the house in the middle, and sitting on the dresser are things wrapped in bright colored paper.

Open them, my big sisters tell us.

I don't know how to, can't find the edge of the box, the lid.

Tear the paper, they say, so we do and the loud sound of paper tearing makes it feel like we're misbehaving.

Yara gets a toy tea set, porcelain or glass or something, gray white, with little yellow flowers. My brother and I get matching toy cars, pickup trucks really. Mine red. His blue. I wish I'd gotten the toy tea set, but I'm not supposed to like girl toys. I'm supposed to like boy toys, so I say Gracias. Yara's and Luis's big brown eyes flicker like candles.

Where did the toys come from? I ask my sisters.

Santa Claus.

When was he here?

He just left.

Why didn't you call me from Tía Eugenia's house to see him? I think to ask, but then I see the blue lights of our Christmas tree. The tree is little, not like Tía Eugenia's that sits on the floor and stands tall all the way to the ceiling. This one sits on the dresser and doesn't go higher than the mirror. This one that I carried home from school, over the bridge, a gift from my second-grade substitute teacher. Strange that she'd give each one of us a gift when she hardly knew us, when she was only there because the teacher couldn't come, but I just said Thank you when she asked me to come up. Thank you, and dragged it to my desk, then here. Amá planted it in an empty lard can filled with dirt. She bought two strings of blue lights at the H.E.B. grocery, four bulbs to each string, eight lights together, each the size of my mother's thumb. Just enough to go around twice. Our own Christmas tree.

Last year I made a Christmas tree cut out from green construction paper, two sheets folded in half lengthwise, stapled, then cut out, then opened like a fan. It stood on its own and I brought it home because I thought this cutout would be enough, would be almost as good as the real thing. But now that the real thing is here with its lights and its strong sweet scent like a song with a long last note, I can see the construction paper cutout was nothing, nothing at all.

Disconnect the lights before getting in bed, says Amá.

I kneel on the corner of the bed. Amá sits on the edge.

Santa Claus never visited us on the other side? I ask her.

No.

Why?

Because he didn't know where we lived.

Why?

Because where we lived there were no addresses.

And I feel bad for the kids that are still over there on the other side, where there are no numbers on houses and street names on mailboxes like on this side and so Santa Claus can't visit them because he doesn't know they are there.

With everybody yawning under quilts, Amá gets up, turns off the ceiling light. I turn around in the dark, and the little lights burn a bright blue, just blue, no hot wires, no center that I can see. So pretty, prettier than anything I can remember. They are like stars that have come down from high up in that huge sky to stay with us this night.

How I want to touch the lights, hold them, but Apá is already sleeping next to me. And I don't want to wake him with my moving around because he gets startled and it scares me. I can't reach the lights from the bed, and I don't want to step on the faces of my sisters lying on the floor. So I grab a hold of the extension cord that connects them to the wall.

The dresser is peeling, but the tree makes you not notice anything but its blue lights. Blue, nothing like the lights at school, the traffic lights up there on the wires, the lights on cars. Blue, more magical than the yellow noonday sun because you can stare at it and not get watery eyes, because you can stare at it and not get the big spots of blindness you get after staring at the ceiling lightbulb.

I pull the cord and the lights go black, dimming like a sigh. I do and the needle leaves of the tree that were cradling the lights also go black. Everything goes that way, sighing into black. I crawl back between my parents under the warm blankets. In the dark I hold my hand before my face, barely making out the outline of it, and think of a blue light soft in my hand that is its cradle, a blue that I see now is not a star but a tiny living thing, a little breathing animal that has landed in my hand because it wants to sleep in it, because it knows I would never hurt it, because it knows I only want to hold it, the glow that is his breathing, the breathing that is his light.

kiss

Apá's back from work and showering in the bathroom next to Tía Eugenia's porch. Yara and I play hopscotch—toss the stone, one-two-three—while the shower hums behind my ears, while the grown-ups talk under a short tree with a rough bark, more aunts and uncles and spouses of aunts and uncles. When the hum dies down, Yara and I stop playing. We get ready to say Hi to Apá because we haven't seen him since yesterday. He goes to work before we wake up for school and doesn't return until the evening when we're out playing. Right away, though, I go to his morral that he leaves on the kitchen table, the nylon sack with the empty stuff of his lunch bag because he usually brings us one orange coated in thin dust from the orchards where he works, an orange larger than my hand, larger than the ones at the grocery store. And whether it's chilled in the refrigerator or not because we can't wait, the orange is always wet, clean, and seedless sweet underneath the thick rind, Amá's fingers splitting it slowly so it won't tear and spill. One wedge of it for each of us.

When Apá steps out of the bathroom, I hug him, his smell of aftershave, his T-shirt clean white and neatly tucked in. His khaki pants are not the ones he wore to work because they don't smell of dirt. They smell of Ariel, the detergent Amá gets on the other side because it's cheaper. Dame un piquito, he says, asking for a peck on the lips. I kiss him, the taste of orange still in my mouth.

twin bed

The money will go directly to the owner, so we won't have to pay any interest, says Amá to Apá, with her hands clasped together like in prayer.

Yeah, yeah, says Apá, slow and hunched over at the kitchen table, the words seeping out.

I've seen it. It's only a few blocks from Tía Eugenia's house, but it's the only house in the lot and it's huge. Two bedrooms, a living room, a dining room, and a kitchen. There are no pipes in it—so the kitchen sink just pours the slop outside, and the bathroom and shower are way out at the back of the lot, and there's no hot water like there was in Tía Eugenia's porch bathroom—but still, it has its own porch and plenty of windows. I feel rich just thinking—walking from room to room.

Bien, bien, I keep hearing Amá say like a chant. But Apá doesn't say much, mostly nods his head.

In some way everything is a sacrifice, says Amá.

My older sisters can also work. I like the idea of pooling your money together to get something you couldn't separately. Eventually Apá says Está bien, and Amá sighs a big sigh.

After three and a half years at Tía Eugenia's little room and kitchen, I can't wait to move out. When we show up at the new house, it's empty except for an old broken radio that's so large it looks like a jukebox and a big console television with only sound, no picture. Both too heavy to move out by the previous owner. We keep the television, place a doily on it and then the small black-and-white TV on top of that.

Everything that seems to never move is now moving, settled into boxes and on the back of pickup trucks. So strange to see beds outdoors under the sun when they've always been in the dark indoors, almost like sunlight isn't supposed to touch certain things. I help with the smaller boxes.

The living room has two pretty shelves like cubby holes in one wall, on either side of the entrance to the first bedroom, and on them are little figurines of dogs and cats that the owner also left behind. The round space above the shelf that looks scooped out from the wall reminds me of the places for saints at the church, statues standing tall and quiet in the walls. Amá takes the figurines, wipes them clean with a rag, and places them back on more doilies. Amá buys curtains at the flea market because the rooms have no doors. My sisters sleep in the large bedroom where you can squeeze in two full-size beds with enough room for the old furniture plus a box for clothes. Amá, Apá, Luis, and I sleep in the smaller room where you can only squeeze one full-size bed for my parents and a twin hand-me-down-from-one-of-Tia-Lydia's-daughters for Luis and me, the head of one bed up against the side of the other. Everything tight like a shoelace but better than sleeping between Amá and Apá.

Two whole windows for this room alone. It isn't any cooler, though, because I'm now sleeping between Luis and a wall without a window. So wet trickles down my neck and for a minute I get angry at the dark that holds only my father's snores, but maybe I'm just acting spoiled because I live in a house with more than one room. Because I share a bed with only one person. Because I'll have the cool concrete porch all to myself in the morning.

part four
1984

andie

My classmate Andie looks clean every day with bows in her hair and plaid dresses with wide skirts. Her cheeks are birthday-cake pink, like a doll's, and her hair is long and big above her face with curls that shimmer crystal black like the women of the telenovelas. I stare at the song of her curls while she says this and that to her girlfriends in an English that rolls soft like marshmallows.

You have such pretty hair, Andie, I say without thinking, knowing right away I shouldn't have said it, because Andie doesn't like me talking to her or even standing next to her.

Get away from me! You're such a faggot! she barks, her eyes tight little slits, her lips pulled back, her teeth hard white, bright like the walls of Mrs. Vasquez's classroom. Andie purses her lips, pulls away, like she's afraid of catching something I have, and swivels back to her friends who murmur with their eyes.

When I say the word faggot to myself it is like biting hard on my lower lip. I understand more English now that I'm in fourth grade, but I'm not sure what that word means, what she's calling me. Don't think I've heard it before, not like this, the way the sound of it feels hot against my face that reddens over any little thing. Something has followed me from the other side.

The classroom windows, metal painted brittle white, frame the trees outside along the chain-link fence. The trees straight and swaying back and forth like dancing a slow dance in place, the leaves shining like wet feathers. It must be warm outside, I think, with a breeze that would mess with my hair, a breeze that would tickle my eyelashes, a breeze that would carry me on to run without feeling tired, to run without sweating, to run away.

From this day on, when the teacher has us get in groups, I make sure I'm not in the one with Andie. Andie who brings a shiny red apple for the teacher. Andie who smiles big at everyone.

turnstile

I'm sick so Amá and I sit in a bus to go see the doctor on the other side. I ask if it'll be Dr. Morton, who gives me that lollipop every time, but she says No. And when we get off the bus there's a bridge, but this is not the same bridge. She says it's also a bridge to the other side, just a different one and this time we walk across. We place the dime in the slot and the turnstile moves. On this side along the river is the tallest chain-link fence I've ever seen with wire similar to the one used to keep animals in one place, except the barbs are larger and look sharp as razors. Also, the wire is coiled, circles and circles that run along the top of the fence. And there's other stuff too, like spikes and more wire piled on top and no longer in perfect circles, just kind of jagged, like the fence alone didn't work and the first layer of wire didn't work and they kept on adding sharp things.

It reminds me of the walls around big pretty houses in México. At first the house has a short concrete wall that just looks pretty, which I think must be to keep stray animals out. Then when you notice it later, the next time you're driving by on the way to visit relatives, the wall is taller. Then later the wall has shards of glass glued along the top. So it wasn't to keep the animals out but the bad people. And I guess the shards of glass are the latest effort. So I think hard: once somebody crosses over when they shouldn't, how do they cross back? How do you go back through the thing that cut you?

The fence is also along the bridge, and I have to stop looking up at the spikes like thorns that never break because I keep stumbling into Amá. Look where you're going, she says, and I stop looking up. Instead I sneak peeks at the river below, slow with swirly spots like dizzy eyes looking up at you, and much wider than the canal in La Sierrita. On the Mexican side of the bridge, we just walk through because we have no bags to be inspected. There are also many shops, like across the other bridge, but there's no canal and no open land, just more shops and hard concrete that we keep walking on and I don't know when we're going to stop. There are many pharmacies, most of them with their doors open, and when I walk by I can smell the medicines but mostly I think of school because their cool air floats out the door. We can't stop though. A lot of people try to sell you stuff, mostly people that look different. I don't know how. Some of them speak to themselves in other languages that are not Spanish, I know, because I can't understand one word. Amá says they are speaking in their dialectos, because they are Indios from far away in the middle of the country who come to the city in search of work. Some of them, dressed in bright skirts and blouses of blue and pink and yellow with lots of ruffles, sell candies and dolls with colorful dresses and dark braids with threaded yarn, dolls that I can tell they've made themselves because they aren't in fancy boxes like Barbies.

Some of the Indios though are so poor that they beg on the streets, mostly women with children slung across their backs or holding their hands. I feel worse for the kid on his mother's back because of the sun hitting his face, the kid who looks like he's got no fight left in him, crumpled into a knot. Sometimes Amá stops and drops a few pesos in their plastic cup, especially if it is an old woman, because if you stop for every person begging on the street, you'll never get to where you're going.

The doctor jots down a note on a piece of paper to give to the person at the pharmacy, some pills for all my snot and coughing. We finally get to enter a pharmacy where, I tell you, it's so cool I could just be there all day—even without a chair. I would just stand.

On the way back we cross the same bridge, but then we enter some other office with heavy glass doors and there are more men in uniforms of the darkest blue, and black guns at their waists, just like the ones in the other bridge. Right outside the office, several rows of cars drive up to booths to be checked by more men in uniforms with guns, a row of them like a dotted line on my textbook that tells me how far up some letters can go. We stand and wait our turn, everybody in line quiet like students in the classroom when the teacher is about to speak.

Amá takes out our little plastic cards and the man takes them with his big hands, looks at them slow, like he's reading the newspaper, and then he turns to us, to Amá then to me, like when you want someone to stop lying and tell the truth, like that, like we've already done something wrong and they're just trying to figure out what it is. Sometimes their eyes stay so long on me, I don't know where to look, so I look in front of me at the turnstile or at the floor of burnt orange tiles or at the kilo sack of tortillas and laundry detergent we carry, and I wonder if I've done something wrong and just don't remember it. His uniform is just this side of black and tight around his wide chest dressed with patches with signs, thick with thread all around the edges to make sure they never wear off, and a badge that I don't want to read because I don't want to make him angry. Sometimes the man is pale with blue eyes like the pictures of Jesus Christ and sometimes he's dark like my father, but always the eyes are the same.

Amá stands next to me, still as a punished student waiting for teacher's orders, until the man puts one card over the other and holds them out between his first and second finger like a cigarette and looks past us at the next person. With his forearm resting on the counter, he lifts his fingers so that Amá can take the cards, like he can't be bothered to lift his arm, like he's relieved to be rid of them, like they were his to get rid of all along. The cards with our faces only lent to us, to carry with us until the next time he wants them back.

like they couldn't make rent

Let's see, she says and pulls up a chair to sit on, stretches out her big arms, motions for me to kneel in front of her and lay my head on her lap so that she may inspect. Her cotton dress that has all the buttons down the front and no waist feels thin and warm over her lap. She parts my hair in several places, runs her hands through it, holds to focus her eyes on my scalp, to look for any white specks that may be lice babies or black moving specks that may be the lice themselves. An itchy scalp can be a sign, and I wonder out loud about lice.

But it isn't lice. I haven't had lice in a long time. C'mon, it's nothing, she says, like she's scolding me but not really angry. It's probably just sweat. I know she's caught me lying, and I'm embarrassed. When we lived on the other side, I didn't mind the lice because I'd get to lay my head on Amá's lap while she picked them out one by one. The feel of her hands through my hair was like her singing. Sometimes, if I closed my eyes and got very quiet, I could feel the tiny legs of the bug walking on me and just at that moment I'd feel the pull of Amá's fingertips pinching it out, the slight sting of the pulled strands of hair, the good feeling when she let go, and it was like she read my mind. Then she'd squish the bug between her thumbnails until you heard the little thing pop. I always got sleepy, not a sleepy-because-it's-so-hot way, but a sleepy-because-her-lap-is-wide-and-softer-than-any-pillow-or-mattress way. And her hands were almost speaking, saying something very quietly.

When we came to this side, the school nurse recommended a shampoo for lice, ordered that we use it, actually, and it worked. The lice were gone, left like they couldn't make rent. And that was that, mostly.

What you need is a shower, Amá says and gets up with a low groan to return to the kitchen, to return to the ironing board, to return to the needle and thread. But I don't shower because I want to remember her fingers through my hair, even though I am nine years old now, a lot older than I used to be, and too old to want that—her fingers through my hair, her gentle hands.

telenovela kiss

I used to think cakes were only made in bakeries in the city. I didn't know the drawer underneath the stove burners could make them, until I saw Tía Jacinta pull one out, all of it pink, and then slather it with creamy frosting. Candy you could spoon. She doesn't make cake every time we visit but there's always a chance she might. And I can say No, thank you, like Amá says I should, and it's okay because Tía Jacinta will still cut me a clean slice. She doesn't believe me when I say no. Even Amá sometimes offers me some. And then the cake tastes even better. I asked Amá why we couldn't make cakes at home and she said Because our oven doesn't work. So that's why the only thing I see coming out of that oven are empty pots and pans.

Anyway, I can't believe my luck that I know someone who can make cakes and share them with me. And it doesn't even have to be a party like at school. So I wait out in the backyard of Tía Jacinta's house in Río Bravo. I wait for the aroma of the oven to flood the backyard because that means she's making cake.

My cousin Jaimito, who somehow has a puppy and has tied a piece of thread to its tail, is having fun watching it chase the piece of thread around a tin tub. Then he gets bored and asks me to help him with something, something about going over the brick fence to look for other boys to play with. I don't know but he says Come on, and I climb over the fence with him. On the other side, he knocks on the back door of the house and nobody answers and I say We should go back. But he doesn't listen and he forces the door open, hurries in, and tells me to follow him. I don't want to but I do, because I don't want to leave him behind, and before I know it, he's on a chair looking over the top of a tall chest of drawers. He finds a jar of coins and I can't believe what he's doing. He tells me to check if anyone is coming. I go back to the door he forced open, and I close my eyes because I don't want to do what he asked me to, but then I get scared that someone might come up and I'll be standing there with my eyes closed, so I open them and see that the doorway is empty. This means I'm helping. And I get the feeling this was his plan all along because he walked in like he knew the place. But I don't really know why he asked me to come with him because he could have done this by himself, I think. Vámonos, Jaimito, I keep telling him, but he won't because he's down off the chair, busy trying to unscrew the jar's tight lid. He can't and he finally listens to me. We leave with him holding the jar in his hands. He closes the door behind him, and I am grateful that he didn't ask me to do that. I cross back first over the brick fence as fast as I can without scraping or snagging my pants because Amá will get angry. When it's his turn, Jaimito lowers the jar from the top of the fence so that I can take it. The jar shines round like a crystal ball, pretty in the sunlight, but I don't want to touch it. Take it, he says, and I do and so I have touched it and it is heavy, heavier than I thought it would be. All the time I think, God is always watching.

Don't tell anyone. If you do, I'll tell them it was your idea, he says.

His eyes have turned to little slits. I believe him. I remember some time back, standing with him in the old house where he and his family used to live, the house beside the canal that feeds the crop. They had a pen with goats and sheep. We were in the back of the pen, just he and I. A little turtle stood, sunning itself, its shell checkered in gray, black, and yellow and beautiful. And my cousin picked up a rock and smashed it against the turtle's shell. The turtle bled, but still it did not move, its blood running down, dripping from the sides of its shell into dry grass. Its neck arched, the top of its head almost against its shell and then it drooped, the eyes blinking slow. Why did you do that? He looked at me and chuckled, and I was scared of him then. I walked away, back to the crowd, back to Amá.

The next time we visit in Río Bravo, I don't want to go to the back because I figure Jaimito is there. Eventually the inside gets too hot and the front is always getting choked in clouds of dust from the passing cars, so I walk out back hoping he's gone, the way he sometimes disappears.

There is a room in the back corner of the house with a separate entrance. That's where Jaimito calls me in. He waves at me, mouths the word— Come—and then I know it's supposed to be something secret.

I don't want to go, but I do. Inside is all drywall, pale yellow like a long bleached Tonka truck, one window with a skinny curtain gray as a cobweb, a concrete floor with crack lines like a map, space enough for a chest of drawers that looks like it's been beaten with a hammer, and a bed so dirty it looks abandoned. He latches the door shut.

Pull your pants down, he says, asking me to do something no one has ever asked of me, not Amá, not my teachers. Once only a nurse at school asked me to take my pants off. I was five years old and embarrassed. Amá was there and she said to just unbutton them but keep them on. And the nurse didn't insist.

I try to walk around him, but he puts his hand on my chest, and says that if I don't do as he says, he'll tell my parents about the break-in and stealing the jar of coins. I begin to undo my pants, but apparently I don't do it fast enough, because he finishes unzipping them and pulls them below my knees, along with my underwear. Then he does the same. We're naked from our waists to our ankles.

Lean on the bed, he says, and I do.

I lean over the edge of the bed and turn my face to the side so I don't get dirt in my mouth and so I can face the window. He parts my butt cheeks and places his thing against my hole. He rubs up against me and I can feel his chest against my back, the dirt-rough sheets on my chest. I don't know how to feel. It's like he finally got me where he wanted but not to throw stones at me or call me names, but to hold me down. To touch me in a way that doesn't hurt.

After more than one moment, he stands up and says, Now you, and he leans like I did. He bends over the edge of the bed and spreads his legs. His butt cheeks feel soft but firm against my palms, my fingers kneading them like a rubber ball. Then I get up and place my thing against his hole. And I press up against him like he taught me. Now we are touching.

A long-legged spider sits fixed in its lonely web up in a corner of the ceiling. Large spiders scare me with all their eyes, but this one doesn't move and I hope that means it is dead. Then I get up and he gets up and we're facing each other again, like in the beginning.

Now kiss me, he says.

I really have to go and they'll be looking for us soon, I say because I don't want to have his face on my face like pushing up to a mirror.

Let's kiss, he says, like he didn't hear what I just said. And he isn't smiling anymore. Let's kiss like in the telenovelas.

Maybe if I make it quick, he'll let me go, I think. He'll let me go and not mind it.

Okay, I say, wanting to get it over with.

And I take a step toward him and lean in to give him a peck on the cheek, hoping this will satisfy him. But he holds me by the neck, pushes my face against his face, and sticks his tongue in my mouth and it probes, rubs up against teeth and behind them and my own tongue that does not know where to be, where to rest. His lips press against my lips, over them, greedy and sloppy. They open and fold out so that the soft insides push against mine, around mine. It feels hot and slimy all around my lips and up to my nose and down my chin, like he's drooling on my face, and I don't know what to do with so much spit. This is also new, like what we did before with our chests and backs and things, but different. My lips begin to quiver, so I tighten them, but I don't think he cares, because he doesn't stop pushing his face into mine. I don't know what to do with his hands around my neck, his chin jutting against mine, his spit soaking me all the way through. Then he pulls away. Then he looks at me and smirks. He's only two years older than me, but he doesn't seem eleven, maybe because he isn't afraid of breaking into a house.

Then I am sweating. Because the room is airless. Because it has always been airless. Well, I should go, I say, thinking to smile a quick smile, hoping this is the end.

Don't say anything, he says. If you do, I'll tell your mom you made me do it.

And the thought of him accusing me frightens me like a monster sneaking up on you in the night, not knowing you turned away from the window in your sleep, not knowing you forgot to keep watch, your ears falling into sleep, too, and not hearing it claw the dark, nothing to warn you it was coming fast, its eyes all anger, and the monster overtakes you and then it is too late because it means the end.

I say nothing because there is nothing to say. He is right. I also did it. I am not innocent. I had wanted to leave quick, to get away after the excitement, but now after his spit and his threat, it doesn't matter. I'll walk out but I'll remember this room so well that it will be like I never left it.

I step outside into the sun and wipe the spit off my face on my sleeve, slick until I can feel my lips dry on the fabric. Tía Jacinta calls out to me and I walk into the kitchen at the other end of the house.

Would you like a piece of cake, she offers.

And the cake sits in a large round plate over the stove, one of my girl cousins almost done coating it with white frosting. I can see the last bit of exposed bread: yellow. About a pinky finger high and perfectly even. I don't say anything. Amá comes up and says it's okay if I want some. She even smiles. Tía Jacinta brings the cake to the table. Up close it is even more beautiful.

No, thank you, I say.

I used to wonder if I said No thank you to food, and I really didn't want it, it might be better. I wouldn't be lying and I wouldn't have to worry about staring. And Amá would be proud of me. But I was wrong. I tighten my lips again so they don't quiver, but they push out. I am tired of my lips that give me away. I run out front and stand by the road, where the dust never settles.

susto

As I kneel before her, she brushes herbs over my face that smell like the air after a long rain. My arms outstretched in the form of a cross, I think of Jesus, but mostly I think that I don't want to be in the old woman's house back here in La Sierrita to be cured of "susto": some ailment that maybe makes me lose my appetite because I may be sick with fright, like something scared me once and I never got over it, some mysterious thing the curandera will heal. I wish I could ask her where she learned her magic powers—In what book?—but I know not to ask. I know because she isn't really looking at me but above me.

Her home is thin and frail like her gray hair. It's got a dirt floor like our old house from long ago, but the walls are not straight like boards or drywall, they're small logs held together with mud and grass. And the roof is so low I think I can almost touch it. The house so small that the prayers she murmurs get squeezed out the open door as soon as they come out of her mouth. When she's done, I think I should feel different, new, like after a bath or a haircut. But I don't. Amá and I walk out to where Apá waits inside the big truck. I ask Amá about the old woman's house, but she says it's just her house, that we used to live in a house like that, all small logs and mud, a long long time ago. You wouldn't remember, she says.

Back in Apá's truck, just the three of us, I like it that I get to sit in the front seat, window down, breeze like a hand stroking my hair.

Back home, I fall asleep on the couch until I half wake up because Amá is trying to carry me to bed. She grunts but it is more in a joking way, like saying, My God, you're getting so big. I am nine, way too old for her to carry me, and it feels strange because I can't remember the last time she did, though I let her. I let her because in her arms I feel light like a bedsheet drying in a slow breeze. And when she lays me down on the bed, I am this cotton fabric brought in from the sun, hovering for a second before landing softly.

saving the orchards

Early in the morning my own pee wakes me before anyone is up. By the time I know to hold it in, it's too late. Summers I also wet my bed but winters are worse because of the cold. So the chamber pot under the bed goes unused. By me, anyway. I thought I'd been warm enough not to pee myself but maybe not. The great thing is that it is Christmas morning and the gifts are waiting. I slide out of bed, careful not to wake anybody else. The jackets we wear when we aren't sleeping are splayed open above the quilts, the morning is quiet, nothing moves. The large cardboard box with clean clothes in it, the one I always fall in when I'm reaching for something because I'm too short for it, is still there in the middle of the three beds, the sides bent, almost caved in. The walls are still dark green, the light fixture naked now without any extension cords to fuel the fans that are tucked away in a corner. The curtain hangs the same but something is different, and I can't quite get at it.

I like the feel of my socked feet on the floor, slippery. I wish I could slide around but Amá says she'll never get the dirt out of them then. So I put my sneakers on. In the kitchen, I grab an avocado, cut it down the middle around the pit. It's harder than I thought it would be. Avocados are usually tender. Maybe it's not ripe enough, maybe it'll be hard to scoop out, maybe I'll have to eat mostly just tortillas. I open the fridge to grab the tortillas to make tacos and when I place the package on the kitchen table, I feel my fingers ache like something is pressing against them tight and rubbing them raw. I haven't bumped my hands against anything, haven't cut myself, but still, it feels like burning and then I remember Amá mentioning the overnight freeze, the reason we all slept in one room, the reason we hammered nails into the window frames to hang quilts over them, hold them up with clothes pins. The reason we kept our layers of clothes on, pushed up against one another to keep the cold away like the dirty kid in the classroom nobody wants around. The reason Apá didn't come home yesterday, the reason he stayed out all night. Saving the orchards, Amá said, when I asked. And I imagined all the oranges freezing, hanging from the crisp branches, and Apá small and hugging one tree to keep it warm.

I turn on a stove burner and place my hands over it, but the flames that are usually enough are not enough today, even when I lower my hands so close I can smell the hair burn. I cross my arms, tuck my hands under my armpits, turn away to look out the window, and the plants are gray statues. That's what was different: this is the coldest it's ever been. I put the tortillas back into the fridge and climb back into bed, thankful that my pee is still in my pants and not wet on the bed. I remember the avocado on the table open and blackening and nearly frozen. I shake, afraid of the cold and its meanness, until I don't.

borrowed faces

We sit out on the front porch, just this side of the sunlight, and she looks long into our faces, like she's seen us for the first time, and says: Your father's eyes, or Salinas snout. Salinas her last name before she married. And so it goes with Amá, a long list of our features, who we look like, like she's doing laundry—Salinas is her side of the family and Rodríguez is Apá's side—what is pretty about us and what is not pretty, like a kindergarten teacher sounding out the alphabet. Yara looks more like Apá's family, more morena with darker hair and thinner lips and curled eyelashes, though, according to Amá, Yara's eyes are small, her nose a bit too wide. Luis has Apá's stock features, the lean body, the leaner face, the thin lips, but he is very fair-skinned and freckly and has the lightest shade of brown eyes of all of us, which tilts toward the Salinas side. Alba and Myrna and Elsa are all Rodríguez, Amá says: darker hair, morenas, thinner lips except for Alba, and Apá's heavy-lidded eyes. Elsa's very pretty, says Amá, and Elsa smiles because she knows it, her perfect lips, her perfect nose. Myrna's eyes are too small, which is not beautiful, which is unfortunate. Beautiful is large eyes like awnings. Norma and Lucía are all Salinas: fair-skinned, round-faced, thick-lipped, light brown hair, though Lucía's nose has a bit of a bump and Norma's face is a little too round.

I look like Amá's family because I am fair-skinned and freckly (mole-ridden really) with light brown hair and a chubby face, though I have Apá's large eyes, and my lips are too thick, like hers. And when she says it, it always feels like she's caressing me with her hand.

At the end she always says, Of course, you're all growing up so who knows who you'll look like when you're big. And it seems then that my face is not my own but somebody else's, and it's not set and settled but changing, moving, as if on a journey.

Then we quiet like we're hiding from everyone that is not us, and Amá looks away squinting under the sun's glare and we look at her features in admiration because of their rarity: red hair, hazel eyes. But Amá says she doesn't like her freckles, her almost invisible eyebrows, her teary eyes, her big thick lips which she calls a pig snout. I think that's why she never smiles around strangers.

When she gets up and moves back into the kitchen, her free time over, we place our forearms against each other's and try to determine who is the fairest of us all, the one with the lightest skin, the most attractive, the prettiest, and every time the same people win and every time the same people lose.

old house

We're driving back from visiting Tía Jacinta and her family and my oldest brothers, Vicente and Pablo, who now live with their own families in the old house in México, the one we all used to live in. Before reaching the bridge that will take us back to the United States, before even reaching the shops on the border, the cactus bushes pop up here and there, and I think of the pencas, the part of the plant that looks like a trunk, and wonder how they come to be. Amá says it's basically an aging cactus pad that grows big and thick and then sprouts other cactus pads. And I ask her if people eat them too. She says some people do, when they're not too bitter, but they're so much work because, in addition to slicing off the thorns, you have to peel off the waxy, outer layer that grows tough with age. So only the poorest of the poor—the worst off—will have a go at them. When there's no other choice, Amá says. Most stick to the more tender cactus pads, like Amá does. And they're so good, the tender pads, de-thorned and diced and boiled until soft and rich with a pinch of salt in a warm taco. I ask her if we ever ate pencas. She says No, we were lucky.

Then Amá says how Tía Jacinta is such a great cook. She'll turn any simple salsa into something delicious, she says, even if it's only beans, her beans always amazing. And we all agree through our eyelashes that are light brown because they are coated in dust fine like flour. We are all coated in dust. That's the way it is around dirt roads when the rain stays away. We laugh at our lashes that must look blond-ish like gringo lashes.

Now the toll is paid on the Mexican side before driving onto the bridge. Past the toll booths, the bridge begins to rise and underneath it are children and really old people with runny noses and always in rags like they're the washboard against which the clothes rub themselves raw. They hold up long sticks with styrofoam cups tied at the end to reach up to the cars and people that walk the bridge, to beg for change. Then the river, the same river, though it looks different here than under the bridge in Reynosa. It is narrower, almost like you could wade across.

On the other side are booths with men, also with guns. One man leans in, rests his arm on the window, asks what we're bringing into the country, asks if we're U.S. citizens. None of us are, except for Amá. Amá just pulls out the cards that say resident alien for the youngest of us. My older sisters carry their own in their purses.

Okay, says the man with the gun and waves us away.

Thank you, says Apá, and we all do the slight nod, almost like a bow.

Right past the booths sit other cars parked under a tall, wide roofing. Apá drives slowly past them. A man in uniform with a gun holds a pole with a mirror at the end of it under a car. Another one lets a big, well-fed dog sniff another car. Looking for something, I guess. The owners stand to the side looking small.

Still, I don't say that I notice this because I'm afraid somebody is watching or hearing, somebody is keeping an eye on me from somewhere inside the offices past the booths, the ones with the windows so dark you can't see in. I look back slowly, like I'm just looking at the back windshield, and the man in the booth isn't looking at us anymore, he's leaning into the window of another vehicle.

I ask Amá to see her card, the one she showed the man. And she pulls it out of her wallet. It is different from mine. There's her photo, her face serious and gray, with green squiggly lines over it, and some small words, her name, but no big letters across the top, no billboard.

How are you a citizen, I ask.

My father was born on this side. That's how.

I don't ask how it happened that her father with his Mexican name would be born in the United States and then end up in México, which is where he comes from when he visits. Why would anyone leave the United States for good? And how would that be? I don't ask because mostly I'm thinking of how that card with her photo makes her different, makes her special, makes her like one of them, like a gringo, the only one who gets to answer yes, when the man asks if we are. And the thought is like an aftertaste, but I can't tell if it's more like the tender pads of the cactus or the pencas.

like a boy

Today it's just me and Mario and Beto in the portable buildings right by the main school building. It's nice here with a couch and soft carpet and spelling books. And they're nice. The teacher, Mrs. Jackson, with her blond hair done up so it looks windswept without moving, has a special record that isn't musical but rather tells ghost stories in a scary voice. It isn't Halloween but I guess the teacher likes that holiday so I don't say anything. That's what we do the whole period, most of it anyway, listening to the stories about ghosts that come back in the night with unfinished business. Always the cackles at the end and the echo. When the record is over, the teacher says, Okay, have a good day, and I get up from my chair, ready to leave, and pick up my books.

Why do you carry your books that way? asks Mario from the couch. I say nothing.

Come on, why? Miss, you should see how the others pick on him.

What? asks Mrs. Jackson.

See how he holds his books like that?

How?

Like a girl. I'm just saying, that's why the kids pick on him.

Oh yeah, Miss, they're always calling him names, Beto chimes in right there next to Mario.

And I just sit back down and stare at them because I don't know what else to do but chuckle. I'm good at pretending like that, like when this girl came up to me during recess one day and said You're José, you were in second grade with me and you peed your pants waiting in line for the teacher to grade your classwork. Then she turned to her friend and they both started giggling. The teacher was putting stickers on every paper she graded, and I really wanted one, a large sticker of a ship with fat sails rushing through rippling waves. Thought I could hold it in until I got that sticker. I chuckled and told the girl my name was José but that I didn't know her, and she stopped giggling, walked away with question marks in her eyes. Yes, I'm good at that.

I've seen them going up to him in the playground, push him around, just cause he's there, Mario goes on.

It's funny though, how he walks and talks.

He should carry his books down here like a boy is all I'm saying.

I look at Mrs. Jackson who looks at them, then at me, like she doesn't know what's going on, like if she looks at me long enough she'll figure something out. My lips begin to quiver and so I tighten them, so they won't stick out, so they won't give me away.

They played together with me sometimes, Mario and Beto, on the monkey bars. I thought they didn't notice because they never made fun of me, but they saw everything. Everybody sees, I guess, there's no running from it. This room doesn't have windows, and I wish it did, so that I could look out, look at the way the wind moves the trees, the heaviest of things.

When Amá makes fun of my lips sticking out, I leave, go outside, sit under the bougainvillea. And then I forget why I went outside, only that I am playing in the dirt. But here, I can't just walk out. The teacher wouldn't like it and she'd tell Amá, who wouldn't like it either. I run my hands over the smooth cover of my book, thick paper folded to protect the textbook that isn't really ours, the teacher says, only borrowed. The covers have ads for Wonderbread, neatly packaged in plastic. When I look back up again, Mario and Beto are walking out.

See you later, José.

The door closes behind them. I mess with my book a little bit to give them time so I don't run into them when I step out.

Why are you all dressed up? asks Mrs. Jackson.

School photo day, I say.

Right. Listen, you look good, except . . . Well, I don't know if I should say.

What?

Well, your undershirt is showing.

And I remember that Amá told me to wear an undershirt under my button-down shirt today for the photo, that it isn't proper to wear a long-sleeve button-down shirt without a white undershirt, a crew-neck specifically. She picked it out for me and everything. We don't have a camera so the school photo will be the only photo for the year.

It shouldn't show, says Mrs. Jackson.

Oh.

If you want, you can change, take it off, and I can hold the undershirt for you until the end of the day.

I don't know about this, but I say Okay. And I think, do I take my shirt off in front of the teacher? As if she's read my mind, she offers: You can change in the closet if you want. The closet that isn't like the ones at Tía Lydia's house, whole separate rooms, but more like a box, a corner of the classroom separated by two extra walls. I step into the closet almost full with boxes of posters and rulers and books. It is dark like at night but it is not hot or humid. And even though this looks nothing like the rest of the room, I'm still in the classroom. Well, more like in and not in at the same time. When I take my undershirt off, I get goose-bumps, the dark like a cool blanket over me.

I roll my undershirt into a tight little bundle. When I step out, I give it to Mrs. Jackson and I know then that I'd rather not. Nobody but Amá touches my clothes like that, separate from my body. I feel like I've done something wrong. But Amá says I should always obey the teacher, and this is what I've done.

See?

She takes a mirror from her desk drawer and props it before me. I can see the V shape that comes together at the second button and my pale skin. No undershirt circling my neck now.

Have a good day, she says.

Okay.

I grab my books and place them against my chest. Then I switch them, bring them down against my left hip, trying to hold them with just my hand, the way boys do. When she opens the door, sunlight floods the room. I step out onto the steps that are always creaky because they're wood.

José, she says. Her voice softer now.

I turn to her.

Don't listen to them, she says quietly, not quite a whisper. And she means Mario and Beto.

There are moments that seem to move really fast like a firework pop or a TV commercial or a car down a neighborhood street, and moments that seem to move really slow like a turtle's steps over a patch of weeds. So slow that sometimes you don't know what you're looking at, the turtle walking heavy with that big shell, its face wrinkled like it's always been old and always tired, and you don't know why and you don't know where it's going and you don't ask because you can't and you grow hot in the sun looking at it walk away to who knows where. And you walk away. This is one of those moments, one long crawl.

I want to tell the teacher, Why didn't you say anything when they were going on and on? Why didn't you stop them? Why did you let them? But I don't. I learned a long time ago you don't make demands on teachers. There's no point now anyway. A gust of wind rushes through us, and her hair again does not move. I turn and go, walk down the covered walkway by the playground that is empty. Recess was over a long time ago and I have another classroom to sit in.

When I get home at the end of the day, I put the undershirt back in the drawer when Amá is in the kitchen, even though I'm almost sure she will notice my neck that feels naked and my shirt stained with sweat. Amá steps into the room, drying her hands on her apron, and the first thing she says is, Where is your undershirt? I tell her what happened, that the teacher thought it shouldn't show. Amá purses her lips, drops her apron over her lap, and her hands smooth it out slowly, like she's not sure what comes next. She is upset, I know, but I don't know how I could have said no to the teacher.

She won't like me in the photo.

The dark kitchen calls her back. She says nothing, which is everything. I close my eyes, the room hot and humid. In my chest, right beneath that bone in the middle, a little feeling of hardness settles like a small stone.

ten

Coach tells us of a project called Jump Rope for Life where students jump rope to raise funds for cancer research. He says that if we're interested in participating, he'll help us gather what he calls sponsors by driving us to different neighborhoods. Well, he won't help everyone, only those who need it, like those who don't have a car or access to one, or something like that. He's nice like that, helping out, like the last time my team was losing at softball in P.E. Bad times because when you're losing, everything begins to feel like crap. The swirling dust felt heavier, the shade thinner. I guess that's what people mean when they say nobody likes to lose. We were down by a lot. I wasn't very good that day—or any day of softball—I just can't hit the ball very hard. I can run fast though. When we do laps I'm usually at the head of the group. Well, I used to be at the head of the group, until some of the tough kids started picking on me because I was faster than them. Nobody likes to lose. They're so quick to start fights, I don't know how they get through the day. Anyway, after a few times of that, I decided to take it slow, let them win . . . sometimes. I'm not stupid. But that benefit, the quick legs, only goes so far in softball. The other kids on the team weren't much better. So Coach did something he'd never done. He went to bat for us.

He assumed the position and looked a little funny doing so—knees a little bent, leaning forward and swaying back and forth a little, like a spring. His short and scrawny legs are hairy as hell, jet black hair, even hairier than my father's legs. Well, I think so. I don't see my father's legs that often because he never wears shorts. Only pants. Always pants, and when he undresses for bed, it is always in the dark.

The team out on the field didn't really like it but they didn't say anything. Who's going to talk angry to the coach, right? So the pitcher forced a chuckle. The team on the field spread out. I wish people would spread out at the sight of me. Still, I could tell we were all curious to see how Coach would do. How strong? How far would the ball go? Would this mean we'd win the game?

Well, it went farther than I'd ever seen. The ball flew high up so fast I lost track of it for a second. And the outfielder took a long time to get it back and Coach ran all around. We cheered. And all the time we were cheering, the dust wasn't heavy and our sweat wasn't sticky and the sun didn't feel all that hot.

We didn't win the game, but it didn't matter. When he reached home base, he high-fived everyone. Okay, P.E. is over, he announced, and didn't let the other team gloat. They were also smiling. I think we were all thinking of the same thing, the ball flying eager for the sky.

I want to spend time with him, so I sign up for the fund-raiser.

Before I can go with him, driving around neighborhoods getting sponsors or people who will donate a certain amount of money for every minute that I jump rope on a set date, he has to get my parents' permission. So he gives me a ride home along with other kids, and he visits each house. I guide him to our house a few blocks from school.

This is where you live?

We're standing outside his car that is still running. The front yard plants flower bright. Amá always makes sure to water them, hibiscus and bougain-villeas and bushes with little roses that fit in your palm. But he's not looking at that. He's looking at the front porch, the cracked cement, the sagging walls, the chipped paint that either flakes off or rubs off on you like chalk dust, the screen door almost all rust. He stares.

I open the front door, the spring making that annoying screeching sound, and I'm enveloped by the scent of ironed cotton. Amá is leaning her weight on the iron over a pair of jeans. Pants and blouses sit in piles around her. I tell her my coach is at the door and needs to tell her something. She lifts her apron and wipes the sweat from her upper lip and comes to the door.

Good afternoon, Ma'am.

Good afternoon.

Amá doesn't invite him in. She doesn't invite strangers in.

I'm one of José's teachers, and I came to ask your permission for José to help me raise funds for a good cause. I would bring him back.

It's strange how Coach speaks Spanish with a gringo accent, even though his last name is Gonzalez.

Alright, she tells him.

Behave, she tells me.

Like I don't already know that. I'm happy that I get to ride around in a car, to not be at school or at home.

When the day comes, the cafeteria is transformed with all the tables folded up against the walls. Many students jump rope, earning money for every minute jumped, while music blares from speakers on stage. Fun. Like dancing. I was able to get several people to sign up to donate cents on every minute so I end up raising something like ten dollars. Depending on how much money you raised, you could get some prizes like a gym bag or a soccer ball. I thought I could get a prize, but I don't. I do get a T-shirt though, which is great because now I have one more T-shirt to wear. And it's new, so it may last longer than my cousins' hand-me-downs.

A few days later I'm playing on the slide during recess, running up the steps and sliding down. I don't stop, don't rest, just go around like a dog chasing its tail. Coach stands under the tree looking after us. There are always adults looking after us, like we're gonna start a fire or something. Every time I run back around to climb the steps, I can see him following me with his eyes, not like upset but more like curious.

I stop at the top of the slide. I sit down, let my legs dangle, and I look at him because I know he wants to say something.

Hi.

Hi.

So how long have you been living there in that house?

Since third grade, I guess.

And how many of you live there?

Ten.

He raises his eyebrows.

Grandparents?

No, just my parents and us.

Ten people live there?

And his voice goes up on "there." Yeah, I say, like it's no big deal. I don't tell him that it's way better than at Tía Eugenia's. I don't tell him how now we have five rooms total and so now it's only six people in one room and four in the other. I only have to share a bed with Luis. So much better than sleeping between my parents, or bumping your head against the underside of the cot when you wake up, or sleeping outside. Okay, sometimes the head bump under the cot was funny. Sometimes we still sleep on the floor—in the living room, actually—when it's too hot to sleep in bed but that's only sometimes and there's no cot to hit your head against. And with the house so close to the front of the lot, the backyard looks big.

I don't tell him that for a while my oldest brother, Vicente, came to live with us with his wife and baby Bernardo, who made me an uncle when I was only eight years old. And that many people, including a baby, maybe wasn't so great, especially when the baby would cry at night. I think he cried because he was hot, because he couldn't sleep. But then Bernardo began to crawl, to recognize the cool of the front porch, and so he and I would lay belly down together afternoons and Saturday mornings and he'd look at me with his big eyes, almost too big for his face, like the eyes of a doll, like glass marbles, the new ones at the store without scratches or chips. Sometimes I'd get to carry him, and I'd ask Amá if I was a baby too once and she'd say, Just like him, crying and wetting yourself but in cloth diapers. Cloth diapers, she'd repeat softly. Bernardo was mostly in disposable diapers, but sometimes he'd be in the cloth kind. And I'd try to imagine myself small in them, soft cotton, pins at my hips. Sometimes I'd sit outside with him on my lap, both of us looking at the hibiscus with its large flower the color of a watermelon heart, and think of me in Amá's arms, all of me, not just my head on her lap. Then it wasn't so bad.

Except one day I got home from school and Vicente and his wife and baby were gone. They left and Amá never said why. Later I found out they had to leave for Dallas to find work. But I don't tell any of this to Coach because all he would think is How many? and who knows what face he'd make then. So I just shrug my shoulders with my best I-don't-care attitude.

He nods, and as he's nodding, his eyes go from looking at me to looking away at nothing in particular.

graduation

They look majestic—Myrna, Elsa, and Norma—today the day of their graduation from high school, class of '84. They're not the same age but they started high school at the same time, after failed jobs that they don't talk about, after having to leave school at the end of sixth grade in México. They picked up English along the way and hurried through high school in three years. Lucía, the oldest, didn't go to school. Instead, she started working right away as a maid to a rich relative of Tío Pedro. She liked it enough, I guess.

But now Myrna, Elsa, and Norma are dressed in sky blue gowns with white collars that Amá ironed for them. They wear thin long golden ropes that hang down the front called honor cords and a pointy hat that looks like something you could fan yourself with, threads called a tassel hanging down one end. When we were getting dressed and ready, they didn't say much because all eyes were on them who looked different in those gowns. They are my sisters, but today they are something else as well.

The ceremony is long because there are hundreds of graduates, but that's fine and the stadium is so big and pretty, you don't even think "hot." I've never seen this much green grass from this view, from up high. The sun falls behind us and covers the field in thin shadow. Everybody looks the same with even the men wearing the same robes. From far away the graduate is not a boy or a girl. And we spend the evening picking my sisters out from the graduating class as they sit, then as they stand up, then as they walk out row by row, then as they walk onto the stage to receive a thing that looks like a leather folder.

I know it's a big deal to graduate because my mother's sisters and their husbands are here. And they have gifts for my sisters. After the last name is called and the final speech made, hundreds of people spill onto the green with balloons and gifts. I hug my sisters and say Congratulations. I ask to see the folded leather thing to see the diploma. There's nothing in it yet, they all say. The folded thing is empty but for a drawing of the high school on the top flap. I don't understand, because the person on the stage spoke in a low serious voice like a priest's about the importance of this night and of receiving their diplomas and they were called up one by one. And there was no diploma.

Back home Amá makes chicken in mole and plenty of rice and beans and buys soda. And we feel rich, feasting in their honor.

silences

Flushed, that's how I know she's hurting, that's how I know it isn't just her eyes tearing by themselves because Amá's eyes are always watery—something about a botched surgery many years ago and her tear ducts growing shut, I heard her telling Tía Lydia once. She always has a tissue tucked in her bra to dab the tears and the goo that collects in the corners. Flushed, she is flushed, and the tears roll freely. I let my backpack fall to the floor, sit gently by her side. The couch cushions are one thin layer of foam and the boards that sustain them give only a little, so I must sit cautiously or risk cracking the boards. I ask her why she is weeping and once again she says nothing. I insist but she shrugs me away like I'm not worth telling, like I'm making things worse by asking, like she's tired of my sitting there, tired of taking up space beside her. Her red eyes tell me she's annoyed at me, and she's weeping. Believe me, it isn't difficult wondering about blame, letting it settle like dust on our beds, the dust that we swat away every night before we fall into sleep, the dust that still grinds between teeth in the middle of the night.

tony

You gotta get in pairs, says Mrs. Dillard to the class with her dress crisp as an envelope. That's how it is, how I first talk to Tony, my friend. Mine. Because neither of us had a pair, like lost socks, and I always sat up front so the blackboard letters wouldn't get blurry. And he always sat in the back corner. The teacher sets up a contest to see who can best re-create the Mayan civilization mentioned in the textbook. Tony and I work together, wiping down a big plastic tray we find in the alley and filling it with dirt and little cardboard pyramids and three plastic Indians. All of them red. We win the contest, the prize a dollar each, and share the walk home. Tony's home, where I keep walking to after school. Tony's home. Tony, with his hands as small as mine, when he rests his head on them when we watch *Clash of the Titans* on his TV.

Tony, who talks to me longer than he has to because he wants to. Tony, who doesn't call me faggot, not even with his eyes. Tony, who lets me take my shoes off like I'm home. Tony, who makes me feel like his brother.

Tony, who waits mornings for me so we can walk to school together. His amá is usually serving them breakfast when I get there, and I feel like I showed up too soon, but they never say so. She always asks if I've had breakfast and I say Yes, though I'm always wanting the buttered toast. There's nothing to see, I tell myself, standing by the door and looking at the linoleum, the stove, the broom in the corner, the trash can, anything that isn't them eating. I have some toast with chocolate milk, she says also in Spanish like my mom. And she's not asking, just saying. The butter she uses is out of a squeeze bottle like ketchup, which I've never seen before, and she uses plenty of it on every slice and I eat it in three bites. The hot chocolate is Quick with warmed milk, which is not only delicious but ingenious.

Tony, who may notice that sometimes I'm still hungry. Like the needy one that nobody wants around. There's a word for someone like that: pediche. To pedir, to ask, to be asking for something that isn't yours. To want something that isn't yours and not having the sense to not ask for it is the worst thing. I wouldn't want someone like that around.

Tony, whose amá offers me a second slice from the plate in the center of the table.

No, thank you, I say, and walk out and wait for my friend Tony to finish eating and think of the toast drenched in butter, think of a slice I might get to say yes to tomorrow if I show up early again by mistake.

93,000,000

Thanks man, you're so smart, says Carlos. Carlos, with his wallet and real bills in it.

Here it is, thanks, he says again.

Yeah okay, I say, trying to sound like it's no big deal, taking his dollar in exchange for a sheet of math homework I did for him because he said Please many times, because he just didn't get the math. It can't be pleasant, not getting it.

We were outside when he asked me, boys and girls squealing on the monkey bars and giggling next to trees and basketball posts. Everything was so bright with sunlight, to look at the sun directly would make your eyes water. Yes, I said in a low voice, like don't get used to this, this will happen just once. Still, it was easy work, and I was already planning the candy.

The teacher steps out of the classroom for something—I can't remember. All the letters of the alphabet are lined up above the chalkboard across the wall. Every letter has the picture of an animal right next to it, an animal whose name begins with that letter. There is a caterpillar next to the letter C and a lion next to the letter L. No chicken or lizard. Above the door at the corner is the flag again that never moves, never sways. I know some of the pledge of allegiance, learning more of the words. I know "I" and "flag" "United States of America" "nation" "under God." The other words like "pledge," "allegiance," and "republic," "liberty," "justice" are a little harder. The teacher says one day I'll know all the words front and back. She says next year in sixth grade everything will be harder, but I will learn new words. She also says I won't have any trouble with sixth grade.

Then somebody behind me calls me the word—faggot—the word that tastes like barb wire, barb wire I've seen on fences keeping things in or out; it's hard to tell which, when you walk up to it, stand next to the lines of it, reach out to touch the barbs thinking you won't get pricked but you always do.

This time it's a boy. When others like him call me first—psst! psst!—I turn and then they say, You're a faggot, right? And that's not good because it's harder to pretend. I have to turn away, which feels already like running. This way, him just saying the word, is better because I can pretend that I don't hear it. He gets angry because I'm not turning so he threatens me with a beating after school. Soon it'll be more than one whispering under their breath about the things that will happen to me. They will tell each other about taking turns beating me up, all the time whispering and all the time saying that word over and over.

I think maybe they're upset because I'm so good in math I can get money for it. Carlos sits on the other side of the room. I won't turn to look at him but I imagine the page on his desk, the one I filled out for him, the way he props his elbow, rests his head on his hand, and leans over the page so that the ceiling lights fall over his back, his tight T-shirt gray—a grown-up color. His hair combed back sleek black like the rock on the teacher's desk. He must be smiling, his large teeth sticking out, like proud. Nobody calls him names.

I think of the dollar and the coins that make up the dollar, the fake quarters, nickels, dimes, and pennies made of cardboard that we used to learn that dollar. They looked real until you held them. But that was a long time ago and now the math I do is big, like a dream with an edge that's difficult to find. Now it's about multiplying numbers, two digit number multiplied by a two digit number and three digit by three digit and I imagine the routine is the same for longer numbers, must be the same forever, maybe, how they each have a place, how they work together to come to some third number. And I look at my long pencil with a number printed on it: 93,000,000 miles. The distance from the earth to the sun. A gift from the teacher, which I would have saved had she not instructed us to use them.

The end of the pencil is dull because I press so hard on the paper, the marks really thick and dark because what's the point of numbers and letters if you can't see them. And the lead glimmers gray and I wonder how it felt for the boy in the noisy house next to mine when he fell and accidentally rammed a pencil into his brain, right between his nose and his right eye. No damage, the grown-ups told each other in tones thick with relief, as in no drooling and changing his diaper like a baby. Lucky stupid boy for running with a pencil. What I want to know is how the lead felt inside his head, if he could taste it or smell it or touch it, if the math became easier, more like hearing music.

The boy behind me pushes me a little because he wants me to turn, and with my elbows propped on my desk, the skin over them folds on itself, pinching me. It hurts and I want to rub the hurt away, but I don't. I don't because if the kids who breakdance during recess on cardboard over cement and land on their backs can pretend that doesn't hurt, then I can pretend this doesn't hurt. What they do is smile. What I do is take out my math book from under my desk, like I just remembered to go over the chapter on long multiplication. But I have to do it so it looks normal, normal, move my head slow like raking my eyes across a page, placing my fingers on the sample problems, turning the pages at that speed that will tell them I'm not here but in the book.

It used to be hard, pretending that you're not pretending at all, thinking of how to sit and move like you do when you're not thinking about sitting or moving, knowing how your legs rest over the seat, how your arms lean on the desk, how your head tilts, eyes looking, just the way you would if you didn't know it. It's like I have to find me outside of me and move myself around like a puppet. Like I'm both of those people in that fairy tale—Pinocchio and Geppetto. And I say nothing, and it feels like a lie.

I used to just freeze when the boys would start in on me, like if I just didn't move, they wouldn't see me anymore, would forget that I was there. But it's getting easier now, moving in place. So easy, sometimes I want to ask my outside self what I look like to him, what he sees when he sees me turning the pages of a math book, running my fingers over the numbers, the sample problems, the others sitting around me repeating the word so many times it becomes more a sound without an edge, no beginning and no end.

dumpster-popsicle-eater

David's shirt looks like a washcloth. David never combs his hair that needs cutting. David likes to wear a Halloween mask when it isn't Halloween. David never plays You're-It. Nobody invites David. In the cafeteria nobody eats next to David. David always eats everything like the Friday bell is about to ring, even the bread with cold cheese and little cubes of sausage that look like vomit. David calls it pizza, then runs to the lonely dumpster behind the cafeteria, the popsicles from the freezer that broke down melting in boxes against a corner. One of each kind for David: Fudgbombs, Push-ups, Drumsticks. They melt half out his mouth, licking them all while he fights flies with his free hand. In class David says, I ate a popsicle, Miss. The teacher blinks. David says he threw up. I'm okay now, David says. The teacher groans behind her desk. David stumbles in the tongues of his classmates like a curse. David writes his name on a piece of paper over and over. David hears the sound of his hair. David didn't see me standing by the dumpster. David was there.

a hollow space

Yara and I lean on the front fence, look lazy at the street, listen to the cicadas get louder as the day gets dimmer. The flies buzz in our faces and we keep swatting them away. The metal outline of a dog sits between us on top of the fence.

On the other side of the street is Tony. He's walking by and hasn't seen me. This is the first time I see him walking by, the first time he'll see me in my house and I feel a little embarrassed and a little shy. But I like that he will see me here, like I will be less of a stranger to him because he will know this much more of me. And I like that.

Tony walks with quick steps, always does, like he can't wait to get to where he's going. His jeans are a little short for him and a little tight. Amá would never let me wear jeans like that. She'd pass them down the line to my worse-off cousins in México. Tony lifts his arm at the elbow, plays with his hair as he swishes his hips. I like that I can see him, and I wait for him to see me. So we can wave at each other. Maybe he'll cross the street and we can talk and it'll be different because it'll be at my house. He's never come to mine. No kid from school has ever come to mine.

That's my friend from school, I say. My friend.

Him? points Yara.

Yeah, him.

She pauses, looks him over, keeps looking. Tony is almost right across the street from us.

She leans over, puts her lips close to my ear and whispers, He's a faggot.

Whispers so he won't hear. Whispers so I cannot help but hear, and remember. Because my chest is deflating, my limbs are floating away, and I am left with no body to claim, only the memory of the word that will never leave me.

I turn to look at her, and when I look away, the evening is darker. Now I know the sun never really leaves, only goes around to the other side of the

115

world. But the dark is the same. The cicadas are no longer singing. All I hear are Tony's soft steps, his ragged tennis shoes with the Velcro tops scraping pebbles as he walks, as he moves away. Tony, who's moving away. Tony, who never saw me. I never called him, and I know now that I will never call him, will never talk to him again, will never sit with him at his kitchen table. I am embarrassed that he was my friend because he is a faggot. That is a faggot and I made it my friend. Nobody wants to hang out with faggots. Nobody likes faggots.

I think of why my sister Yara didn't want me playing with her hand-me-down Barbie dolls, combing their ratty blond hair. I think of why she only let me play hopscotch with her in our backyard, never at the school playground. But the thoughts are growing quiet with the night growing louder.

the sky beneath

I'm old enough to know the sky reflected in the puddles by the street curb is just that, a reflection. But it looks so real, like another sky is peeking through the water, like the puddles are not puddles but places where the other side shows, the world beneath the streets and the houses and lampposts. Large and empty with a few clouds floating like jellyfish in an ocean I saw in a documentary once. Sometimes, walking home after school, I crouch, straddle a little puddle and stare at the sky between my feet and the clouds moving inside it, and I swear sometimes I'm afraid I'll fall in because if you look at it long enough, you can't see the concrete underneath. It's like looking up.

It does seem fun, though, a fall that is not a fall if it lasts forever. I'll be lost to my parents, my family. Where's José, they'll ask. And nobody will be able to answer. I saw a boy by the curb, a neighbor will say, and then he was not there. And that will be all. They'll wonder if I got lost. No, he couldn't get lost, they'll correct themselves, not so close to home. They'll wonder if somebody took me away, pushed me into some old rusty car. They'll stop asking after a while. And they'll never know that the streets and houses and schools and everything is sitting on top of a sky, floating, clues of it peeking through the puddle that lasts only until the sun and wind whisk it away, all only nothingness and everybody thinking everything sits on solid ground.

the call

The title *The Call of the Wild* glides across the book cover, and I sit down at my desk and read because I'm done early with classwork. It has lots of words and very few pictures, which means it must be a grown-up book, and I feel proud that I can read it even if it takes me a long time. The book belongs at school, so I return it to the teacher and she keeps it for me until I have more spare time for the story about a dog named Buck—Buck, a name short and sharp like a cap gun pop—that gets kidnapped and taken to a land far away that is different from anything he has known. And in that faraway land he has many adventures and feels new things like "yearnings" and "stirrings" and "desires," and when I ask the teacher what these words mean, she hands me a dictionary. When I look up the words, I feel like I'm learning something mysterious, a secret. When I say them, they feel slippery and sweet before they dissolve, like ice cream melting in my mouth.

What's funny is that all through the story I keep thinking Buck's master who loves him will find him and take him back to his home because everybody has to go home sooner or later. But this never happens. Buck stays in that faraway land. Forever. Though, when he hears the howl of the wolf that calls to him, it is "mournful." And when I look up the meaning of that word—mournful—it feels like I always knew it. And when I finish reading the last page, I get sad, and my lips tighten, but I'm not sure if it's because of the story or because the story's over.

I put the book down and stare at it without blinking because boys aren't supposed to cry or feel sad over stories. Then I get up, take the book back to the teacher at her desk, and ask her where the Yukon is because that is the place where Buck stays forever. She points to the map on the back wall, behind her.

On the laminated map of North America, the Yukon doesn't stand next to any of the U.S. states. It is way up there by itself on a far corner, that place Buck can't return from, that place that must become home.

part five
1985 *to* 1987

cockroaches and diplomas

A woman from the front office who looks like she's in charge calls Amá in for a meeting. Amá walks to school with me, umbrella in her hand to keep the sun from her face. Amá keeps stealing glances at her dress that she hasn't worn in a long time. She always wears dresses but hardly ever this one with little faded yellow flowers. I think she's looking for cockroaches that might have died and gotten stuck to the skirt of the dress when it was folded up. Cockroaches do stick but they're as big as a thumb. No way she would miss them. Still she keeps looking.

The chairs in the office are soft like a mattress, cushioned like the chairs of Tía Lydia's dining room set. The walls are heavy with framed certificates and diplomas, so white, straight and clean. In the corner is a bookshelf but there are no books in it, only photographs of the woman with other people, sometimes with kids. I guess it's her family. So much space for the things she likes, a cubby hole for everything. Nothing is cramped or crumpled up to fit.

The woman with a dress that looks like a suit sits behind her big desk and speaks a soft and slow Spanish.

Your son has qualified for the school program for gifted students.

It is beautiful Spanish, like the one spoken in telenovelas. Amá nods her head. She is sitting at the edge of the chair, her back impossibly straight, her hands still as doilies on her lap. And Amá keeps rolling her lips like my sisters do when they apply lipstick. But Amá doesn't use lipstick. She does her lips that way because she's nervous. She does it when strangers come by the house like Jehovah's witnesses or salespeople. I don't think Amá likes strangers. After the long speech by the woman in charge, Amá speaks.

Well, that's wonderful news, that this child has been chosen.

She's using her best Spanish.

The woman congratulates Amá on my admission to this program, which means I get to go to a new school.

A few weeks ago I had to take a test in the school library with a bunch of other students, a very long test that was all about picking out the missing shape from a lineup of patterns. I guess I won. I feel like doing cartwheels all the way home.

On the way back, Amá smiles at me, says I've done well, that I should keep it up so I won't end up like her, a burro who only went up to sixth grade, or like my father who only went up to third. I ask her why she or Apá didn't keep going to school, and she doesn't answer, only saying, This life is not . . . Then she stops herself and turns to me, looks down and says, Where there is a will, there is a way.

We keep walking. I don't like imagining my parents as burros, as dumb asses, but I do like feeling smart. Special.

The program means I'll have to go to another elementary school that's not close to where we live. This time I will have to take the bus, which means I will have to get up very early, but I don't mind. I don't mind as long as I get to leave this school and everyone in it, leave this school for another one where I haven't been called a name, where I can be special and learn special things and go to that tree in every school, the one out back that no one goes to, and sit under it to think of all those special things I know and will know because I will learn so much that I'll become gifted, become a gift, like a book with great heavy words that I will want to read.

orange

Sometimes it was just that I needed to pee, sometimes it was the roar of a fast car, sometimes it was the light from the kitchen spearing itself through the curtains that woke me. When it did, I could hear Amá and Apá murmur. It was always early, four or five in the morning. Amá making breakfast and lunch-to-go for Apá—sometimes chicken or ground beef but usually potatoes and eggs with hot sauce, or chorizo and eggs with hot sauce, or beans with hot sauce. It was the tortillas that looked prettiest, the way she'd stack a few of them and wrap them carefully in a cloth napkin with bright flowers that she'd embroidered herself. Then she'd wrap them a second time in aluminum foil—to try to keep them warm longer, though the warmth wouldn't last, I knew—and place them in the nylon bag along with the food thermos and the coffee thermos. And I'd imagine unwrapping the leftovers like a gift when Apá came back from work.

Sometimes I'd stay up to watch a pickup come for him. He'd climb up on the back with the other men, his bag down at his feet. Usually though, I'd go back to sleep before then, before he was done drinking the last of his coffee at the table. By the time I woke again for school, Apá was always gone.

One of those early mornings I heard them talking about work. He said it was dying, that there just wasn't enough anymore. The orchards froze. That was it. That he'd heard there was work in Florida, large farms. Amá said nothing and I knew this was her way of speaking.

Soon after that he bought a used suitcase at the flea market, dark brown with a strap like a dog leash and little rust-specked wheels. Amá packed it tight with most of his clothes. Most of his cowboy shirts, thin like butterfly wings from so many washes, and khaki pants frayed at the seams. He never wears jeans.

This time it's a car driving up early in the morning dark, and we are all up. He kisses me on the lips the way he used to when I was little, tells me Pórtate bien, but I know he's only saying it because he has to, because

I always behave and he knows it. He kisses Amá on the lips, not long like in the telenovelas, but short. It is the first time I have ever seen them kiss. The first time I have seen them touch, other than when he tries to get her to dance in the kitchen, when she always says no. He's at the front door, and I think he's crying, but I'm not sure because he clears his throat and turns away. He says Buenos días to his driver friend. He looks smaller.

The next morning, when I get up, there is no murmuring from the kitchen, no coffee and tortillas, and I know he won't be coming back in the evening. Amá sits at the table, the kitchen light on but nothing warming on the stove.

When will Apá be back?

December, God willing.

God willing. This time there is no other side, no bridge, just far away. But it's just the same. He's gone and I have to imagine a place where he is, even though I can't see him, a place where he smokes and laughs. And I want to imagine a place he comes to after work, but I can't, and I wonder if he packed one of Amá's embroidered napkins, the ones with the bright flowers, if there is anyone there who will wrap him a few lunch tortillas in the morning. And what would the kitchen look like? What would that place be like without Amá? Without us? Who would he bring the orange to? So much sweetness and no one to share it with.

not yet, i think

Not yet, I think, standing on the porch saying Bye when Alba leaves for Austin to be with our sister Myrna and study after graduating from high school, taking Lucía with her even though she's not studying. Not yet, I think, counting the number of people left in the house: Elsa, Norma, Luis, Yara, Amá, and me. Not yet, I think when Amá says Luis and I get the small room all for ourselves, each a twin bed. Not yet, I think, trying to sleep with little ants that get all worked up crawling on the sheets, maybe because there's so much room in the bed.

One day I will leave too, but not yet, I tell the morning dark, waiting for the school bus. And there they are, others who are waiting too, others with wrinkled pants and uncombed hair. The ones who look angry, though they joke and laugh, like they can't stand anyone and still find each other. If nobody's bothering to iron their pants or bothering to let them know their hair isn't combed, I don't blame them. I hope they're not in my class.

When the bus arrives, it seems to bring with it all the yellow in the world. I let the others go ahead of me because I want to know where they will all be sitting before I choose a seat. Fortunately, the bus isn't very cramped, which makes me breathe a little easier. I take a seat at the front, close to the bus driver. Soon, though, the bus is fat with boys and girls from different pickup spots in different neighborhoods that look the same, with homes too tired to stand up straight and the empty lots overgrown next to them. So fat, the bus wobbles along never able to pick up speed, big and round and mustard yellow. Inside it older boys sit, slapping each other's wide shoulders and half-saying the words that chuckle out of them, words suddenly loud and angry like fireworks exploding inside a tin can so that the bright lights are snuffed out—just a small explosion and the trailing stench of it—because I don't know why and all this in the seat behind me and I can't get away. They remind me of my old classmate Andie from way back but bigger and stronger. The roughest looking ones with snarls instead of notebooks like it way in the back.

I keep my first-class-day notebook on my lap, keep looking at it like it's a door I could run through. Or I stare out the window, like the road is the most interesting thing I've ever seen. When the bus finally rolls onto the school driveway, my head is pounding like something wants out. I think about taking this trip five days a week for the rest of the year, and this makes everything go quiet, even inside, like I have forgotten all words. I think of my old school, walking to it, not having to share some cramped space with people who cannot help but look at me on the front seat when they get on the bus, so many of them carrying anger with them, as if it were homework.

The bus driver says Come on, time to get off. And I go.

I'm inside the school, which smells of chilled air and looks new—bright lights that don't make you squint, floors glossy like hard candy, wooden doors smooth as table tops, white tiles dressing the walls, and rounded corners. No hard edges.

Then I'm inside the classroom, smaller than the one from fifth grade, with desks that have no writing on them, chairs without scratches or wobbly legs, and a red carpet so clean and pretty I want to lay down on it and close my eyes. My class and the other one next-door are the only two classes in the school that are called gifted-and-talented. The students in the classroom come from all over town, different schools, names I've never heard of. And they don't seem like the angry type. As we tell each other our names, Mrs. Johnson realizes there are two José's in the class, me and a José Pereira who has even bigger lips than mine and a chubby face.

One of you will have to be Joe, because it will be too confusing to have two José's, she says.

José and I look at each other confused. How will either of us be anything other than what we've always been? How does a name-change happen?

Don't worry, we'll just be calling one of you Joe in the classroom.

I guess I can be Joe, I offer.

Alright, then. Joe Rodríguez.

Mrs. Johnson says that we'll be learning subjects like English and Social Studies with her and Math and Science with Mr. Gonzalez next door.

In line at the cafeteria, I mention the chocolate milk to another boy from class, and the woman handing out the pints of milk scolds me, that I shouldn't speak Spanish, that this is America. She wears shorts and a whistle around her neck. Then I think this school isn't so different from the last one. This one is far away but it's almost like the coaches all went to the same training school where they were taught to tell kids to speak English only. Except now they're in the cafeteria too, not just the playground.

After lunch, we switch rooms and teachers with the other group of students next door. As we're walking across the hallways, I see Bob who also got good grades at the old school. Great, he's here too. He's always so cheery, like he owns the damn place, it makes me want to shut him up.

Mr. Gonzalez smiles by the door to his room, like he's happy to see us. Wearing sharp dress pants and a long-sleeve shirt that looks just-pressed, he takes long steps to the front of his desk, sits on it, his long legs dangling, and says Welcome, I'm glad you're all here. And he does seem so glad, talking about all that we will learn this year, that it makes me happy to be here. So happy that I forget all about the bus trip back.

'Buelito

There on the table is the recorder with the cassette reels turning and a little red light. And there's 'Buelito, Amá's father, sitting by it with his dented cowboy hat on his lap, his face busy with wrinkles, his eyes taking in the light from the window. Sitting next to him is my sister Elsa, who had to buy the cassette recorder just for this, an interview of him as homework for one of her classes at the university.

Once, when I'd mentioned to Amá the Great Depression of the United States that I learned about at school, she told me her father had lived through it, how he was already married with children, earning one dollar fifty cents a day working in the fields in this part of Texas, how one day his boss told him he'd be earning fifty cents a day and that was that. No warning. Anywhere you go, the boss told him, you'll get paid the same rate. What did he do? I asked. He left, she said, went off in search of more work. The family could not live on fifty cents a day. Eventually he and his family ended up leaving the United States altogether, settling in the state of Nuevo León with grandma's father.

And there's the red light, his words being recorded because they're important enough for a grade in a class. He speaks of being a boy of maybe ten on the Mexican side of the border and how his father took him out of school to help him take care of cows, other people's cows. He had to take them out to graze and make sure to herd them all back. Once, he lost track of a cow and went back looking for it in the brush and bumped his head against the feet of a hanged man, the rope braced around some low branch.

I'd never seen anything like that, he says. Eyebrows raised as if in disbelief, even now.

Terrified he ran to tell his parents what he had seen, what he had touched, what had touched him. Soon the people of the village knew of this and were alarmed. What happened then, what did they do? I want to ask 'Buelito, but I don't have to.

And that was it, he says, there was nothing anybody could do.

His words hang in the air, like the dead man's feet, which I imagine were naked or dressed in sandals or boots and swaying just a little, slowly coming to stillness.

At the end of the interview, of his stories of the Mexican revolutionaries harassing his family and his meeting my grandma on this side of the river and getting married and the Depression and moving back to México then and coming back again, I ask 'Buelito who hanged that man.

Los rinches, he says.

Before I can ask who they were, he says it was the law on this side of the river—la ley. This makes me think of police officers, as if long ago, the police officers were the rinches. Then I don't know what to say because this sounds wrong, because lawmen are supposed to be good guys because the law is good and the men who make the law their business are supposed to be even better, and good guys aren't supposed to hang people and leave them out for children to run into. And what was la ley doing in a whole other country, anyway? This I don't ask because 'Buelito isn't looking at me anymore. He's looking away past the window, the sun growing tired and slowly leaving us in the dark.

Gracias, 'Buelito, says Elsa.

I look down at the tape recorder. The red light is no longer on, and the cassette reels are still. The interview was already over.

No thanks needed, says 'Buelito, putting his hat back on, standing up in that slow way that old people do, like being extra careful to keep his balance. Then he walks out to the front porch where he stands for a long time and doesn't speak.

hamburgers and fries

Mr. Gonzalez's dress pants are always snug, tight around his thighs in that stretchy polyester. And the long-sleeve button-down shirt always matches: navy blue pants with sky blue shirt, black pants with black-pinstripe shirt, brown pants with beige shirt. Today it's gray pants with gray-lined dress shirt. He has jet black hair and large dark eyes with long lashes that say Look at me, aren't I sad and pretty. A face that smiles, even when it doesn't. And I stand by him as he sits and grades my math test. The way it works is that each of us works at our own pace with the math textbooks from sixth, seventh, and eighth grade. If we have any questions, we can go up to him and ask or ask each other. If enough people are having difficulty with the same or similar subject, like the significance of zeroes after the decimal point, for example, he'll stop everybody, do a mini-lecture on the issue, and then go on with the grading. The books sit over a wall-length bookshelf, color coded according to grade level. Most students are moving at about the same pace. I'm working on my seventh-grade math book. Once we've read and understood the chapter, we ask for the test that matches it, which we take, which he then grades.

But I can't help staring at his front pant pocket, the white fabric sticking out a little bit. More than anything, I want to reach out and tuck it in for him, but I just smile and think of a question.

How does my test look? I ask.

Good, good. You've passed and are ready to move on to the next chapter. He smiles.

The next day, he invites Mr. Rivera, Bob's father and a math teacher from the high school, to come and invite us to join a team for math competitions. He has all these tricks and techniques to solve problems very quickly, and he's willing to teach us if we'll devote some time to it.

The best part is I get to stay a little longer at school and get a ride from Mr. Gonzalez and get to hang out with my friends on some Saturdays. It's also okay to love numbers and okay to try your very best to get the gold star on the poster-board chart glittering so bright you want to wear it on you.

And even better than the ribbon at the meet is the free lunch afterward at Burger King or Whataburger.

Before now, the only times I ate at Burger King were when my sister Norma took me along with her and her boyfriend. She'd scold me under her breath because I wasn't eating one French fry at a time, because it embarrassed her that I was eating like a starving animal. She'd warn me to leave some fries on the wrapper to throw away so people wouldn't think that I'd never eaten out before.

Now, I eat everything and more than one French fry at a time, and Mr. Gonzalez doesn't say anything, not even with his eyes. And I wonder what it would be like to be his son, to do math with him always, eat hamburgers and fries with him, to come home to him.

the sex education of joe

This is the male reproductive system, says Mr. Gonzalez, pointing his pen at the transparency on the overhead projector, his voice serene like reading a newspaper. And we know not to giggle in the darkened classroom, even though the magnified outline of the organs looks more like a cartoon than a real body—no hair, no wrinkles, no sweat. When the male is sexually excited, Mr. Gonzalez goes on, his penis fills with blood, lengthens, and hardens and then is able to penetrate the female's vagina. After that comes more about the orgasm, the vas deferens, semen, and lots of swimming, and one gets through, and fertilization happens.

He switches transparencies and places, on the overhead, the one with the female organs. He goes on to talk about ovaries, and fallopian tubes, and trips up and down to wombs and vaginal canals, and after nine months, birth. This is the way we are born, says Mr. Gonzalez, standing in the half-dark room, the light of the projector bright on the clean white screen, some of the light falling on his shoulder, some of it falling over all of us. So this is the way we become. From nothing, to this.

Any questions? asks Mr. Gonzalez. By now we've been separated for the question-and-answer part: all the boys with him and all the girls with Mrs. Johnson in the other room, so we can feel more comfortable, the teachers say. There's more from him about puberty and fantasizing and waiting until marriage.

What about men's nipples? Why do we have them? I ask him.

If all parts of our bodies are there for a reason, then what's the reason for men's nipples, I wonder, though I'm not really interested in the answer. I'm asking to ask, because everybody else is asking. And Mr. Gonzalez says No reason, really, and starts moving in his chair like he's getting ready to end things.

I look down at the blue carpet in his classroom, think of the names I've been called in English and Spanish—joto, jota, marica, maricón, vieja, puto—Spanish, which somehow hurts more than English. I think of being little back in México and running home from the store, and standing next to Amá sitting on the bed—the metal footboard dark with rust—and asking her

How did I get here?

When?

The first time.

You came out of me.

How?

Through a tear in my belly.

A tear?

Yes.

Is it gone now?

Yes.

Did it hurt?

Yes.

Then I didn't ask anymore. But it didn't answer anything, nothing about this. This thing that boys are supposed to do with girls, supposed to want with girls—wanting to be so close to them, that both bodies do things together. This wanting that I think is what I want with boys. This that I think is why they call me names. This that they see, that they saw, that they could tell even before I could.

If you have any other questions, maybe you can go to your fathers, says Mr. Gonzalez as he stands up and begins to gather the transparencies of the sexual organs, a thin white sheet separating one from another.

matchstick boy

You wanna come?

He's not really my friend.

Who cares, says my friend Arnold. I guess it's settled.

This is my first invitation to a birthday party. We walk half a block to his friend Josh's place, and all I can think of is cake, hotdogs, chips, soda, bean dip, and everything else that goes with a party. On the outside Josh's place looks pretty, what looks like a house with a long front porch turned into two apartments. Old wood just like my house, but with a level porch and walls that are half white and half pink, like cake layers, straight because they sit on concrete.

Come on in, Josh says when he hears Arnold knocking. Amá's voice keeps ringing between my ears: Pórtate bien. And I keep thinking of my hands not touching anything they shouldn't, my eyes not staring, my waiting to be offered food, not just going for it. Arnold walks in first and I follow, stopping right inside the door.

Hi, says Josh surprised, his yellow blond hair even brighter up close.

Hi, I say, trying not to stare.

With the windows dressed in droopy curtains and one wall windowless as a closet, only a little light falls on the flattened couch cushions, the scratched up chairs, the dirty dishes on the coffee table. No other friends are here. His mother, with long hair as gray as her eyes, hurries him: C'mon, cut the cake already. In a corner stands his older sister with the same yellow hair, but she's got the eyes of someone who isn't all there, who is tontita—slow. I think of Lily, our grown-up neighbor, who comes over all the time to tell Amá all about the trips she's taken with her family. As she's talking she keeps remembering something she bought or was bought for her, a pair of earrings, some barrettes, and decides to walk two houses down to her home and pick up the earrings to bring them. Then, as she's showing them to us, she remembers something else and goes back to get that. And that's how it goes. Amá oohs and aahs at everything Lily brings and smiles at her and laughs at all her jokes. Lily, with her curls tight like her giggles. Amá says Lily is like a child, and she says it like she's confiding in me, like Lily must be like a child who is younger than me.

Josh's sister must be like a child too, but she doesn't talk a lot or show us shiny trinkets. She just stands in a corner shifting her weight from one leg to another, and it must be a lot of weight because she carries that big pregnant belly. I know now how babies are made so I'm confused that someone who is like a child could have sex, that someone could have sex with someone who is like a child. The belly is large and looks like something that's always getting in the way, and it makes me sad, but I'm not sure how.

I said cut the cake, here's the knife, Josh's mom commands.

His mother keeps looking my way. I don't tell her that I see her and Josh every morning through my window as she walks him to school, as they move through the tall grass of the empty lot. I forget anyway when I see the cake, how it gives under the knife. It's lopsided with frosting that is more gray than white, homemade. A two-liter bottle of Sprite stands next to the cake that celebrates Josh's eleventh, I think. The cake is so soft and sweet, I think about getting a second piece, but then I'd have to ask for it. Instead, I just eat the one piece that's been offered really slowly.

And all the time I think of the first time I saw Josh at the old school, remembered him from my window. His and his mother's skinny bodies drifting by. His mother grumbling and scolding in short spurts like spitting: Damn it! and I can't believe this! and Hurry up! And his talking back: Jeez! and I'm going! and Gosh! Their voices always ending low, like their back-and-forth were the leftovers of an argument, the simmer of an earlier boil. When I saw him, he was at the far end of the playground, kicking dirt. Then another boy, angry for who knows what, went after Josh, tackled him, pushed him into the ground, into the grass. Eat it! he yelled. Josh got red like the head of a match, which is what Amá would say he looked like, a match, because she too saw him in the mornings through her window, saw his thin stick of a body and big mop of hair. Josh kept yelling Get off me, Get off me, until Arnold walked up and pried the boy off of him. Josh got up, shocked red, said Man! and walked away. He didn't cry.

After gobbling up his slice of cake, Josh opens his mom's gift—an orange nerf football. Thanks, he squeals, his eyes fixed on it, like he's thanking it instead of his mom. She says nothing, keeps turning her eyes to Arnold and me, eyes gleaming fierce like precious stones.

Wanna throw the ball around? asks Josh.

Sorry, we gotta go, says Arnold.

Josh's sister still stands, her belly so very round. When I leave I think I'll see Josh around, maybe run into him at Arnold's house, since he doesn't go to the new school Arnold and I are in. He still goes to the old one where I know he still stands out with that pale face of freckles, that mop of yellow hair.

Okay, see you guys, he says, squeezing the ball in his hands.

As soon as Arnold and I are outside, Josh and his mom begin to argue.

Gosh! I didn't even get to play with them!

You can play on your own!

Then a door slams, and I wonder what it must be like to talk back to your mother that way, like whatever she says back to you can't be worse than you keeping your words inside, than you saying nothing at all.

stripped

I'm the last one eating and Amá has heated the last of the tortillas. She sits down at the opposite end of the table. The sun is almost gone and there is only a half-lit window behind her and a naked lightbulb above us. She groans, bends down to rub her calves.

What's wrong? I ask.

Tired, that's all. Life, she says.

She gets like this sometimes. Tired. I always wish there was something I could do or say to make her feel better. I keep eating.

Children, I should have never had so many children, she says.

The lightbulb flickers, and I drop my tortilla on the plate, gets soggy with the watery refried beans and salsa, and I don't like to use a fork because it's one more thing to wash. I am the last born, child number 10, and I know of regret, but not like this. And if she could take back her children, undo them, how many would she undo, how many would she cast back to that place where nothing is? Nine and keep one? eight and keep two? seven? . . . The numbers trickle away into some quiet dark like what you see behind your eyelids when you close them without falling asleep, a dark swirling without direction.

But your father didn't believe in preventing pregnancies. To him, only loose women were interested in that, she says like I've just asked why.

And her lips are pursed like they always are when she is upset, her eyes hard and fixed on something not on the table, something not in the kitchen, something far away from me.

I think of the slip of paper she signed, the one giving permission for my sex ed at school. There it was, the secret of what my body could do, that that was for more than just peeing, that it was for making more of me. Then when I came back from school that day, I felt weird knowing those things about my mother's body and knowing that she knew I knew. But what was there to say? She swept the floor. I did my homework.

Now, none of that matters, because she wanted to use birth control and Apá would have none of it and she ended up pregnant time and time again. Maybe he didn't want so many children either, maybe he just didn't want his wife to be called anything other than his wife.

And now I know what the telenovelas never showed. Now I know why my sisters wouldn't answer me when I asked them how it was that the leading man believed the villainous woman when she said her child was his. They'd just keep looking at the TV. If he didn't love her, how could the child be his? How did a child become? The children in the telenovelas always came from love and love for them or something like it, some want for a child. That's how it had to be.

And though I would see moms and dads sneer at their children outside my window or at the grocery store, I always figured they still loved them because they were there. They'd been born to them. The pinching and the shouting and the shoving wasn't so bad because the child sobbing after her parents in the parking lot would always reach them, even if she had to run to keep up with their long strides, even if her tears ran all the way down her face and settled like melting candle wax at the edge of it, at the jaw line where they start to itch a little, and nobody bothered to wipe them away, she'd still get back to them, and they would take that child back, let her climb clumsy into the backseat because it could not be otherwise. That's how I thought it was, but I was wrong.

It turns out all it takes is for the man to be excited and for the woman to let him. Having children doesn't need love. Children can be made without want. Maybe when the parents walking away in the parking lot let the child straggling behind climb into the backseat, it isn't out of love but out of something else. This makes me sad, but a new sad with a new name I don't know, a sad like when you find out that Christmas trees don't live forever even if you plant them in a can of dirt, that they die, browned and shriveled and stripped of their blue lights, and are thrown out in the back alley ugly and forgotten.

One lonely fly sits at the corner of the stack of tortillas. Long ago, back on the other side, the air hummed with flies. They rested on your hands, on your face, and if you closed your eyes, you could feel them tickle all of you with their little legs. It was like the air itself was alive and breathing, your hands swatting this breathing air away. They'd lift and scatter but they would always come back. But here, now, the screen doors keep most of the flies out. There is no humming. Nothing moves, nothing tickles you, nothing is there that you can swat away.

rock hudson

Rock Hudson has died of AIDS. I don't know who he is, but there he is on TV, his name said over and over. They keep showing photos of him; he looks like he's ninety and in great pain, darkness around his eyes—like bruises, like it hurts him to open them, hurts him to see. I go to my oldest sister who's sitting at the table filing her long fingernails, the bright red polish bottle next to her.

Lucía, what is AIDS?

She looks at me like she's angry I even asked the question, like just asking it means I've done something I shouldn't have done and should have known not to do.

It is God's punishment for doing what they do, for being perverts, it's in the Bible, she spits out, pointing the nail file at me for a moment, then going back to her nails. And I don't want to ask any more, don't want to know any more.

Amá is always saying that I shouldn't do anything wrong, like lie or cheat, because God will punish me, always saying Diosito te castiga. "Diosito," little God, little child God can't help but punish. Some punishments must be small, for little wrongs, and some must be harsh, for big wrongs. And this is what "harsh" must mean, a thing that eats at you from inside, makes you grow old so fast you end up looking like him. But what could be the punishment for asking a question you shouldn't have asked?

convert

Mrs. Johnson, in her squeaky clean glasses and high heels, says the conquistadors came to the New World for the three Gs: Gold, God, and Glory. She says they conquered and settled everything from Canada to the tip of Chile, like it was one big goal and Columbus was the first, the one who said It's safe, come on in. The Portuguese settled what is now Brazil, and that is why the people there now speak Portuguese, she says, and the British settled what is now America, and that is why we speak English, and the Spanish settled what is now México and Central America and some of South America, and that is why everybody there speaks Spanish.

And the missionaries, which sound like they were priests but not really, came with them to spread Christianity so that the Indians could be converted and form part of the new civilization growing around them. And I want to tell her that when Amá and I walk across the bridge to the other side to go to the doctor or the pharmacy, we see many Indios. So I raise my hand and tell Mrs. Johnson that I've seen Indians on the other side in Reynosa. And she says, Yes, there are Indians living among us. And then I tell her that they dress differently and don't speak Spanish. And she says, Yes, they often speak other languages. And she's speaking in that calm tone, like I'm not saying anything new, like she already knows this, so I don't say anything else. I don't tell her about the Indian woman sitting on the steps outside the big church in front of the plaza in Reynosa, the Indian woman leaning against the front wall of the church in the shade, with her dress like wet newspaper, her black hair blowing in her face, her lips gray and dry, her hand outstretched, and a baby in her arms with a gummy face and eyes like droopy curtains. And how people dropped a few pesos in the plastic cup at her feet, a cup like the disposable ones used in school birthday parties, and walked into the church with its door always open, the church that is air-conditioned. I know because Amá gave me a few pesos to give the woman, and when I ran up the stairs to drop them into her plastic cup, I felt the cool breeze from inside reach me. So cool it felt wet. I wished I could stand there a long time. It had the tallest ceiling ever and some big colorful altar at the end. That's all I got to see, because the cool air and shade and quiet were so great, I felt like I was being bad just standing there at the lip. Women with shiny shoes and men dabbing their upper lips with pure white handkerchiefs walked past me, stepped inside. And I at the lip, enjoying what wasn't meant for me, like I was taking what wasn't mine. So I ran back. Why wait to be kicked out? That's what Amá says and she's right. I don't tell my teacher that I asked Amá why the Indian woman couldn't beg inside the church where the floor is surely cooler. And how Amá said the woman wasn't allowed inside and hurried me along.

Maybe Mrs. Johnson already knows because she knows so many things. But right now she's busy teaching us all about history—her eyes blinking wide behind those glasses, gold dangling around her neck—all important and grand things like the lives of the brave conquistadors sailing the rough Atlantic, not peaceful and easy like the Pacific, saddled with ideas heavy like a suit of armor, ideas that make sense because who wouldn't want to have money and fame and the love of God. So much love and so sure of it, you would never fear losing it, because you had found some Indians and changed them from loving something else into loving God, a God that punishes you when you're bad but leaves you alone when you're good, a God that lets them into the new civilization growing around them. And I wonder if the woman outside the church has been converted or would like to be converted, if a missionary with a serious voice has offered God to her, if the offer is still open, if she hasn't said no yet, if her baby could sleep inside the church then, get away from sun and sweat into a quiet cool place.

cougar

Amá who's in the passenger's seat says The nice things you want you can get when you go to school and study hard. And I can't wait to be grown-up, to graduate and go to college and have the good life with the rolled-up window and everything hot on the other side of it, like it is here in the backseat of my sister Myrna's Cougar. This is what it must be like to feel like those people with money, driving down the hot interstate through Austin or through any town, with the windows up, untroubled by the heat and wind and traffic noise, their hair like a helmet, their collars unruffled. I let myself be taken wherever Myrna wants to go—her long black hair shimmery as black feathers—whatever errand she needs to run this weekend we've come up to visit. The little window for the backseat is in the shape of a fang, and through it I can see the eyes of other drivers in older cars sad and wrinkled.

Sad and wrinkled cars, that is what Apá drives when he comes down for the summer from Florida, that is what we will be riding back in, the windows down and roaring, the heat, and a couple of gallons of water in the trunk to replace the water that will steam out of the radiator when it overheats somewhere along the six-hour drive. This almost always happens, and we have to stand out on the side of the highway and wait until the motor cools down, Apá nothing but a bent back under the hood, Amá in the passenger seat looking at her purse in her lap, always in her lap because it's bad luck to place it on the floor. The cars rush by, the drivers staring as long as their speed will allow. When it is buses or eighteen-wheelers, I cover my ears. When the car is finally ready, we stuff ourselves into the backseat and notice the heat bending the air up ahead. And Amá remembers the men we sometimes see walking al norte, a jug of water in their hands, the ones we can never offer a ride to because the car is already packed. They must be ilegales, making their way north looking for work, Amá usually says and Apá usually nods. And then she tells us we have no room to complain because at least we have a car and don't have to walk in this over-ninety-degree heat hoping for someone to give us a ride. I don't say anything, thinking about not complaining, thinking how school can save me from a highway and a jug of water. That is how it will be, so I always hope for a cloudy day.

The sad cars fall behind Myrna driving fast down a slope and saying something to Amá that makes her smile as she says it, a smile big as the highway, and I turn away from the sad car's driver's tired hair, his sweaty forearm on the window frame. I sit in the middle of the backseat so I can scoot forward to feel the cool breeze from one of the AC vents that I used to think were only for decoration because all of Apá's cars never had a working air conditioner. The air rushes through the vents and cools my face. I think of the cool church in Reynosa, but this time, I'm not anywhere I'm not supposed to be. Nobody will come kick me out. I could sleep here. I could wake up here. That is how it is in the backseat of Myrna's Cougar.

for good

On the way up to Austin on Highway 281 we had to stop at a checkpoint, a little shack with a guy in uniform with a gun. Seemed like the shack was always closed, which meant you just kept driving, but this time it was open and you had to stop or else. The man asked if we were U.S. citizens. We said no and showed our cards, which was strange because there was no bridge, no fence, no flag on a pole to tell you this was a new country. Still, there was some line we could not cross without permission, some other border that doesn't show up on any map I've seen. But maybe that's just the way it is, maybe leaving home is like leaving a country and entering a new one.

It's a huge house that we move into, one that my sisters Myrna, Alba, and Lucía picked here in Austin where Myrna was the first to live, the first to say yes to a world full of strangers.

Now we all live together again, like we used to, except for Pablo and Vicente. I thought the house in McAllen was big, but I was wrong. The kitchen here is huge with all those cabinets that fancy kitchens have and a stove with an oven that works, which means we can bake cakes, my sisters say. And I can't wait for a birthday. There are also glass doors that slide open into the backyard, like Tía Lydia's house. There's also a garage. There's indoor plumbing, with showers and hot water. There's even two bathrooms, not just one. Three bedrooms, each with a closet and a door that shuts, and Luis and I get a room to ourselves. This time, without ants stinging you out of sleep.

ventriloquist

Can I dream? asked the little girl and the woman said Yes, all the way home—says my sister Myrna in the bedroom with one fancy window that opens sideways. In that cool movie she saw last night, the monsters that burst out of people's chests to be born, the monsters with a tongue that's also a stiff angry set of jaws like a mean fist, the monsters that are nothing but bad die, and the little girl gets to not be scared anymore and we get up off the bed 'cause it's Saturday and we can't be in bed all day. And I ask Myrna what's the name of the movie. *Aliens*, she says. I like the word—steely. *Aliens*, I say, and then I remember the TV commercial for the movie—the woman that looks like a boy, the little blond, blue-eyed girl with her piercing scream, and the monster with an angry face without eyes, so the anger is all in the tight lips that pull back to reveal sharp translucent teeth. The soundtrack like train wheels against tracks, all grinding effort, and then the title: letters tall and lean, the "I" an open slit like a cat's pupil, a tear in the dark universe behind it.

I ask Amá if I can see my pasaporte, the card I need to come back into the United States.

It's in my purse, she says, and then, Don't lose it.

I search through her purse, find the thin two-pocket wallet with our pasaportes, and pull mine out. There it is: Resident Alien. I know "Resident," as in residente, as in reside, as in residence, as in residencia, as in a place to live in. I never really thought of the other word. I don't know the exact word in Spanish, something like stranger or foreigner, something not from here. It's not like I haven't heard of things from outer space before, but E.T. was cute, an Extraterrestrial, and Martians are skinny people with big heads and little voices. But this one's a monster. I knew the words on my card meant me, but I didn't know exactly what, and I wonder if someone made a mistake, putting that word over my five-year-old face, the one sucking in the lower lip and loving the shirt snaps, putting that word that also means this.

At night, on a twin bed all to myself, the air conditioner murmuring, I dream that the streets are empty. The world is quiet, so quiet I can hear the lamppost light pulsate like it's alive. Then I'm at school standing alone in the middle of the courtyard. When I open my mouth to call out for someone, anyone, I feel my tongue not as a tongue but as a second mouth, like I am my own ventriloquist, and when I speak to the nothing in the courtyard, it isn't me speaking but my tongue hidden behind my teeth throwing its voice.

an empty house

We're moving back to McAllen. Nobody says why. Maybe it was Amá, who couldn't talk to any of the neighbors because nobody spoke Spanish. Maybe it was my sisters, who couldn't make rent anymore. Maybe it was Apá, who . . . I don't know.

One semester at the junior high school. That was it.

It is dark and drizzling when we arrive at our old house. The place is empty. A friend of Luis and his family rented it while we lived in Austin, but it's as if they never lived here. It looks abandoned. I felt rich, or rich-like, because we had a house rented out, like Tía Lydia who has houses for rent. It didn't last long, but it was fun thinking about it.

We unload only the necessary things to sleep through the night—pillows, blankets to lay out on the floor. We don't get enough of them out because most of them were packed first, way in the front of the U-Haul, and I don't think any of us sleeps tonight. It's so cold, only the side of you that touches the blankets gets warm, so you have to keep turning to warm the other side. It doesn't really work, but you're only half-awake, so you don't know to give up. Nobody murmurs, nobody whispers. I shiver, but it's alright, because I'm back sleeping on the linoleum I know, the one that creaks like it's talking to you, glad that you're back. The little shelves built into the wall stand guard, empty and ready to hold the knickknacks we've brought back with us. The sun will be coming soon, because that's how it is with days. Soon it will be January, and I'll go back to school, another new school, a junior high where my friends learn new math that makes them smarter, faster, able to win the weekend competitions, I'm sure, able to celebrate afterwards with burgers and fries.

alamo

Look at this, students, isn't it beautiful? says Mrs. June.

It's a pencil drawing by a student from last year of a defender of the Alamo who sits on a hill with his head down, saddened by the fall of the fort that smolders in the background. The figure wears a beaver hat so it could be David Crockett, but then again, it could be anybody because the face is hidden behind the arm in shame and sorrow.

Mrs. June passes out blank pieces of paper, since all we have are ruled paper and that's no good for drawings, so that we may offer our own rendering of the Alamo. Just use your imagination, she says. Something to remember from the time we've spent listening to her talk about this important part of Texas History, the heroes like William B. Travis and Crockett and Bowie, and how they and a small group of Texans defended the fort from the bloodthirsty invading Mexicans led by General Antonio López de Santa Anna. They were very brave, she says, because they figured they would lose, being far outnumbered, and still stayed to fight for what they believed in. And besides, Santa Anna was defeated a few weeks later by Sam Houston, and Texas became Texas, independent from México. But I wonder if Texas wasn't Texas yet until Santa Anna was defeated, then how were the defenders Texans? And if they weren't Texans, what were they? And why did they fight so hard to be independent to then become one of many states in America? It's all confusing, but what isn't confusing is that the defeat of Santa Anna was a great thing because otherwise Texas would still be part of México. And I figure if my family wanted to come to the United States, we would have had to travel a long ways to get out of México then.

I figure all those guys must have been brave and honorable men because several local schools in town are called Houston, Bowie, Travis, and Crockett. I didn't know it before, but now I do, and now every time I say the name of the school I feel like I'm tasting history. And it tastes fancy and foreign, like a telenovela where everybody is handsome and noble and fighting for their big hacienda. This time though the names are all gringo names because it's an American telenovela, and the only name that sounds familiar is Antonio because that's my middle name but he's the enemy.

I try to draw something as artistic as the example she showed us, but I can't. All I keep seeing in my head are the photos and pictures in the textbook, the front wall of the Alamo, Bowie's huge knife, and Crockett's beaver hat. I also imagine bayonets because legend has it that the Mexican army was so savage that they bayoneted people mercilessly, even babies, but I don't want to draw bloody bayonets. I stare at the white paper.

The next day Mrs. June talks about the new state of Texas and how the frontier was still very much unsettled and lawless and so the Texas Rangers were created to help keep the peace and protect Texas from Indians and Mexican bandits. The rangers were also honorable and respected and still are because they exist even today.

But then I remember 'Buelito being interviewed and talking about the rinches and the hanged man he ran into when he was a child. And I think I want to ask Mrs. June if the rinches were the Texas Rangers, but I don't.

fake tree

Joe, would you mind stepping into my office, asks Mrs. Resendez, one of the counselors.

Take a seat.

She closes the door. I've glanced into her office before, but now that I'm inside, it looks even cozier, lots of certificates on wood-siding walls with writing like that on money and family photos in frames. She sits, her tan pants pleated and matching her blouse of red and tan squares. Red shoes, red lipstick, red.

Joe, there's something we need to talk about.

It can't be good if she can barely look at me. I nod. Adults nod a lot. I'm good at nodding.

There's no easy way of saying this. There've been some complaints from some of the students and teachers.

What is it that I do that more than one person would find wrong? Talking too much maybe? Some not-funny joke? Maybe something else? Sometimes I look at boys that way, the way boys look at girls. I try not to be noticed, to not get caught, just the briefest of glances, when they're walking away. The way they move. Nobody can read my thoughts, but maybe they can read my eyes. Too loud, my eyes.

Don't say it, I want to tell her. This will be too embarrassing, I want to plead with Mrs. Resendez. I'll have to come to school knowing everybody sees, in spite of everything, sees. I start biting my nails, and she says Don't bite your nails. Then I'm embarrassed at my fingertips red and raw and bleeding a little. So I hide my hands under me. I pray inside where my heart is pounding like the ants found their way in while I was sleeping and are now feeding on what is left of my organs, ants everywhere inside me. I smile. I nod.

Mm-hmm.

There seems to be a body odor problem. Some people have come to me, asked me to speak to you about this, she says, and her forehead goes a little wrinkly. Concerned.

Well, it's not my eyes betraying me, I think, relieved.

Alright, I say.

She pauses. Be careful when adults are being careful about what they're going to say. It is never a good sign. I take a deep breath, imagine my chest filling like a balloon, like the coyote in that cartoon, when he realizes he won't catch the roadrunner that day. I look down because I can't stand seeing her pressed pants, her perfect hair surely curled with rollers. I have grown-up sisters. She's always walking around the hallways with her hands in her pockets, like a model in a magazine.

Do you bathe often?

Like what?

Every day?

I don't tell her the bathroom is way in the back of the house and it's dark because it has no electricity. A wire runs from the front all the way to the back to light a small foldout mirror with little bulbs, which is the only light and when it's on, it's so murky that it's almost worse than no light at all. And my sisters usually go first. So I want to ask my brother to shower with me but he's always busy. And even in the warm weather the water is really cold and my sisters take forever and I always have to go at night, and I feel strange being naked in a tiny room surrounded by darkness. So sometimes I don't. And that's when it's warm. When it's colder you have to heat up the water in a tin bucket on the stove, which has four burners but you can't use all four burners at the same time because four people can't bathe at the same time so the water will get cold, and besides, Amá needs burners for dinner. And you don't know how long it takes to heat so many gallons of water. And getting the scalding hot water off the stove is tricky in itself. Water weighs so much. So one bucket of hot water, diluted with cold water, may be good for two buckets of warm water, good for two people to bathe. Then, you have to carry that bucket of warm water to the back of the house. And in the cold months, the bathroom in the back won't do because it's one layer of plywood. You have to bathe in the kitchen, which is warmer once you move the space heater over and private once you hang a quilt over the doorway, clothespin it to corner nails. But you have to be careful not to trip and burn your face off when you move the space heater because it is heavy and has no handles and the gas hose is made of tough rubber so it's not very flexible and the ceramic bricks are so hot they glow red. Then you have to bring in the washtub Amá washes clothes in. It is too small, and you have to be careful not to get the kitchen floor too wet. Every bowlful of water must be poured over the body carefully and deliberately. You can't sit and you can't stand, so you have to crouch the whole time and the whole time watch your elbows because water runs down them and out, and the linoleum is already peeling. And you have to watch the side of the tub that's closest to the heater because sometimes it can burn. Then after you're done you have to empty the washtub outside, which usually requires two people. And you can't do it yourself because Amá says it's not healthy to go outside into the cold right after bathing. So you have to ask two other people to do it. Then you have to mop the floor. Then more heating of water, then it becomes late really quick because all this started after dinner, once the kitchen was available. Then I am too tired.

And what does it matter anyway if even after I shower, sometimes I go a little in my underwear because I try to hold it in because I'm scared of the dark because I'm an idiot. I know I shouldn't be but when I'm walking to the bathroom in the back of the house I'm always thinking someone's gonna jump out of the shadows, someone with angry eyes and hands, though I don't know what they'll do to me. I never get that far, only that they jump up from behind and grab me. And the odd thing is, when I was little in México, I wasn't afraid of the dark. The moonlight was enough and the stars were so many. I didn't know of monsters then. So maybe if I can just go to the bathroom when I need to, if I can be the big boy I should be and not be afraid of the dark, I won't need to bathe too often.

So no, I don't bathe every day, I bathe on weekends mostly and I don't know why you had to tell me, why you had to care this much, if Amá hardly gets after me about it. This is what I want to say. But Amá is always only at home, and this here is where I am, speaking to a grown-up in a language Amá doesn't speak. And I feel my face tightening because all this is pouring itself inside. My hands tingle now resting on the sides of the chair like they want to move, but what I really want to do is unbutton my pants a little because they're tight at the waist because they're girl pants. They're okay around the hips and they're black so I figured I could wear them when Amá pulled them out of a garbage bag and showed them to me like a long lost gift, but every once in a while when no one's looking, I unbutton them so my stomach can rest a little, so I can rub my hands over the pinched skin at my waist. That's what I want to do, but there is Mrs. Resendez, her large eyes confused and maybe a little angry because I haven't said anything.

Yes. I'm sorry, I say.

So, as I was saying . . . Do you use deodorant?

No.

I say it like I've just realized this, not because I could never remember to use it but because it just never occurred to me.

You might want to use deodorant. Some brands are better than others. Mitchum is a good brand.

Oh. Okay.

Are you alright?

Mm-hmm.

The ants did not seize the night to crawl inside me. I should be happy, really, because no one's complained about my wandering eyes. I should.

In a back corner of her office is a plant, a fake little tree. I used to think those things in offices were real, because why wouldn't they be. I touched one once, looked at it closely, saw the stitching, felt the rubbery surface, the leaves' rough edges, the color that never changed. They weren't real. This one looks hard, stiffened by the thin layer of dust that accumulates, the air whirring softly but constantly, rotated by the air-conditioning unit outside, the machine in charge of what we breathe in and out. The plant looks withered, even though it can't be.

You've taken this very well, she says a little surprised.

I smile because that always works.

I'll look for that deodorant. Anything else? I ask.

No, I guess not. That's all. Enjoy the rest of your afternoon.

Okay.

The class period is over, I can hear the student traffic between classes, the shuffle of sneaker soles.

I'll see you tomorrow, I say.

See you tomorrow, Joe.

The next day I show up in my best clothes, those saved for visiting relatives on the other side: navy blue dress pants and a sky blue button-down shirt and black belt that came with the pants. And my brother's cologne. I'm anxious for Mrs. Resendez to see me.

Oh, you look so nice and smell so nice. Is that cologne? she asks in a big way, her eyebrows arched, straight set of white teeth shining between her wide smile.

Yes, I say proudly. And then something happens. Mrs. Resendez walks away and I'm left in the common area alone and feeling dumb, like a dog getting a treat. I thought taking the most advanced classes and earning the best grades would be enough. All the teachers smiled at me because I was so bright. I didn't mind waiting for the school bus after school, because this made it so I could stay longer, walk the wide tiled hallways when they were vacant, visit some of my classrooms and talk to the teachers about nothing, watch them gather their papers into their big bags. Then when they turned off the light and locked their room, I'd say bye and make my way to the sunken library in the center of the building, carpeted and bordered with glass windows. From outside the glass, the carpet looked soft, so soft I imagined I could sleep inside, no need for blankets, just my backpack for a pillow and my dreams that would become the books all around me. I wouldn't be afraid of the dark then.

But I can't come dressed like this every day. And I'm too embarrassed to ask Amá to buy me deodorant. My navy blue sneakers have holes in them, right above my big toes that push up and I only have two pairs of dark socks to match the sneakers to camouflage the big hole. You get what you pay for, Amá said of the shoes.

The other counselor comes in, sees me, and asks What's the occasion? I say No occasion, and go back to stapling handouts.

part six
1988 *to* 1991

older

Vengan a comer, Tía Jacinta yells to the men outside. They amble away to go sit at the dining table while I stay behind, stand just outside the doorframe admiring the results of Tía Jacinta's green thumb. Ven a sentarte, says Amá from the doorframe. I turn and stare, not sure of what she's implying. Ven a sentarte con los hombres, she says, serious. Then she returns to the kitchen. So I obey and sit down to eat with my father and Luis and uncle and guy cousins who are all older than me, because I am now too old to sit with the women and children. I am fourteen, and I get to eat before they do. I think this has something to do with the idea that men do the "hard labor" and so must get their fill first to keep their bodies strong, while the women, who stay at home, can make do with the leftovers. Except I don't do hard labor and my grownup sisters work outside the home. But I don't say anything.

On the couch and chairs at the other end of the room sit most of my sisters and girl cousins, the ones who aren't serving in the kitchen this time, all of them older than me. Before I can think that they will never be old enough to be served before I am served, before I can tell whether they are looking out at the beauty of the flowering plants or just looking away, before I can see whether Yara is staring at me or staring past me, my uncle asks me how I like the meal. Todo muy sabroso, I respond digging into my lowest voice, trying to sound like a grown-up, trying to sound like a man.

josh

I am standing on Tía Lydia's driveway. Next door is a house made of brick, with tinted windows to keep out the heat. It looks abandoned but I see it isn't, because there's Josh outside. Josh of the mop of yellow hair, the birthday party with the nerf ball, the angry mom. I never saw him in middle school, haven't seen him in high school yet. But there he is next door helping his mother with what look like grocery bags. They must have walked to the store, because I see no car.

I stand for a long time because I want him to see me, remember me who came to his birthday party, come up excited, surprised at the coincidence. I want to ask him where he goes to school. I want to tell him the great news—that my sister Myrna graduated from college and is now a State Trooper way up in the Texas panhandle. That she makes a lot of money and is helping my parents build a new home. That someone bought the old house, ripped it up from the ground and took it, leaving one big empty space. That looking at the empty space felt like looking at a book with all its pages torn out. I've learned houses can leave too. So now we're staying with Tía Lydia, again. Like when we first got here, I want to say. And even though Tía smiles a lot, Amá only wants to cross her arms and legs, to make herself into a little knot of a bird, to show us how to behave in a place that isn't ours.

Josh, I want to say, the house will be a real dream once it's ready real soon, just in time for Christmas. It's way smaller than Tía's house, but it's just as pretty, with a real sink. No more emptying the bucket of slop. New linoleum flowery like a quilt. An electric outlet on every wall, not like the old house with the ceiling light outlet and the extension cords all tangled up. The bathroom indoors. No more running in the dark. No more heating water. Windows that stay up all by themselves. A whole separate room with just enough space for a washer and dryer and all the necessary hookups for hot and cold water. So Amá can finally use the washer that Myrna got her long ago, the one she's never been able to use. She won't ever have to wash by hand again.

And, Josh, here's the best part: an indoor air-conditioning unit and ducts to all the rooms, every one. The house will be air-conditioned.

But Josh doesn't see me. Josh, with his long skinny legs and pants still too short for him, disappears into the dark behind the front door. And I dream of a house that won't fight me anymore when I sleep.

sinks, doors, hot water

December, we move in.

Amá gets her own room. Elsa and Yara share a second. Luis and I get the third. And I feel rich.

With the walls that are layered—brick, wood frame, insulation, drywall—the winter night is nothing, nothing at all. We still need quilts but just a couple.

Then spring comes and it turns out this house is hotter than the old one. The brick walls act like an oven. I ask Amá if I can turn the air conditioner on, but she says that the outside unit, the motor that is the source of the cooling air, is not included in the building of the home. It costs seven hundred dollars. So no central air yet. Anyway, she says, if we had the unit, the light bill would be crazy high, so maybe it's better this way.

At night we open the windows all the way, the bedroom doors as well, the floor fan whirs, and I keep reminding myself: closets, electrical outlets, shiny linoleum, sink, indoor bathroom, fancy windows, straight walls.

Mornings, we move the floor fan to the kitchen. We say nothing about the heat.

parking lot

You wouldn't think parking lots could speak, or buses or cars. But they all do. Many things without voices speak. At the junior high most of us take the bus or walk away and a few, only a few, are picked up by parents in nice sedans.

At the high school the doors of the main building exit out to a long driveway where the buses park, load students, and rumble away, making room for more buses to park and do the same. Beyond the driveway is the student parking lot, fenced with chain link and large and filled with the cars of students who drive themselves to school.

Inside the bus we wait until it is filled to capacity—two, sometimes three per seat. The windows often don't work, haven't for a long time. We've stopped trying. Out the closed window, all the students with their own cars—and they must be their own for how could a borrowed vehicle sit all day unused—walk through the lanes, their gait soft and sure. As they say good-bye to each other, heads disappear between rows, their keys in their hands, as if they have always been there dangling from their fingers all day long in the classroom, in the hallways, in the bathrooms, the playing field. Many of their names sound like the names in history books, presidents' names, writers' names, important sounding names. They come from that junior high that is so far north I've never seen it, nobody I know has ever seen it, that junior high that doesn't know where my old junior high is either. They are the ones who don't eat cafeteria food because they buy their lunch every day at the annex.

The thing is, they aren't being chocantes when they buy their food from the other set of cooks, when they float over to their cars; they're not rubbing our noses in it, I can tell, because they move like every person around them has soft drinks for lunch instead of milk, move like everyone is friends with the teacher, move like everyone owns a car. Move like they don't see the buses, don't see the students lined outside, don't see me inside. They don't hear the old coughing motors, don't smell the exhaust. They smile always, always smile, and I wonder what it must be like to float like that across pavement.

A car roars by, the profile full of smile like it's something that feeds you. A boy crashes into the seat next to me. Sometimes the boys are stout, strong, dressed in tight jeans and button-down shirts unbuttoned to show off their chests. And they walk like they own the bus, their girlfriends tailing them. But this boy is all long lanky arms and lean legs, his face and forearms glistening. He reminds me of the boys strolling through the neighborhood who look at you like they already carry in their pockets a lifetime's worth of anger. They wear undershirts like my uncle's, without sleeves, with scooped necks. Their arms marked with tattoos. I imagine the needle, the little stabs, the blood, and I wonder what drives them to do that to themselves, to go look for hurt. It is then that I am glad for fences. But here in the bus, knees bang against knees. The boy's furrowed brow lets me know he's not in the mood for chatting. I know to look away out the window.

But, really, there is nothing new to see, so I step off the bus, because today I'll walk home. By the time I get there with the sun heavy on my back, I'll be so dehydrated my piss will be yellower than a pineapple snow cone. I don't care. Anyway, I'll take a break at the cool grocery store, read magazines about the lives of famous people all big hair, draped shoulders, and candy smiles.

The parking lot simmers with bright cars and big hair, a parade of the sun's glare on metallic reds and blues, boys in jeans washed into that worn look on purpose, sneakers with loud laces and soles hardly worn down. Girls with purses bigger than books, with blouses like billboards with names like Esprit and Guess written in pastel colors. All of them moving slow, unhurried, as they ask each other what's going on, what are you doing tonight, what are you up to. Every question an invitation.

I follow the railroad tracks south, and I imagine the lot empty behind me.

now distant and wordless

The guy behind the cash register at KB Toys hands me a job application. Soon I'm sitting in the store's backroom with the manager and his huge belly that I'm trying not to stare at. Why should I hire you? he asks, like he's not really interested in the answer. I want to say Because I want the money to have something in my wallet, because my mom needs the money to help with the bills and blood pressure medication, because getting hired is what you gotta do when you grow up, because it's time, but none of it seems like the proper thing to say. So I say I like working around children. He rolls his eyes. Are you reliable, are you punctual? he asks exasperated. Yes, yes, of course, I say.

It's minimum wage, part-time, and some nights you will be closing, which means vacuuming the entire store, straightening up the aisles, making it look new again for the following day. We'll get out at around midnight or one those nights.

Okay, I say in my most enthusiastic voice, though I'm nervous as hell. When I got about as tall as Amá, I figured I should work, but Amá said No, study, hold off on that. And I was secretly relieved because the truth is I didn't want to be in a workplace, another place to have to watch my hands, my voice, my eyes. And I still am scared, but I'm sixteen now.

The first few days, I work in the backroom—which looks like a big dumpster, waist high with opened boxes—pricing boxes of new toys, mostly action figures. First, the price on the price sticker must be slashed with a red pen and relabeled with a lower, discounted price. Then that sticker goes on the new toy. After that, I'm moved to the floor for customer service. Weekends suck with so many children, it's almost unbelievable. The droning of the hive never stops and we're told that sometimes kids try to take stuff without paying so we have to keep an eye on the entrance, like a cop.

Years ago, Luis and I walked to the mall. One of the smaller stores had a whole bin of little Transformer-like toys, little robots that turned to jet planes. They weren't Transformer brand so they were cheaper, but it didn't really matter because when you have no money, you have no money for anything cheap or otherwise. Walking back from the mall, Luis pulled out of his pocket one of those little robots and it looked even prettier in the sunlight. I was shocked and delighted, and judging by how Luis kept shifting his eyes, I knew he'd taken it without paying. I imagined a cop sneaking up on us and telling us what Luis had done was wrong and telling me I was guilty too for letting my hands hold it. But just then, Luis said Let's go back. And I knew I wouldn't get to play with it after all. He snuck it back into the store, dropped it back into the bin.

As Christmas approaches it becomes almost silly to pick up toys and place them back on the shelf because three seconds later they're back on the floor. The store seems more a preschool because children roam unattended. But their behavior isn't much different even with parents by them. And when they leave something on the floor, or scream their heads off in temper tantrums that last for aisles, or drop their popsicle on the carpet, the parents don't correct them or scold them for being unmindful or careless or spoiled. We're leaving, is all they say and walk away from the mess their child created.

The only thing the rich are interested in is becoming richer, so never expect any kindness from them, certainly not any disinterested kindness, Amá always says. And what could I expect from those who spend hundreds of dollars or pesos on junk with a look that says Serve me. They can't even stand waiting in line, keep rolling their eyes and pursing their lips, especially behind someone who's buying a cheap toy, one toy, paying with a five.

What are you gonna do, says Amá, that's the rich. And the Mexican rich are worse.

Maybe she has a point, Mexican rich people have a particularly blunt way of thumbing their noses at the poor or the poorer. They want to move ahead in line because they're buying more expensive things. They talk in loud, full voices like they've never been told to quiet down. They move through the mall like they have no time to spare for anyone but their own kind. But maybe they're not really different from the American rich. Maybe they just don't care to hide it, their scowls that say Why do I have to share this space with you? Why must I be reminded that you exist?

At night, when Luis comes to pick me up, I think of Elsa who worked at Chick-fil-A for years, of how Norma would come pick her up and I'd tag along for the ride, hoping Elsa would have some leftover waffle fries. If you ate them right away, you could catch their last bit of warmth.

When I get my first paycheck, I feel like a man, and when I look at the stub and know taxes, I want to tear up the check and go home. But I don't. I give some to Amá, which she tucks in her bra, as she lowers her eyes and says timidly, You're hardly keeping any for yourself. The rest I keep for my expenses, like lunch during my break, which is lunch at the mall, which makes me feel fat with success because I can take myself out to eat now. I don't have to wait for Elsa's waffle fries or math competitions with Mr. Gonzalez, I can go get some myself, hot out of the fryer. When I am eating, I am like everyone else eating at the mall, and this feels like the beginning of something big, something important, something like a long journey, one that goes uphill so that at the end you're looking down at the world that's now distant and wordless like a landscape photo.

open house

It is a strange sight, the school at night, aglow with light emanating from all its open doors. Amá, Luis, Yara, and I walk toward it, together. Amá begins to lag behind. We slow our pace and she catches up but eventually lags behind again, like she prefers to walk one step behind us.

In every room, we find a corner to stand in, Amá wringing her hands like she owes the room money. I tell her about how crowded the school is, built for half the number of students that now live a third of their lives in it. The teacher walks to us. In every room I translate for the teacher. In every room I translate for Amá. In every room I am a gran estudiante. The Spanish reminds me of church. The Spanish sounds foreign—talk of literature, talk of math, talk of science. In every room the white students marvel at my perfect Spanish, my Spanish without an accent, avert their eyes from my mother's lack of English.

In every room they harbor the suspicion, hear the language, my first tongue, the telling sign that I could not be from here, that I could not be American. How they look at me, see someone they didn't imagine.

statue of liberty

Once I had a student who didn't like it when I mentioned the KKK and racism in the same sentence, says Mr. Williams who is taking a break from his lecture on American history because it's a good class and we all pay attention.

Mr. Williams, with his short mustache and long comb-over, whistles while he pages through his notes, enjoying what he talks about like wars and nations and the branches of government and the pilgrims. Mr. Williams, who carries our papers in his leather satchel. Mr. Williams, who I imagine walking down the hallway at the end of the day, into his car, onto the street, into his home, a home I imagine furnished with a desk and a plush chair, and his favorite books on the Bill of Rights—the great men who thought them up, so wise their words are still with us, so great we still love them for what they said. On a wall, a large photograph of the Statue of Liberty, that tall woman with a crown that reminds me of Jesus's crown of thorns, a lit torch held high, and a face that doesn't look friendly at all, a face that makes me wonder whether she's aiming to light Ellis Island or burn it down. Though I wouldn't say that to Mr. Williams in that home where he is happy and fed because what he loves is how he makes his living. What he loves feeds him. I imagine knocking on his front door and smiling when he says Hi come on in, in that voice light and friendly like a father in an American sitcom. And after sitting with me by the window, he'd say If you want this, you could have this, you could teach history, too. And then he'd mess up my hair in that both rough and tender way fathers do to their sons right before they hug them in movies.

In the classroom, Joe Pereira, who used to be José in sixth grade while I became Joe, sits in front of me. Yes, he became Joe too. Eventually every José becomes Joe. Right in front of Joe is Mr. Williams's desk.

Sitting on his stool and tipping his head forward to peer over his reading glasses, Mr. Williams continues: So this student, she said the KKK wasn't about lynching blacks anymore, that her father was a member of the KKK and that it was about family and picnics and barbecue, and I said, Yeah, about barbecueing blacks.

And he chuckles, amused with himself. And the class exhales a Whoah, like Them's fightin' words. And then we all chuckle hesitantly, not sure if it's out of actual delight or simple politeness.

Seriously though . . . , he continues, as he scans the room to his right where most of the girls sit, to his left where most of the boys sit, and in the middle where I am.

Seriously, racism is bad. It's like a disease and you have to be careful you don't catch it, like with homosexuality.

The classroom falls silent, not like when the teacher enters the room at the beginning of class, slow and smooth, but like when someone opens the door in the middle of class, sudden, breathless, like we might get a chance to leave, like we've always been wanting to leave.

It's like a disease and so it's something that can be cured, he adds in that white boyish voice of his, laid back, flippant, free of all uncertainty.

He looks at everyone and he looks at me and I think his eyes fall over me for more than a second. But I must be getting paranoid because there is no way he would know. I'm very good about limiting my comments in class so as not to call attention to myself, particularly from the football team to my right.

And so he ends his aside, the little anecdote to punctuate the lecture. The bell rings, and we stand up in a hurry because the day is over. Have a good afternoon, he says, as he grabs his leather satchel from his desk.

In his home in my head Mr. Williams was always wearing his reading glasses and smiling, loving the world entirely, like it was his book to teach. In my head he never said Watch out for homosexuals, because he just never thought of them. And sometimes I think I could ask him if in between his talks of countries being born and countries dying, he imagines a country where all homosexuals are sent, a country apart from all other countries, some space where they won't infect anyone with their sickness which is them—a nation of Rock Hudsons groaning in a pain that is long past the point of tears, so they don't cry, only shield their eyes from the harsh light of the sun with their clumsy bony hands almost already ash. I wonder if this means México is better off since I left it.

We pick up our spirals and textbooks, make our way out of the classroom, less murmurs and grunts and squeals than usual. He didn't call homosexuality an abomination, I think. At least he didn't call it that. At least a diseased person deserves some compassion, though probably not enough to let him sit in your home and follow in your footsteps like a son. It is obvious now that the dream of befriending him is mere fantasy, an illusion, something I shouldn't waste time with anymore, something I should bury underneath a heavy object, an object that will never be moved and so never show its underside, something like a stone or one of those monuments to great men, those who inspired others so much that their statue is never moved so that nothing else can take the place of what they stood for.

scarlet

Reading about history or algebraic equations is great fun, but reading novels is something completely different. And there are so many of them, I had no idea. When I was little I thought it couldn't get better than pop-up books, the ones I leafed through at the book fairs and old torn ones I checked out from the school library, but I was wrong.

The Scarlet Letter is certainly not pop-up, has no drawings even like *The Call of the Wild* did back then. It's so many pages of words, but they add up to something I want to hold with me all the time in the hallways and at the public library and walking home, which is my favorite part of the day, because I can be alone then. I know the railroad tracks so well, I can walk on them and read at the same time and when I am reading, there's no traffic, there's no sun, there's no nothing. It's like I disappear into the words and the world they conjure, like I fade away into them. Nathaniel, Nathaniel—I let the name linger on my tongue like candy.

The way Hester Prynne is branded with that letter sucks because then everybody knows what she's done and what she's done becomes who she is. And before she even arrives, she's already been judged. She's everywhere already, not her really but the idea of her. And how do you escape the idea of you? How do you introduce yourself to someone when they already have a letter for you? How do you escape the letter? And yet by the end of the book, she has. She's turned that letter on her chest into something else, not through fighting or fleeing but simply through living, through the work of the every day. She just keeps on breathing. And it feels like a fuck-you to everyone, but one that is quiet because it isn't about showing the other that you are not ashamed, because it is not about the other, it is a fuck-you that is serene and essential, that breathes like the waves at the shore where she lives in that house at the edge of town. Her letter becoming something else, something unforeseen, something unimaginable, something beautiful.

I've only seen the ocean once, as a kid, when I went to South Padre

Island with a friend and his family. It was messy and enormous, looked like it wanted to come swallow me. I walked up to that thing that was like a universe and let it wet my feet. It felt like eternity touching me. I ran back.

When I imagine Hester in a little house by the sea, I imagine the house I was born in transported to South Padre Island, and Hester in it. The other people at the beach look at Hester weird every time she steps outside because she's in that old-style dress, and the letter is still on her chest and she's not wearing sunscreen on her nose or holding a beer can. But she doesn't see them, doesn't care that they are there. For her, they are not. I imagine her stepping out to the shore, wading into it, the water lapping up to her thighs. The ocean swells and heaves, but she does not buckle, not even inside, just stands there, her entire body one big yes because she knows she is the ocean.

At home, Amá sometimes leafs through my books and always says the same thing: It doesn't even have drawings. I tell Amá the books don't have drawings because they're stories. The stories that matter, the ones that have remained this long it seems just to find me, to be read by me. The ones I wish I could write because to write them would be like commanding the ocean. But I don't tell this to anyone, not to my mother, not to the teacher. No, because it is a fool's dream. The kind of dream that is so impossible, so very distant, you wonder how it is that you even think it. Because it is foolish that you do, foolish that you think you have any right to dream this dream. This dream that doesn't belong to you but to others, people you'll never even get to meet, people who lived a long time ago and in faraway places where snow is falling, making everything romantic, falling over them with their handsome names like those of presidents. Nathaniel. Nathaniel Rodríguez—just listen how stupid that sounds.

Even so, I don't know why sometimes I dream that I've written words printed in bound pages that nest inside people, inside their chests, and when they are reading them, they are reading me, and when they hold them, they are holding me.

part seven

1992 *to* **1993**

beginning

This time my family is here to see me. I am the last one to graduate from high school. This time I'm seeing the seated crowd at the stadium from the green field.

I stand up, walk down the row that stretches out across the front of the stadium, alphabetical order. So like kindergarten. My friends do the same. Everybody is here, the ones who didn't drop out, in their caps and gowns, in rich purple and gold, as if at least this evening, we are all the same. And I wish life were this, every day a ceremony, every day rich in purple and gold.

After the last person gets their fake diploma, after the last old man and his words, the families flood the field—grandparents, neighbors, everybody. Our neighbor Lucy is here, too. Tía Lydia is here. Tía Eugenia is here. We take pictures. My friends and I say We made it. More pictures.

Amá's made a dinner in my honor: chicken salad, potato salad, chips and dip, and some chicken in mole sauce and rice. When she hugs me, she holds me a little tighter, a little longer. Felicidades, she says. Muchas felicidades, m'hijo.

The high school has organized a celebration at a sports center to offer a "safer" alternative to the partying going on tonight. The high school has been touting it heavily, promising door prizes, free food, a pool. I told my mother before tonight that I wanted to go. She said Okay, as long as you'll spend a little bit of time with family, with your tíos. I said yes. After an hour at my own party, I leave for the sports center.

The door prizes are CDs by foreign artists nobody knows. All the food is already gone. The music promised is a band made up of high school students—rich kids with expensive hobbies.

One of those rich kids was in class once talking about the GPA rankings for the graduating class of nearly seven hundred students. After naming the valedictorian and salutatorian and so on, he came to number five and didn't know who it was. That's me, I said. Oh, he said, and walked away.

I regret coming, feel bad for ditching my party at home, but I don't say it because it wouldn't be cool to admit how much it means, even if I knew. After walking around the gym complex, my friends and I end up in an empty aerobics room, the music blaring from the speakers. We take a few mats leaning against one wall and spread them out, lie on our backs, and stare at the ceiling. Nobody wants to say it, what a letdown this party has been, what a sad way to end the night.

Some of my friends are leaving far away to college, leaving the state entirely. It's a good thing, and I am proud of them. I hope tomorrow, the day after graduation, means something new, something better, even though I am not leaving. Even though I am staying. I hope tomorrow means I will one day be better, one day be new. Maybe if I keep reading, keep studying, keep working, keep earning money, keep behaving in that way the world wants you to behave, keep being good, maybe one day all this will be enough.

siren

The library at the college campus is the largest one I've ever seen. It is four stories tall and I want to tell Amá all about it, except for the books I read there. I've found more books on human sexuality, more than at the public library.

They look like textbooks and they usually have a chapter on homosexuality grouped with the unit on deviant behaviors like bestiality and sadomasochism, and I learn all about homosexuals and porn theatres and bathhouses during the seventies and eighties, about how they're becoming a thing of the past as homosexuality becomes more mainstream in larger metropolitan areas. The chapters also talk about cruising and popular gathering spots and subgroups. All this reminds me of that video store at the edge of town. It's called Dollar Video and I never really thought too much about the fact that it never advertises new movies or has any windows or many cars in the parking lot during the day. At night, though, the parking lot is full.

One night I drive by and a cop car idles outside, its lights bright like fire. What's going on inside? What else do I not know? What else do the books not say? What other library is out there with more to learn? Because knowledge seems to come in doses, like mathematics. When you're little the teacher says only even numbers can be divided by two. Then the next year you learn about fractions and realize odd numbers too can be divided by two. So fractions exist but negative numbers don't, there are no numbers smaller than zero. Then the next year you learn about negative numbers, so there's an X-axis. Then you learn there's also a Y-axis, but that's it, you're told. Then later it turns out there's also a Z-axis, and together the three axes correspond to the three-dimensional space we inhabit, but that's it. Then you study matrices and it turns out that mathematically there are plenty more dimensions, except only a few gifted mathematicians claim to sort of visualize them. And by the way, you can very much take the square root of a negative number. But all along you think, Well some things still hold, like the fact that the sum of the angles of a triangle always add up to 180 degrees, no exceptions. Then the university professor says, well, high school geometry doesn't account for the curvature of space, which is a reality of the universe. For example, take two points along the Earth's equator and draw a line to form the base of a triangle. Now, draw a line from each point to the North Pole and you have a triangle; the base angles are each ninety-degree angles, which is already 180 degrees but you still have to add the third angle at the top. So that high school lesson was also a kind of lie.

It's the same with sex. At first the penis is only for peeing. Then it turns out no, it's not only for peeing, it's for making babies too, but love has to be involved in it. Then it turns out love doesn't really have to be involved, but it's still mostly to have kids so it has to be a guy and a girl together and don't think about the other stuff. Then, it's yeah there's other stuff, other thoughts and fantasies, but they're mostly transitory. Then when they're not transitory, it's yeah for some people it's not transitory, but it's different because they can't have children so it doesn't count and anyway they're so few of them you can't really see them and besides they're all gonna get AIDS because God hates them. Also, they're not really around, except in large cities. Then it turns out they may be around except only at the edge of town and only at night and only for one thing because that's all they are. And by the time you figure there are others like you, you don't even know how to speak it, how to breathe it, because you weren't even supposed to be. For so long, you didn't even exist.

I think that's why so many kids fail in math, because they so internalized the earlier rule, that they can't accommodate the later one that breaks that rule. And just when they're internalizing that second rule, allowing for that exception or that new aspect of numbers and the mysterious ways in which they work, here comes another rule to break that one. Every time your heart's broken a little by the lie, until all of you feels like a stress fracture. But maybe that's just me.

Here's the thing: I figure every line in the universe eventually intersects. It doesn't matter that they're parallel or on different planes, like the high school teacher said, because everything shifts. The planet rotates and orbits and turns on its axis, so all the lines traversed through the surface will intersect with the same ones made a season later. And you have to figure the sun is also turning on its own axis, so that has to shift the entire solar system. And you don't think the galaxy is shifting? So I figure, when all lines eventually intersect, when all that crossing creates a chaos no mathematician can decipher into order, when everything comes crashing into each other, is it like a black hole or a supernova? The end of a universe or the beginning? The day dawning or the day dying?

The lights above the police car whirl without the siren, and it seems like a contradiction, a warning that isn't fully uttered. I wonder if there are men in there doing the thing I dream of when I let myself dream of it, if that thing they do mends the heart or further breaks it.

the three enemies, or, bridge

The pen is in my hand now. On the other side of this moment is the college scholarship from NASA, an opportunity I am almost certain the scholarship-selection committee will see that I deserve, once I become a U.S. citizen. The interview is over and the man waits for me to sign the form and so surrender all allegiance to México. This surrender is supposed to be a good thing.

Maybe if there were no flags or bridges or razor-wire fences or birth certificates, you could love a place and it would be just that, a place, not a country. And then you wouldn't ever have to say good-bye to it, even if you left, because leaving it would be different. It would not be this, a good-bye that feels like a wall rising.

I sign.

Congratulations, he says. Expect an appointment for your certificate in a few weeks.

He smiles politely. I do too, and we shake hands. Then I turn fast and walk away because I don't want to be here anymore. I'm done.

made natural

Weeks later, as promised, I get the appointment to pick up my naturalization certificate at the Holiday Inn. The ballroom is full, hundreds of people receiving theirs. I thought it would be an individual thing in a mousy office and a man in another short-sleeve button-down shirt visibly tired from long hours with people with divided families and questions and barely-okay pay would hand me the certificate, saying Here you go and wave me off. Thanks, I'd say politely and turn to go, then find a moment out in the parking lot so no one would see me pull it out of the envelope and look at it, my photo floating in it.

The stage, the flags of Texas, the United States, and México, standing solemnly at one end, the old man speaking in that measured self-important way, all of it reminds me of my high school graduation. He speaks of America, how great it is, how being naturalized means falling under the umbrella of American laws and rights, privileges and responsibilities. And that isn't all of it amazing? I am reminded of one of my history teachers in junior high and his lecture on Manifest Destiny, the belief that America was meant to extend its young borders all the way to the Pacific. He made it sound noble and patriotic and almost inevitable. That the country, with its current borders and traffic and factories, was precisely the way it was meant to be. So that young America and present America were kind of like the same thing only young and old, the way one looks at a child and dreams not of all the things that it could be but of all the things that it should be, all the things that it must be, all the things that it will be. And that was the doctrine that made this country what it is, he proclaimed, smiling wide because it was a grand thing.

I am certain now that I will get that NASA scholarship. Just look at me.

I imagine graduating from college, getting the bright house with perfect right-angle corners and the car with the cleanest carpet and coolest air conditioner and the shoes with the softest insoles. I'll eat out every day and never have to use coupons. And I'll never have to remind myself to slow down while eating in public, because I will never feel bad about leaving food on the plate.

My name is called, and I go up to receive my certificate. When I walk back to my chair, I look down at it and it has a border with squiggly lines and some fancy font that reminds me of the perfect attendance certificates I was awarded as a kid, sometimes for the entire year, sometimes consecutive years. I'd bring them to Amá and she'd look at them thoughtfully until I told her what they were for and then she'd go back to staring at them but smiling big this time. I'd let her put them in a safe place where maybe the mice wouldn't get to them. I thought those certificates were almost magical, like they were made in some special factory in some secret room of the school. But then one day at Wal-Mart I saw the office supplies aisle, all the little plastic containers you saw on teacher's desks were there, the pencil holders, the staplers, the stacked paper trays, all the things that made order a virtue. And next to them was the thick certificate paper, blank with only the fancy border. Big packets of them, some opened, some bent. They weren't magical at all.

When I look up, the old man is facing the American flag, hand over his heart, reciting the pledge of allegiance. Everyone is standing doing the same. I get up and join them and the words are no longer phonetic and no longer just big words. Now I know them all, the sounds round like gold coins, all our voices chanting, the chant more powerful than the voice, like the words themselves don't even matter anymore.

Now, when I cross the bridge back from the pharmacy on the other side, I won't have to show any identification card or passport at the checkpoint, won't have to surrender them to the officer, won't have to wait for him to hand them back. I'll look straight at him and say American Citizen, like I've seen others do, and like the officer does to them, he will smile at me politely, almost friendly, and wave me through, because I will be so convincing, he will have no choice but to believe me. He will see it in my eyes. He will hear it in my voice, the tongue trained for so many years, it won't even have an accent.

the other side

The car ambles along the dirt road that leads to the village, the same dirt road. Apá's driving. Amá's in the passenger seat.

Tía Jacinta and her family are living back in the village. Every time I cross the bridge to come back here, my uncle asks me the same question: How are you doing, Josesito? and I say the same thing: Doing well, uncle, going to school. Then he and Apá start talking about crops and irrigation ditches, and I walk off. I want to go see the goats milling around the old house, the chickens looking for bugs, the mesquite tree, whatever may be left of it. I always feel that I stand out around here, but I figure if anyone notices me, they will notice the good things: my clean, bathed body, my combed hair, my sneakers, the good kind that aren't fake like the ones at the flea market that come unglued right away, and my new shirt and jeans from JC Penney, all bought with my part-time work in my old high school—where I proctor GED exams and type up transcripts with carbon copies and answer the phone and never sweat—and what remains from the NASA scholarship after tuition and books. Astronauts smile at me from space.

People will peer from behind their windows and doorframes and guess that I am probably not from here, that I have come from some faraway place with someone else, that I've walked off on my own because there's nothing else to do here but walk off. Maybe some gray-haired woman will see the boy behind my face and remember: Es Josesito, hijo de Esperanza y Perfecto. Josesito, tan grande.

Yes, grown-up, all nineteen years of me.

A house stands closer to the road, in front of my old house. It has always been there and some other family has always lived there. I know this because the few times I've come here from Tía Jacinta's, the little front porch is always swept. And I think maybe a woman will walk out wearing an apron and holding a broom or a load of laundry to wash by hand in a tub, and she will see me. I will tell her I was born here, inside that house, and she will be impressed at how well I've turned out. She will eye me up and down in a subtle way that I will still notice.

That moment when I stand before the house, the remnants of it, that moment will be beautiful. So beautiful, in fact, that if this were a novel, that would be the ending, the one that justifies everything that's come before it, gives centering meaning to all the details, becomes something so great you can almost sink into it. Yes, that ending, like standing before the ocean.

But when I get there, the goats and the chickens are gone. Everything is gone. It's like nothing that lives shelters itself there anymore. Everything is weeds and brush that tower above me. The house is surrounded by them, and all I can make out are crumbling walls, rot, no longer useful even for goats. I try to make my way through because I suddenly feel the urge to go up to the door, to touch it, maybe even open it, see what has become of this place, but thorns scratch my arms. The brush is too thick, and I don't know how that can be when it hardly rains here. I step back. The makeshift kitchen assembled with little logs is crumbling because the logs are being pulled out by people. One day all of it will be gone, rotted away or turned to kindling for someone's cooking or warmth.

I think of closing my eyes to see it new again, how it used to be when I was little, but it isn't necessary. I see it now. All the brush is gone. A train whistles in the distance. Children giggle behind trees. The pig sleeps in the pen. The mesquite sways tall, its glossy leaves thrashed clean by a hard wind. The walls of the house are not rotting. The door opens and I expect my mother. But it is not my mother. It is only a room in shadow, welcoming, like a cool shade.

And then I see it—what it is. The brush is once again eating away at the walls. The railroad sleeps, the mesquite sits bent like an old man, and nobody giggles.

Nobody from the neighboring house with the swept porch comes out, and it's okay. Instead, a chicken unexpectedly steps out of the brush, pecking at a small clearing because it sees nourishment where I see only dirt. When it sees me, it doesn't startle. It stares, perfectly round eyes steady, wings folded in, soft as pillows. I want to hold it, but I know it won't let me, so I still myself before it.

I turn to leave and notice a faint yellow through the brush—the neighbor's house, the one with the line of pines, the one with the potted plants out front and the burning garbage out back. But everything is gone, again, the house sits abandoned. I walk around the shrubs to get a better look and see that the house wasn't so different from ours after all, maybe just a little larger, maybe one more room. Most of the paint has flaked off, the screen door long gone. In fact there is no door at all. The only thing that remains of the potted plants is the sculpted rubber tire. It wasn't plant pots at all, just old tires packed with dirt.

I could walk up to what's left of the house, touch it, move into it, but I don't. It doesn't feel right. This wasn't my home. Instead, I stand at the edge, stare at the front yard and from some place deep inside rises the image of a toy horse rocking in the wind, the one I waited for day after day in that pile of ash and debris. My eyes scan this desolate place before I realize I'm looking for him. And I don't know why I would still want him, and I can't believe I still do. I imagine the back corner where the garbage used to burn, where the ashes used to lie. I imagine whatever is left of him is there, sun bleached white now, cracked and missing parts. I walk to the place where the fire left behind what it couldn't claim. I imagine him there and I imagine picking him up, wiping away the dirt that cakes itself to the surface of things after the morning dew, after so many morning dews. I am holding him, beautiful, like I always knew he would be.

Broken but finally mine, I tell him about it all—the kids with their stones, the fire pit, the hungry chicken, the refrigerator, the school with heavy doors, the floorboards outside, the plastic giraffe, the mice in the traps, the onion fields, the earaches, the peaches, the pink walls, the Christmas tree, the cardboard cornflakes, the frozen avocado, the bridge, the men with guns, the razor wire fence, the Indian mother outside the church, the classroom closet, my mother weeping, my father leaving, the beans, the broken oven, my aunt's cakes, my cousin's spit, Tony across the street, the slice of buttered toast, the bed with the plastic sheet, the bed with ants, the soiled underwear, the fake tree in the counselor's office, the gray face of Rock Hudson, the monsters chasing me, the video shop in the dark, the having to say No, thank you, No, thank you, No, thank you.

Then I open my eyes. Then I turn and walk away. The road feels hard under my feet from lack of use, no dirt ground to fine dust. Nobody stands under doorframes. Nobody peers through windows. Actually, most of the houses don't even have windows anymore or doors. I see now that they are empty, abandoned. Even the railroad looks abandoned—the beams not gleaming warm but dull. The passenger train doesn't make a stop here anymore. Only a few gray-blue stones linger. When I get back to Tía Jacinta's house, I stand under the doorframe, tell Amá sitting on the couch that the old house is all covered in brush. Tall, I say. So tall.

Yes, son, without animals, everything becomes overgrown.

Of course. It makes sense that the animals, the goats, would have kept the plot clear, that without their grazing, everything grows back. I ask her then about the other houses around here, where everybody went.

They left, she says.

Where?

Where else?

And she says it in that way she speaks sometimes, where the last of it grows quiet, like she's talking both to me and to herself, like she's sad but from far away.

I nod like I understand everything and walk out. My aunt's potted hibiscus blooms so many threaded vivid reds, so many hearts. The soft light of dusk murmurs something like a prayer for everyone gone, for everyone going. I imagine them crossing a bridge—a bridge they first imagined, like a totem to guard them against a future with an uncertain name—and hope they find what they're searching for on the other side.

In the distance a goat bleats its song.

In this book I have recounted events to the best of my memory, employing the elements of craft necessary to turn life into a literary work, including occasionally condensing time. Fragments of this memoir have been previously published in slightly different form. Addresses and names of individuals and schools have been changed. Memory is, as Mark Doty says, a "transforming, idiosyncratic light," so the thoughts and feelings I express are only my own.

Because of the opportunities that authorship provides, I encourage all women to write, especially if they're at a crossroads or are beginning a new chapter of their lives. Having a book gives you credibility and establishes your authority. It gives you confidence—something I was sorely lacking before becoming an author. Due to childhood medical trauma, including painful tests done without anesthesia, I'd felt unsafe in the world and even in my own body for the longest time. I didn't even realize how much it affected me until the feeling subsided and I started to feel comfortable in my own skin. Moving through my healing process, doing the writing, and promoting my book was part of it. The other part came from the unleashed Kundalini working on my lower chakras, especially one associated with safety and survival.

While this was occurring, I found strength and comfort in the goddesses, who, strangely, seemed to be one and the same as my teacher, whom I'd been told was really no different than me. How was I to understand that? Who were the goddesses, really? My experience was that they represented higher forces I could call upon. Establishing a relationship with them on the outside allowed me to access their power on the inside. By the way, none of this seemed incompatible with any other spiritual beliefs. And apparently others felt the same, because I even saw Catholic nuns at the ashram.

While escaping my marriage and during my divorce, I resonated most with Durga, the warrior goddess who gives a person the strength to rise up and say, "Enough!" when they've been pushed around too long and have finally learned their lessons. Calling upon her power was what allowed me—with the aid of my one small female attorney—to face

down and defeat one of New York's nastiest law firms and its nastiest lawyer. Like a thunderbolt, Durga has the power to destroy anything, including toxic people or influences in your path. Not that it happens all at once. She's the power of perseverance.

You can call upon this invincible mountain goddess within yourself to escape abusive situations and find your strength again when you feel weak. Durga breaks the shackles that bind you and gives you the endurance to bear your trials as you walk the path to freedom. She reminds us all that we're equal to anything, that we all have a tiger inside of us, and that we *are* that tigress when we need to be.

Write

Travel wasn't the only thing I did to get better. I'd spent six years going to therapy three times a week and seven years going to esoteric healing schools, plus I'd spent thousands upon thousands of dollars going to every doctor and quack on the planet trying to heal myself. But none of it worked.

Because I'm a writer, I naturally turned to writing. When I got home from traveling the globe, I began pouring everything out on paper to try make sense of the trauma I'd been through. I wrote about my painful experience, just letting it out on the page and trying to shape it into some kind of narrative. And something really interesting happened. When I finished a third book about my experience and closed that chapter on my life, the chronic fatigue and fibromyalgia disappeared. No one could explain why. Some said it was a miracle, because doctors had told me that there was no cure. I'm not saying that writing is a panacea, but when I started teaching writing workshops, I was struck by the breakthroughs many of my students were having. I knew

there was something extraordinarily powerful about the writing process, and when I started investigating it I found that starting in the 1980s, research was done on writing as a healing modality. It led one expert at the University of Miami to say that although initially skeptical, he later came to believe that it could be as useful as psychotherapy.

But not just any kind of writing. The only kind clinically proven to improve immune function, for example, was expressive writing, which involves writing about personal traumas. This is not just venting on the page, and it's not just the kind of journaling that people do before breakfast. It's a specific type of writing where you write in depth about a disturbing incident or trauma, digging deeply into your thoughts and feelings, including how you felt when it was happening and also how you feel looking back upon it from a distance. Expressive writing helps release negative emotions so you don't keep recycling them, repeating the trauma, or making yourself ill.

Why is writing so powerful? One reason is that your brain is a narrative organ. It understands things in terms of stories. Think about how important stories have been to human history. Think about how important they've been in your life. In layman's terms (at least the way I understand it), if your brain can't make sense of a trauma, like loss, abuse, illness, or an accident, it will churn it over endlessly in a vain attempt to make the story come out right. But if you can construct a thoughtful story around what happened, you can view it from a more empowering perspective, lay it to rest, or even find the silver lining in it. Then you can start writing better scripts for yourself and happier endings.

This was what I'd been doing through writing without even realizing it, because I had to find the meaning in the

madness I'd experienced. And guess what? Writing a book, becoming an author, and going out and speaking to inspire others helped me make my own story come out right. But not only that, healing my soul, arriving at a more powerful place, and assisting others who were stuck, suffering, or desperate to arrive in a place of beauty, peace, and sanctuary made my own trip through hell worth the journey.

Just to underscore how powerful the writing process is, one of my clients shed tears of joy and relief when she wrote a chapter for a group book I put together. She'd never written about the loss of her husband or what she'd had to go through to get her life back after his untimely death. She was amazed by what a cathartic experience it was to put everything down on paper, and it was especially important to her because she knew she would be helping other women with what she wrote.

Writing your story elicits emotion. And emotion causes motion. It helps get the pain out of your head and onto the page, so it's not just swirling around inside of you. Your story wants to be told. Like the ghost of Hamlet's father, who torments his son over a wrong that must be righted, writing thoughtfully about your experience helps to right the wrongs in your life by giving them a voice.

And in my case, something else really important came out of writing. The desire to serve others and do the things necessary to market my book created in me a level of confidence I never even knew when I was running around the world as a reporter. And that's why I'm so passionate about helping other women heal their pain, write *their* stories and become bestselling authors so that they can step into their power, share their gifts, and have the same experience.

My muse during the writing part of my journey was Saraswati, the lovely goddess of music, wisdom and the arts, whose name means "essence of oneself," or "the one who leads a person to the essence of self-knowledge." When we tap into our own essence, we no longer have to comply with the scripts forced down our throats by bullies and abusers, and we stop resonating with any suggestion that we're stupid, ugly, or worthless. The essence of Saraswati was the encouragement I needed to have enough self-regard to follow through with my desire to apply myself to my chosen art, which is writing.

Writing really is a gift of the gods and goddesses, as the ancients believed. Years of teaching writing and of writing myself have shown me that no one can adequately explain how an idea gets from your head onto paper. It's a complicated process, which I appreciate every time I see a writing student struggle to express what's in his or her heart. Our ancestors must have considered writing to be a miracle—literally a thought in frozen form—which gave them the power to transcend time and space and preserve their ideas for the future. Writing even granted people a form of immortality, because their written words had the ability to live longer than their physical forms.

Being able to put myself out there as a writer required the healing of my solar plexus center, or chakra, which is linked to a person's perception of who they are, their self-esteem, personal power, and self-discipline, all of which are necessary for becoming any kind of communicator, free agent, or leader. Because like it or not, writing books casts you in a leadership role. Notice how the word "author" is contained in the word "authority."

Speak

Writing lays the foundation, but your finishing school culminates in sharing your written story through the vehicle of speaking. The way that played out for me was that my heart was opened so that I could put aside my small self and its petty concerns and excuses, recognize my role within a larger reality, and find the depth of spirit necessary for connecting with an audience. It takes courage and authenticity to be able to speak honestly about your life, without judgment, shame, or candy coating. And it's important because it's often the difficult parts that people most need to hear.

They don't want to be impressed. They don't care about your degrees and accomplishments. They want to know that you've been through something like they have and that you understand and care enough to help them with their problem. They reach this place of trust when you share your story. Being willing to share your story through writing and speaking is what allows you to turn your pain into power and your "mess" into your ultimate success.

Back when I was so traumatized on the witness stand, the judge kept having to tell me to "speak louder," so it's a miracle that now I can speak comfortably in front of hundreds. Or thousands. And I don't think it would matter if it were millions. Here's the really interesting part: I didn't try to make that happen or go through rigorous training to manage my fear. It just "dissolved" and got swallowed up by my vision. Meanwhile, the Kundalini was clearing out my throat chakra, and one day I just woke up and noticed I was no longer afraid. Instead, I was excited, and that was astonishing. It's something I want to pass on to others, because speaking is supposedly the top fear of human beings.

Before you get nervous, let me add that "speaking" doesn't have to mean public speaking. It involves all the layers of owning your voice, including how you speak to yourself. But once you write your story and discover your message, you may want to share it with others, even if you don't want to now. That overflowing desire to share is characteristic of Lakshmi, the goddess of wealth and abundance. Freeing yourself to speak is a priceless gift. It could mean sharing deeply with just one person. But if you're like me and most of my clients and you've been through the mill, you probably *do* have something to say, and you get to claim it! You're a warrior and a goddess. You've fought hard for your freedom, and you deserve to be heard!

Speaking of which, the Dalai Lama rightly stated that the world will be saved by the Western woman. It's already happening. Women are making a tremendous strides, but my friends in the speaking industry tell me there's not a big enough feminine presence on world stages. That needs to change, because 1) we need female role models for a new kind of power, and 2) women need to make more money. Profit speaking is one of the highest-paid professions in the world, so get your book done and get onstage!

If you're wondering, "Who am I to be that visible?" I have to ask you, who are you *not* to be? If you have a message to share, you *need* to be out there. As a teacher of mine once bluntly put it, "People are dying because of you!" Yeah, if you have a gift, it's your responsibility to get off your assets and make it available. Forget about what others think. Lakshmi is all about beauty, radiance and brilliance, and shining your light so your tribe can find you.

If any of this resonates with you—if it stirs your heart and lights a fire—you might want to consider joining one of my

programs, which are designed to help women like you step up, share your gifts, and shine your light, especially if you were ever sold the lie that you had nothing to offer.

I'm going to be taking a small group of women to Bali for a Triple Goddess "Heal, Write, Speak" Retreat. Would you like to be part of it? It's going to be a safe, nurturing, feminine experience, where you can heal your pain, claim your voice, and write the story you really want to live. It's going to be luxurious, sensual, pleasurable, and fun—a celebration of everything feminine! You're going to feel like a goddess, and by the end of the week, if you choose to play along, you'll have material for a chapter in one of my bestselling books, so for the rest of your life you can walk around as an international bestselling author. And no one can ever take that away from you.

How do you think you'll feel when that happens? How would it feel in just one week to blow through some of the things that have been holding you back for years? What could that do for your life? Your business? Your children? Your romantic self-esteem?

If you're feeling the call, give yourself permission to do this. When a woman takes care of herself, when she says "Yes!" to her dreams, it's the best thing she can do for herself and everyone around her. Come with me on this sacred journey back to wholeness. It will change your life.

If you feel a full-bodied "Yes!" for Bali and you're super excited about being a bestselling author, sign up for a free assessment call at www.healwritespeak.com, and let's see if it's a fit, because this is an intimate experience and I can't take everyone.

Whether we decide to play together or not, you will get a lot of value out of it, and after your session, you'll know your very next step!

Jill Hendrickson

As the world's No. 1 "Writing as a Tool for Healing" mentor, author and speaker Jill Hendrickson, MFA Columbia University, helps women turn their challenging experiences into stories—and best-selling books—about power and transformation. When Jill began her career as a reporter on Capitol Hill, one of her first stories was featured on *Good Morning, America*. She was the first woman to sit on the copy desk of *The Japan Times* newspaper in Tokyo, has reported for the Associated Press, worked in radio and TV, and taught writing at the university level. Jill's mission is to help one million women worldwide turn their pain into power and their "mess" into success using writing as a tool for healing.

www.jillhendrickson.com
and
www.healwritespeak.com

22

Your Body, Your Teacher

By Claudia Castillo Holley

I **NEVER CEASE** to be amazed by our bodies' loyal commitment to heal, repair and regenerate when given the right resources. It is truly magical.

There are defining moments in life when the opportunity to grow and become more wholesome individuals leads us to completely unexpected and far-reaching possibilities, impacting not only our lives but causing a powerful ripple effect. At forty-seven years of age, enjoying vibrant health and energy, I glance back in awe at all the turning points in my life and how each one of them has validated a notion that started very early on, taking me on the most profound journey of trust and love towards my best health and wellness teacher: my body.

It all started back in the early 1980s, in a little Venezuelan town called El Limon. I grew up surrounded by the freshness and flavorful abundance of my family's garden, with all the delicious tropical fruits and vegetables, fragrant herbs, with summer weather and lushness all year around. Our way of eating, like any other family in town, also included a good dose of fried foods, meat eight to ten times a week, all sorts of beans, white rice and "arepas," a Venezuelan staple, which

is a muffin-shaped bread made from refined corn flour. And cheese—tons of soft and flavorful Venezuelan white cheese. Life felt so good!

Growing up in a small town, the youngest of five, with both parents hard working professors, I became a very resourceful and independent young girl. At thirteen, I had my own business, supplying avocados to small grocery stores in town. These avocados came from my family's backyard, where we had five trees of the biggest, most creamy and tasty variety of avocados. You could feed a whole family with one avocado! I was making great money for a thirteen-year-old and I was creating a business that contributed something unique to my neighbors. Achieving this at such a young age was one of the most empowering things I ever did. But in the midst of my satisfaction, something happened that destroyed this picture of entrepreneurial glory. My once smooth and clear complexion started breaking out, almost overnight. It became ravaged by cystic acne, robbing me of my joy and confidence.

As excited as I was with my new business venture, I really wanted to run away and hide. I didn't know what to do about it. Every day it got worse. It was traumatizing, and I felt hopeless, ugly and not worthy of love.

Things did not get any better. I carried on, hoping my breakouts would go away, but they never did. And then one day my dad, moved by compassion for me, said, "Why don't you try to eat more fiber and drink more water?" As a young teenager, I thought that sounded really weird. Nevertheless, his suggestion sparked some interest in me. I quietly watched for days and saw how my dad almost always chose what he ate with some kind of health related purpose in mind. I started thinking I had nothing to lose if

I tried switching to whole grain bread or eating our yuca-based cracker, "casaba," and drinking more water. But more than that, there was something inside of me telling me to keep paying attention. And I did. I became fascinated by the connection between what I ate and how I looked and felt. The benefits surpassed the way my complexion looked. My digestion improved as well. And although I was too young and distracted to be consistent with this awareness, I knew I had to continue with this new way of eating as much as possible.

Fast forward twenty years. By the time I was in my early thirties, I had the chance to travel around the world as a British Airways flight attendant and build my own graphics design business, while at the same time developing a strong spiritual way of living and taking the first steps towards a clean, vegetarian diet. I went from acne prone skin to having a flawless complexion. I turned towards hiking, paragliding and swimming, always living life with health and spirituality at my core. Then, right before I turned thirty-three I became a momma to a vibrant happy baby girl, Sabrina. And a year later, my daughter, her father and I found ourselves making our way to California's holistic corner of the United States. Sabrina's dad and I agreed that we didn't want our daughter to grow up in Venezuela, where social, economic and political unrest was on the rise. We were looking for the healthiest environment possible to grow a family.

We arrived in California in December of 2001. We were happy and so excited. I was ready to take on the world in our new home country and in our new business venture as the owners of Curves for Women in the city of San Rafael, where I could devote myself to learning more about healthier ways of life and help others do the same. The only problem

was that in order for me to work, my daughter had to go to daycare. And it was there where she tried, for the first time at the age of two, green and blue frosted cupcakes with golden sprinkles from one of those big chain grocery stores. Sabrina couldn't have enough. She was absolutely hooked on the new flavors, colors and smooth textures. And I couldn't have been more devastated. Six months later, after who knows how many cupcakes, pieces of candy, goldfish crackers and ice cream pops had made their way into her tummy during playdates and birthday parties, this once vibrantly healthy toddler became dangerously allergic and highly asthmatic, requiring six to eight nebulizer treatments daily to stay alive. She could barely breathe on her own.

As this was happening, we were just beginning to adapt to our new environment and culture. Our Curves business was booming and the learning curve was truly exciting *and* very steep. Long hours were required from both my husband and I. We hardly had a community or support at this time, and even though we were both doing our best, our relationship was incredibly challenging. At the same time, as terrible as it sounds, the thought, "I don't need a sick child!!" was constantly on my mind. Fear and anger took a big toll on me. My health started declining and my back problems and acne came back, plus this time I developed crippling digestive issues. I lost twenty pounds I couldn't afford to lose and the ability to absorb nutrients from the good foods I was striving to include in my meals. I not only had a sick child, but her health issues were enormous and so foreign to me, and I didn't know where else to go but to a pediatrician who gave me no other hope or option than medication—for life. Meanwhile I had a business and hundreds of clients needing my time and support. My stress level was off the charts and

my marriage and business partnership was in jeopardy. I was terribly homesick for my family and friends back in Venezuela. It was a nightmare.

After lots of tears and a tough period of wondering why this was happening to me, I pulled myself together and realized that something *had* to shift. Conventional medicine was telling me my daughter would have to rely on breathing treatments daily in order to survive. Even though I was deeply grateful for the medicine that kept my daughter alive, something deep inside told me there *had* to be another way, and it kept nudging me with the idea that our bodies were doing nothing else but giving us big SOS signs, and it was up to me to figure out what they were desperately asking for. I became fiercely determined to find out.

From then on, other than making sure my daughter could breathe, my priority became learning ways to help our bodies heal and thrive. I needed to become my daughter's and my own health advocate. I was called to do it for my own physical well-being, for my family, for my sanity, and for the hundreds of clients who relied on me for guidance on healthy living. My hunger to learn more about healthier choices, lifestyle, foods and healing practices immersed me in studying and applying different strategies that allow our bodies to do what they know to do so well: heal.

I then completed studies in diet consulting and obtained my certification in nutrition education at Bauman College. I attended clinical aromatherapy workshops through the Institute for Spiritual Healing, where I learned about therapeutic grade essential oils and their extraordinary capacity to support the body in its own healing. I learned about Emotional Freedom Technique, a process that uses

tapping on various parts of the body in a specific sequence to help alleviate emotional disturbances and their physical manifestations. I also studied Raindrop Technique, a method that utilizes therapeutic grade essential oils applied in ways that support the energy centers of the body in coming back into alignment. I read books on natural health and started to follow expert holistic healing supporters such as Dr. Christiane Northdrup, Ed Bauman, Linda Page, Dr. Colin T. Campbell, the Weston A. Price Foundation, Dr. Gary Young and so many others. I have collaborated with and learned from holistic practitioners throughout the San Francisco Bay Area who offered allergy relief to my daughter using NAET, Nambudripad's Allergy Elimination Technique, helping her body reprogram reactions to benign substances which had become toxic and life-threatening to her system. And to this day I continue to research and experience the power of immune-enhancing and energy-supporting foods, lifestyle choices and therapeutic grade essential oils as the foundation of a wholesome life, great health and overall well-being. This knowledge has proven extremely powerful in maintaining the quality of life of my daughter, myself, my family and all those I have had the privilege to serve.

This is why today our lives couldn't be more fulfilling. My now fifteen-year-old daughter is healthy, vibrant and as happy as a teenager can be, literally allergy and asthma free, without the use of any prescription drugs or allergy shots. She's been a vegetarian since the moment she was conceived. She has never been vaccinated, has never had a cavity or an ear infection. She has never taken antibiotics, not only because our choice is to stay away from pharmaceuticals, but because her health is generally so vibrant and her natural immunity is so strong that when she does get sick,

she doesn't require any medication. She has three years of competitive dance under her belt, winning a national title in the category of musical theater in the Summer of 2014, at the Spotlight National Dance Competition in Seaside, Oregon. She is a walking testimonial of what it really means for we women to become our own family's' best health advocate.

As for me, one of the most rewarding aspects of this journey of mine has not only been seeing my daughter thrive and be naturally allergy and asthma free, but also witnessing how the women I have worked with have shifted towards healthier, more fulfilled lifestyles, and the tremendous impact that has had on their families.

When I first met Annie, she was fifty years old and carried thirty pounds over her ideal weight. She also suffered from excruciating structural back issues, including a herniated disk and three bulging disks. To minimize pain, her life revolved around activities that required a minimum physical movement. Her doctor had been suggesting exercise for a long time, to develop muscle in her lower back and legs to give her some core strength, and to alleviate the pain. But she lacked the support and motivation to do it. As she eased into our session, she finally said to me, "I am here because I want to make sure I can still walk when I am sixty."

She had a long way to go, however she was now ready and had the guidance to make that one-step-at-a-time shift towards the health she knew had to happen, but it was so difficult for her to do on her own. Annie's story was so similar to that of many of the women who came through the doors at Curves and it felt truly amazing to be able to provide answers and support to those who had so little hope.

With the right modifications, we tailored our regular routine to one that would accommodate Annie's fitness

level, yet make it challenging enough for her body to become stronger, more flexible, and more stable. Once the habit of physical activity was created and her body gained strength, we introduced diet modifications that addressed inflammation. With a slow but steady transition towards a whole foods approach, increasing her hydration and adjusting to a more effective eating schedule, her body continued to flourish. Annie gradually went from skipping breakfast and lunch, and eating a big dinner later in the day, to having a few power snacks throughout the day plus an earlier dinner. Nutrient-rich foods supportive of her body's anti-inflammatory response were introduced in smoothies and broths. Power-foods, such as miso, flax and chia seeds, leafy greens and wolfberries became part of her kitchen staples. Some other local and seasonal whole foods slowly replaced the choices she would have previously made. We incorporated the use of specific therapeutic-grade essential oils, which provided an additional sense of ease and comfort to her back and increased her overall sense of well-being.

Annie's was an example of team effort, some trial and error and adapting the resources we had available to meet the needs of the individual. Over the course of two years, she achieved her ideal weight and added a daily power walk to her exercise routine. Her back became stronger than ever. She looked great and felt even better.

The life enhancing results she experienced reached beyond her own health. Her husband Rick, who smoked and suffered from diabetes and excess weight, also led a sedentary life. Rick has stopped smoking, and he now takes daily walks and enjoys power smoothies with his wife every morning. He buys mostly organic foods, and to this

day, his and Annie's eating habits have remained within a healthier rhythm.

While working with Annie and hundreds of other clients, I realized very quickly how incredibly resilient our bodies are. There is an inherent healing and survival force constantly present. Even if we wanted to, we couldn't prevent a cut from bleeding, or our nails from growing. How many times have you tried to hold your breath for as long as you possibly can, only to give in to your body's unstoppable urge to take air in? And why does your body take such intense control over your conscious mind at that moment? The only explanation I can find is that our body's instinctive wisdom is the spark devoted to keep harmony and balance in the preservation of life. And it happens effortlessly.

But what disrupts this natural state of equilibrium? Why do we become depleted and suffer from disease? I believe that a source of adequate nourishment particular to the individual must be available regularly. And the proper state of mind must be present for our bodies to be able to fully receive it and utilize it.

When it comes to nourishment, there are three fundamental pillars that fuel our healing ability. These three building blocks are sleep, exercise and food. And yes, other things do make a big difference in our capacity to heal, like being happy and fulfilled, believing in ourselves and in something greater than us, feeling loved and connected, and having a sense of purpose and contribution. You can probably think of specific things that apply to you which provide you with a sense of well-being. That's what sets the foundation for the best state of mind, which is so critical for sleep, exercise and proper nourishment.

We all know we need to have adequate sleep on a daily basis, right? But do we really listen to our bodies when they are exhausted? Do we stop and rest, or do we keep going, thinking we can push through? Can you relate to "I can do this! Just tonight... I'll catch up on sleep tomorrow!" And then you would have the same thought the next day. And the next?

I have found out the hard way how adequate sleep is critical for me to simply function. Bottom line, sleep provides a unique, irreplaceable opportunity for our bodies to heal, regenerate, and repair. No matter how much you invest in healthy foods and exercise, if your body is sleep deprived, well-being will be unattainable. The body will sense danger, and stress hormones will be released. This is an incredible mechanism to help the body cope, but it becomes a problem when you constantly keep running from the tiger. In addition, sleep deprivation can lead to poor food and lifestyle choices, compromised decision making, and our ability to be tolerant, all of which highly interferes with quality of life in general. Yours, and everyone else's.

Now, when it comes to exercise, our lifestyle has sadly become more sedentary, making our bodies weak and prone to disease.

When you exercise regularly, so many wonderful things happen. Your lungs and your motivation expand. Your heart and thinking become vibrant, stronger. Your metabolism and those feel-good endorphins get kicked in just right. The ratio of muscle mass vs fat becomes more balanced, helping you tone up and achieve healthier body weight. Your blood circulation improves, transporting oxygen and nutrients throughout your body, giving you that healthy glow. You look and feel better, and you love it! We can say that exercise

makes us healthier *and* happier. And if on top of that you choose a physical activity that brings joy and excitement, you'll not only add years to your life, but they will be so worth living.

Let's move on to food, as the third building block for well-being. I believe in fully loving our food experience, and our life experience for that matter, while at the same time getting educated about the healthiest options, so that we can choose wisely. I am not a food police. My philosophy is that meals should not only be nourishing powerhouses but also should delight our senses. And with this in mind, as a student at Bauman College, I was completely overjoyed learning about a unique food group that is easily incorporated into *any* eating style, making a super healthy-and-scrumptious meal experience much more possible. This food group is called SOUL foods: Seasonal, Organic, Unrefined and Local.

Why are SOUL foods so critical for well-being? Regarding seasonal foods, there was a time when our meals were based on what Mother Nature provided at any given time of year. But today, we have access to anything we dream of at the grocery store. The problem is, when we eat out of season, the foods need to be kept in storage and are often transported from many miles away, which greatly diminishes their nourishing capacity, flavor and texture. Including seasonal foods in your meals provides the freshest, most readily accessible ingredients at their nutritional peak, with the perfect combination of nutrients and flavors that will best support your body and taste buds at that time of the year.

Organic foods are well known for being the cleanest, most wholesome and flavorful form of nourishment, exuding purity and integrity. When you choose organic whole foods, you're not only paying for high quality food with a

higher nutritional value, but you are supporting cleaner air, waterways and soil. You are contributing to your health as well as the health of the planet, a legacy we are passing on to future generations.

Unrefined foods provide all the good fats, phytochemicals and fiber that Mother Nature intended to work together, in a harmonious ratio, with proteins and carbs, vitamins and minerals. In the refining process, a lot of these critical parts are removed or altered, depleting the nutrient content and denaturing the therapeutic property of these foods. The addition of other refined or even artificial substances to the final product to enhance flavor and promote shelf life is a common practice, which has a negative impact in our body's metabolic processes. Including whole, unrefined foods whenever possible offers a unique platform for efficient food digestion and nutrient absorption, plus adequate food transit time through the digestive system so that nutrients and waste can go to where they are meant to go.

Last but not least, local foods are not only the freshest and best tasting, but they are also available at their peak of ripeness. Consuming what is grown locally offers a much higher nutrient contribution than consuming foods that have been trucked or flown in from far away and picked way in advance, sometimes being confined to storage through their ripening and transportation process. In addition, local foods will inevitably be seasonal, and these two deliver an incredible platform for sustained well-being.

You can find SOUL foods at a local farmers market, or you can sign up for a Community Supported Agriculture (CSA) basket that comes straight to you. Some grocery stores support local farmers and will even label local produce, so it's easy to spot. Organic produce is now available in most

grocery stores in California and Hawaii. If your lifestyle allows it, growing your own fruits and vegetables is one of the best, most rewarding ways to have SOUL foods at your fingertips. There is nothing like picking your own greens minutes before creating a salad.

Now, even though SOUL foods have such a positive impact on our health, specific ones will provide *you* with superior health, based on your personal requirements, circumstances and preferences, according to your biochemical individuality. In addition, recognizing which SOUL foods you find delightful, exciting and energizing, and which you find depleting and unappealing, will bring you closer to tapping into your body's wisdom, which greatly contributes to expanding your nourishing experience and to becoming your own health advocate.

As exciting as this all sounds, I understand that this journey can be quite confusing and overwhelming. It took a big investment of time and money, and a tremendous amount of trial and error for my daughter and I to enjoy optimum health today. It is a powerful journey. It's a path we walk daily, and I'm here to tell you that it's so worth it, and you don't have to do it all alone. The body, mind and soul benefits will greatly impact the quality of life that you long for and deserve, as well as your family's, creating the most amazing ripple effect around you.

 **Claudia Castillo Holley**

For over 35 years, Claudia has been studying the effects of foods and lifestyle in the way our bodies thrive, integrating deep spiritual energy and creative style in her approach to health and wellbeing.

A Nutrition Education graduate of Bauman College, and a student of clinical aromatherapy at the Institute for Spiritual Healing, she became the owner and manager of two successful Curves for Women fitness studios in San Rafael, California, where for five years she had the phenomenal opportunity to help thousands of women achieve active and healthy lives.

Growing up in Third World South America, moving countries with her baby, and starting a fulfilling career while overcoming serious health and personal challenges have all contributed to shape her unique approach to healing and purposely living. She is passionate about sharing this knowledge with exhausted moms who need to balance family, work, and self-care so that they can become all they crave to be and have the life they dream of.

www.facebook.com/ClaudiaCastilloHolley
www.ylwebsite.com/claudia

Creating a Business You Love

By Dr. Kimberli Law

MY JOURNEY TO owning my own business started when, as an educator, I often found myself helping and inspiring people to find success in their careers and at school. I kept noticing that many women were struggling with needing to make a living while also wanting to start their own business. It was significant to me, because I was raised by a single mother. Throughout my childhood, I was not only able to see the sacrifices my mother made for me, but also the sacrifices other women made for their children. I saw that, like my mother, so many women set aside their careers and dreams to take care of their families. I can still recall my mother talking about her dream to become a college professor. As I got older, I would often encourage her to go back to school to pursue her dreams. However, as a single mother, who worked full-time and who was devoted to helping me do well with my studies, my goals and extracurricular activities, she often mentioned she did not have the time or the energy to return to college. She felt it was more important for her to be there for me 100 percent as a support system so I could achieve the education and have the same opportunities that other children had.

The more I worked with women who were attending college to achieve their dream jobs, the more I noticed a common theme among them. Many of these women were not only passionate about graduating and pursuing their dream jobs. Many also had the desire to start and own their own learning centers, schools, and retail businesses. But like my mother, they were unsure of how to make their business ideas come to life, especially while working full-time at other jobs. Their plight touched me deeply. And it has therefore become my mission to help as many women as possible to start and grow the businesses of their dreams!

Although my mission developed slowly over time, I truly believed it could be achieved. I knew there were many women who wanted to start and own their own businesses. They were just confused and unsure of how to make their ideas a reality. However, I knew that with a viable business plan, key educational coaching services and the right products, I would be able to inspire, guide, and lead women towards creating the businesses of their dreams!

As a career coach and educator, I have had countless opportunities to work with women who want to have a successful career or business. What I find is that women entrepreneurs often have brilliant ideas, but they feel stuck, overwhelmed and confused about the next steps to take in order to make their businesses thrive. They are not only unsure of how to make this happen, but they also lack the confidence, knowledge, skills, and detailed plans to make it a reality. What they really want is to have a roadmap with clear directions and the tools they need to build, launch and grow their businesses to the levels of success that they desire and beyond.

In the course of working with women in search of their dream careers, the mission of my own business shifted from simply helping women find a career into the direction of inspiring women entrepreneurs to build and grow their businesses to extraordinary levels of success through education, coaching, planning and the development of a winning mindset. I feel fortunate that I am able to help women accomplish their goals by incorporating multiple strategies into my coaching business. These strategies include developing and teaching classes in the areas of leadership, strategic planning and small business startup. In addition to teaching classes, I also provide individual coaching and consulting services to women entrepreneurs who want the support of one-to-one coaching and/or a group experience. I have found that some people love private coaching services because they get lots of personal support and attention when trying to start and grow their business. Other people enjoy the group experience atmosphere, because they love receiving the support, feedback, and level of accountability that members can only receive from participating in a group experience.

Starting a business can trigger a variety of feelings in women. Many of my clients and students describe it as a challenging and frightening experience. In my own case, starting a business felt exciting, challenging, rewarding, and, at times, in the beginning, nerve-racking. On the one hand, it was an exciting experience, because it gave me the opportunity to become my own boss while developing a viable business model I knew would produce results. On the other hand, starting a business as a solopreneur was challenging, because I did not have a business coach to hold me accountable to my goals.

I remember experiencing feelings of nervousness, especially around whether my business would be able to meet my financial goals. These feelings of anxiety would often wake me up in the middle of the night, and the frequency of these sleepless nights caused me to search for strategies and solutions to help build and grow my business to extraordinary success. I knew I needed to develop a business plan and a viable business model that would produce results by generating a steady stream of income. However, although I knew that my plan and business model needed to help me generate a steady stream of income, I also knew that the strategies and solutions I selected needed to be things I could successfully implement and enjoy.

Now my viable business model consists of a detailed plan or roadmap for generating service and product ideas. To make sure these ideas were solid before marketing them to potential clients, I made sure each had three to four potential income streams. A great example of this is my small business startup program. I offer small business startup services to individual clients, groups and in academic settings. Looking back on my experience, I can see that it would have been great to have had a business coach to hold my hand and guide me through the startup phase, and that's why I am so passionate about helping other women through coaching.

The most rewarding part of my own journey has been my ability to contribute to society by helping hundreds of women entrepreneurs achieve success in their businesses. For example, I once had a client named Victoria who contacted me to help her pursue her dream of starting a consulting business. Although Victoria was excited about the prospect of finally being her own boss while pursuing her dreams, she felt nervous and unsure about her decision

to leave her job, which provided the cushion and security of a guaranteed paycheck as well as benefits. She knew she needed a coach. But not just any coach. Victoria knew she needed a coach who could hold her hand and direct her through the process of starting her business, because at the beginning of her journey, she felt confused about how to do that. She knew she not only needed a clear plan, but she also needed a coach to hold her accountable to the goals she was making for her business.

Looking back after her business got off the ground and began to thrive, Victoria expressed how appreciative she was that I'd provided her with the level of accountability she needed to start and launch her business. Through individualized lesson plans geared towards helping her implement the essential keys of a successful business, Victoria was able to achieve clarity around what she was doing on multiple levels. She said it was important to her from the beginning that I listened to her story about why she wanted to start a business in the first place and what type of business she wanted to create.

She also felt it was important that I helped her to identify the challenges she believed were stopping her from launching, building and growing a successful business. In addition, Victoria said that she valued my guidance in helping her construct a plan that was unique to her business needs and which gave her the confidence and the level of accountability that were necessary to move forward. The business plan also provided her with detailed data points on the essential tools needed to plan and actually launch her business within a period of five to six months. Although her coaching sessions are now finished, Victoria told me she believes that the strategies I provided her with to help her

identify her ideal clients and promote her business through networking and branding with her company website and multiple social media platforms were invaluable.

Keys to a Successful Business

As a career coach and an educator in the areas of business and leadership, I have often been asked by students and clients about the essential keys to creating a successful business. To begin with, it's important to have a viable idea. Then you must have a clear plan for starting and growing your business. You must know your competition and you must know how to market your business. Plus you must understand the power of a positive mindset and be able to avoid the detrimental influence of negative people.

Having a *viable idea* is the first key to creating a successful business. Although your idea should be something you are passionate about, it should also have the potential to attract a big enough target market to generate revenue. Without the right idea, you will feel frustrated and will experience difficulty in generating money. Another client I worked with initially struggled with the process of developing a viable business idea. Jocelyn believed that entrepreneurs could just start a business without having a clear plan. She believed that the only thing a person needed was to have an interesting business idea.

Although having an idea is a great first step in starting a business, I explained to Jocelyn that creating a business plan was essential for many reasons. First, a business plan can help an entrepreneur to develop a clear purpose for their business. Second, it can help them identify the goals for their business. And third, a business plan can help an entrepreneur identify their target market and the services

and products they need to incorporate to help them to achieve the purpose, goals, and vision of their business. As I worked with Jocelyn to help her create a business plan, she quickly began to see its usefulness. She now sees a business plan as an effective tool that can be used as a roadmap to help guide an entrepreneur on their path of success.

After you have identified your viable business idea, the next step is to create a *vision* for your business. Having a vision allows your target market to understand why your business exists. As an entrepreneur, if you have not clarified the purpose of your business, then it will be next to impossible to attract your ideal clients. Put simply, a vision or a vision statement helps entrepreneurs identify what they would like to achieve in their business. It helps to paint a clear picture of the type of business they would like to build and have in the future.

Another important component of a successful business is a sustainable business model. Having one is important because it helps entrepreneurs identify the key components of their business. It provides them with a visual design that illustrates the steps needed to successfully generate revenue. This includes entrepreneurs discovering new ways to identify key resources to help them make a profit and convert potential prospects into paying clients or customers. What happens if you don't have a clear plan for your business? It will fail because there is no direction for it to go. When there is no clear roadmap for how to move your business forward, not only will it fail, but you will also experience frustration, anger, and a hit to your self-confidence due to the loss of the time and energy you invested in trying to make your business a success.

I had a client, Mary, who was also unsure of how to start her business. Like many women entrepreneurs, Mary had a great idea. She knew what she wanted to do, but she was unclear about how to build her business. Thanks to our coaching together, she started to feel secure about the future of her business because she knew where it was going. Mary felt that I'd given her the essential tools she needed to continue to incorporate not just in her business but also in her thought processes. She had a sustainable business model and her coaching sessions with me provided her with a clear direction in which to guide her business. She said that the clarity she was able to achieve around the purpose of her business was extremely valuable. And most importantly, I was able to help her generate streams of revenue by identifying ways to leverage her existing skills and talents so that she could contribute maximum value to her clients in the marketplace.

Another important key to the success of any business is to "*know your competition.*" Knowing who your competitors are and how they are doing is crucial, because it provides you with an idea of how you measure up and alerts you to the "must haves" for your area of business, such as some of the different tools and strategies your competitors are using to achieve success. Many times people do not understand the importance of knowing their competition.

A strategy I often use to help clients I work with to gain a better understanding of their competition is a SWOT Analysis. A SWOT Analysis is an assessment tool used to help analyze the strengths, weaknesses, opportunities for improvement and potential threats that can exist in a business or organization. The purpose of using this assessment tool with my clients is to help them not only to

assess where their competitors are but to also assess where they are in comparison to their competitors. This is often an eye opening experience for clients that helps to increase their awareness of the strengths that already exist in their business, including their existing knowledge, skills and background. On the other hand, clients can also become more aware of the areas in their business that need more attention and what training or skills they need to develop to improve those areas or whom they need to hire. A good example of a client who learned the benefits of incorporating a SWOT Analysis was Victoria, whom I mentioned earlier in this chapter.

While conducting a SWOT Analysis for her business, Victoria quickly learned the value of getting to "know her competition." Through an analysis of her competitors' businesses, Victoria was able to identify who her competitors were and what they were doing to leverage their businesses. During our final meeting, Victoria mentioned that incorporating the SWOT Analysis into the planning of her business was a powerful and eye opening tool. It helped her not only gain a better understanding of her competition, but the SWOT Analysis also helped alert her to the weaknesses that existed in her business and identify the "must haves" she needed to integrate to make her business a success.

Marketing your business is crucial. After an entrepreneur or business owner has a viable business idea, a vision for their business, an identified target market, a sustainable business model, and a business plan, they must determine how to market their business through different platforms. During this stage, business owners must decide which strategies will best promote and deliver their marketing message to their target audience. They should also know

which strategies will best help them leverage their product or service.

For example, common online strategies entrepreneurs use to market their businesses are websites, social media platforms, and webinars to name a few, as opposed to traditional offline strategies that include attending networking events, joining business chambers of commerce and other organizations, attending conferences, and public speaking. I have found the marketing phase to be the most frightening experience for many new entrepreneurs because they don't want to spend the money necessary to start or grow their business. It has been my experience that most people need to spend money in their business. This is something that they need to know and plan for accordingly.

Another area of utmost importance that I emphasize to my students and clients (because it is often overlooked) is the power of maintaining a *positive mindset*. Through my own success in education, my career, and the work I have provided to others, I have discovered that a person's mindset strongly contributes to their success. If an individual believes that he or she will achieve success and actively visualizes it happening, then that is the outcome that will result. On the other hand, if an individual believes he or she will not have success and actively visualizes a negative outcome, then that is the outcome that will result. Before I was introduced to *The Secret* by a colleague, I often had negative feelings about giving presentations in class. I didn't take it seriously until one time I noticed that my negative thoughts about not giving good class presentations were interfering with my being a successful presenter and a student. Of course there are other components that also come into play, such as setting goals and attracting the results you want. Goal

setting involves the process of an individual identifying the goal that he or she wants to accomplish and then creating a step-by-step plan or course of action to implement it. Doing so will inspire an individual to achieve his or her goal.

I believe that another important piece of the success puzzle is what's known as the "Law of Attraction." For more than a decade, the Law of Attraction has attracted many supporters, thanks in part to the creator of *The Secret,* Rhonda Byrne. *The Secret* is largely based on what is known as the Law of Attraction, which relates to an individual's ability to attract what he or she wants through the power of their thoughts, beliefs, and actions. It is the connection we make through positive thinking (our thoughts/beliefs), our emotions (feelings), and the actions we take, which produces an outcome.

According to the Law of Attraction, an outcome that results is always in support of our thoughts and beliefs. I was introduced to the Law of Attraction by a former colleague. After putting it into practice, I saw it really does work! A practice from the Law of Attraction that I utilize on a regular basis is the process of visualization. Personally, I have found visualization to be the thing most effective in helping me to achieve my goals thus far in my life. As a doctoral student, I would often visualize myself preparing for and delivering successful class presentations. And that would be the end result, time and time again. For my qualifying examination, I would often visualize myself preparing for and then passing my qualifying examination on the first attempt. Guess what? I passed my qualifying examination on the first attempt!

I have also used the Law of Attraction's visualization process to help me attract the type of clients I would like to have in my business. I believe the visualization process

is effective because it helps people to become more aware of what they want. When people become more aware about what they want, they are automatically thinking about what they want. According to the Law of Attraction, when people constantly think about what they want, they are also producing the feelings and results that reflect their thoughts.

Lastly, I really need to mention something that's often discounted or overlooked entirely by business owners and entrepreneurs, and that is the influence of *negative people*. Due to their negative outlook on life, negative people can destroy any positive progress you have made in your business. Therefore, it is best to quickly identify such individuals and determine how to keep them at a distance. Unfortunately, I have had more than my share of dealings with negative people. From my experience, I have found negative people to be toxic and they often work very hard to shatter the confidence level of positive people. Therefore, over the years, I developed the philosophy to only surround myself with positive people and not allow negative people into my life.

Granted, there is a lot to know about starting a business and also about what happens if you try to start yours without knowing all these things. It all may seem a bit overwhelming, but let me assure you that when you take things step by step it's very doable. It can also be tremendously helpful to have a coach as a professional ally to help you and cheer you on through the various stages of the success of your business.

As with most business owners, coaches and consultants are most successful when they provide service to people who fit their client profile. For a potential coaching client to achieve success in their business, a client will need to find a coach who has a clearly defined ideal client profile.

In other words, a client will need to find a coach who knows who he or she works with best. This provides potential clients with the insight they need to determine, in advance, if the coaching relationship will be a success. To know if our coaching relationship will be a success, I like working with women who are enthusiastic and passionate about their work—women who not only want to start their own business, but women who are determined to put in the hard work that is needed to plan and launch their business. Although starting a business can be exciting and rewarding, progressing through the different stages of planning and starting a business is often challenging. Therefore, most of all, I like working with women who have a positive mindset and are determined and willing to persevere to make their business a success.

If this sounds like you and you fit my ideal client profile and would like to have me as your coach, please do not hesitate to contact me. I am always dedicated to helping my clients achieve great success in their businesses. And I know that as your coach and professional ally, I can also help you achieve the success that you want in your business. Don't wait another minute to turn your dream business into a reality. Go to my website at **www.ctcforwomen.com** and enter your name, email, and phone number for a free twenty-minute Business Breakthrough Consultation.

Dr. Kimberli Law

Certified career coach and educator Dr. Kimberli Law is the founder of Career Transition Coaching For Women (CTC For Women), dedicated to helping women entrepreneurs achieve maximum success in their businesses.

CTC For Women helps established business owners — especially those who feel stuck, overwhelmed and confused about the next steps to take — grow their businesses to extraordinary levels of success by helping them maximize their talents and skills.

Throughout her career, Dr. Law has discovered that many women she encounters have brilliant business ideas, but they do not know where to begin to bring those ideas to life. At CTC For Women you will not only learn how to launch and grow your business, you will also learn strategies to grow it to extraordinary levels of success.

With over ten years of experience in leadership, professional speaking, and professional training for educators, business leaders, and clients, Dr. Law brings a unique set of skills to her work. She has dedicated her life to helping others persevere, succeed, and find balance in their lives and businesses. She looks forward to helping you, too.

www.ctcforwomen.com
info@ctcforwomen.com

Name Alchemy

By Barbera Ammahlia Schaefer Berdner

WHAT IF YOUR name held the answer to all your woes and all your potential success? People rarely consider the importance of their name, but what if ... hidden in your birth name is the spiritual map of your life? That is the foundation of my life's work, and it took a big knock to the head for me to discover that. Literally.

One day, while driving a team of eight sled dogs, I got thrown from the sled and—boom—life was never the same. You've heard of the proverbial two-by-four from the Universe? Well, mine came in the form of the entire planet hitting me smack on the head. Thank goodness it finally knocked some sense into me! Because I was heading down the wrong path, and it just might have killed me.

Fast forward eighteen years, and now, as a Soul's Wisdom Muse and motivational speaker, I get to share all the gifts that the two-by-four gave me. I'm passionately doing my life's work. As an Advanced Divine Healing Practitioner and Lightbody Surgeon, my deep joy is to support people in rediscovering their wholeness.

But my life was not always so joyful and whole, and there were times along the way when I could easily have checked out. But I chose not to, no matter how fragmented and fractured I felt. Something kept me going, and that something

is what I want to share with you today. Because I don't want you to have to struggle and take eight years to discover your true purpose, like I did. And it was hidden in my name.

I was born into a military family. An absentee dad and a rage-prone mother ensured an uneasy start to this world. At school I felt like an outcast. I just didn't fit in, despite my good grades. That sense of separation was only exacerbated by a date rape at the age of sixteen. Shortly after that, while floating in my mother's pool, I read the book *Jaws* and immediately developed a shark phobia. I was easily startled and I regularly jumped "out of my skin."

Apparently I still wasn't getting the message the Universe was telling me about my disempowerment around men. I promptly decided to study engineering back in a time when very few women went into that field. Then, of course, I chose to work for a utility company in a male dominated construction department.

I do have super achiever tendencies, and back then as a young, cocky thirty-five-year-old, I decided the corporate world was to be my oyster and stepped into a high position at one of the largest utilities in the country, overseeing 300 engineers. I was on the fast track.

Yet here was the dilemma. Outside I was doing great. Progressing. Stepping up. All that good stuff. But inside I was wasting away. I felt like a fake. I could never show my true self. I always had to hide behind the strong, corporate façade. I had the car, I had the house, I had a good-looking husband, and my life was crap. My nerves were at an all-time high, our marriage was distant at best, and I was still jumping out of my skin all the time—in other words, on high alert. The distance in our marriage was so severe we separated and three times nearly divorced.

I was numb to my emotions and at the same time living in fear that one false step, one stray emotion, and I could lose my job.

I really didn't know who I was. There were so many rules at work and at home related to how I was meant to be that I lost myself. The only way I knew to receive love was through achievement. But it left me hollow.

The only time I was happy was when I was shopping, so I spent all kinds of money to try and fill the bottomless pit inside of me. I didn't feel safe and I didn't trust that people would be there for me, which of course led to total exhaustion.

I quit my job, but I didn't change the way I was doing things. And the Universe came along and said, "Barbera! How many times have I told you?" So it arranged for me to hit my head and I had a near death experience. I was out of my body for seven minutes. I remember it and that's a whole other story – an entire book – and when I came to, I couldn't do math anymore, so I couldn't be an engineer. I had impaired vision in my right eye, impaired hearing in my right ear, and horrific migraines. I couldn't even walk ten feet without passing out. Basically I could barely take care of myself. So things were more than crappy.

What I didn't know then was that this knock to the head was about to lead me on a healing journey that would change everything about my life.

But first I had to go through the pain. It was horrid being so brilliant and self-sufficient one moment and then the next needing so much help. I was not accustomed to asking for help and didn't know how to receive help, and all of a sudden I was forced to ask for it. I could barely walk, I couldn't focus, and I felt like crap all the time.

Now, being forced to receive was part of the huge, huge lesson. I had always loved taking care of other people, but I never let anyone help me. And I was denying them that gift. It took me a hit on the head and about four years to figure that one out.

Traditional medicine wasn't offering me very many solutions and it wasn't getting to the deep core part of my problem. Five element acupuncture was somewhat helpful in shifting the energy. But what really stopped me falling into the abyss was the deep drive I had to take care of my dogs. I didn't know why, I just knew I had to.

When I think back to that time, it appears gray in my mind's eye. I was barely there. Just getting through the day was work enough. I had lost touch with my hopes and dreams. I just wanted the fog to go away.

Then, one day back in 2004, I met a healer who offered me the first glimmer of hope I'd felt in seven years.

He put his hands on my head and the fog and the pain simply lifted. And it was gone, magically, for three whole days. For the first time in seven years I could feel that healing was actually possible. I felt as if I had accessed the core of healing my wound—the piece about worthiness and being whole. I got a taste of it and it was exquisite. I finally had hope that in this lifetime I could really feel like me again—a "me" that was so much more brilliant than I had ever remembered. Some people get miraculously healed; you hear about that. That wasn't my path. (It's in my name and soul contract – and I'll talk about that later.) My path was to try out and learn many different approaches so that I could teach people like you who have also tried all kinds of things to heal yourself, with only limited results.

Here's how stubborn I was. Even though I had just been given the gift of a lifetime, a true glimpse of heaven, I still had to go through the learning curve of pushing myself way too hard with my leadership training company (using sled dogs) that I drove myself to the point of exhaustion.

Thank goodness for serendipity. Quite a few years after the healing experience, I met a gal on Facebook, and she became my spiritual mentor and a very good friend. She showed me a brochure for "soul contract" training. I had no idea what it was but felt a deep resonance and a strong desire to take the class. In the class a light went on for me. I remembered something else that had happened when I hit my head. I'd seen the place where soul contracts are held, and it touched me deep to the core. I know and remember that place.

Suddenly, everything started to make sense, and I began to explore this soul contract work very deeply.

Here's what it's all about: You have a name, you are born with it, and you think you're stuck with it (or you change it). You use it day in, day out for decades, never really knowing what it means or that it holds the Signature Frequency of what your soul wanted to experience in this lifetime.

Your name is like a GPS, or guidance system. But it doesn't work if you plug in the wrong coordinates. Then you find yourself going in circles or feeling that there's something missing in your life. Zeroing in on your correct name can profoundly affect your happiness, as well as your success in life.

As I studied deeper levels of soul contract work, I also received powerful initiations and training in a very precise form of vibrational alignment called Divine Healing. I was

thrilled to notice my health and clarity improving by leaps and bounds.

I call this work Name Alchemy. It's based on the sounds of Ancient Hebrew, one of the seven sacred languages of God. It empowers you by revealing your soul wisdom and describing your challenges, talents, goals, dreams and soul destiny.

Knowing my soul contract gave me the comfort that there was nothing wrong with me and that my life really was meant to play out like this. It was both a comfort and a confirmation. I could now look at my life in a more objective way. Instead of worrying about "woulda, coulda, shoulda," I was able to see that my life was playing out just as planned and that before, I just hadn't been plugging in the right coordinates.

Connecting with the map of my soul wisdom has helped me be gentler with myself and really pull back the layers of armoring and bravado, revealing how things in my soul contract play out with other people. I was able to see my mother's issues around trust and my father's tendency to abandon as all part of a greater plan. I felt instantly more compassionate and loving towards both of them.

I began working with friends and then eventually taking on clients. After years of wondering if I'd ever work again, here I was with a newly blossoming business.

I reflected on a major turning point in my life—getting married to the love of my life, John Berdner. But why had I chosen not to share his name?

I never quite understood it at the time, but when I finally found the Name Alchemy work and looked into it in more detail, I realized more clearly that I had experienced disempowerment by men throughout my life and had feared

that by sharing John's name I would be giving away more of my power.

But now, steeped in Name Alchemy as I was, I began to consider sharing John's name. When I mentioned it to him, his eyes got big and his face lit up, and he surprised me by saying, "Well, then, the next time we go to Hawaii we will have to get remarried."

I took that as a sign from the Universe that sharing his last name was going to be a nice big piece towards deeper connection in our marriage. So now I needed to find the right name combinations that would hold the signature frequency of my life goal and my desired life. This new name would need to help me work through all the abandonment, mistrust, and disempowerment I had experienced.

After a bit of noodling, I finally landed on the perfect name: Barbera Ammahlia Schaefer Berdner, a name that would bring balance and help dissolve the disempowerment and abandonment issues. It was a name that would support me in being my authentic self in the world, ready to be seen. It was also a name that would bring unity where I had experienced fragmentation and trust where I had experienced disappointment.

Soon after claiming that name, I noticed my relationship with John improving. Also, many positive things unfolded in my business. I know the new name is a mouthful. But don't worry. When you decide to optimize your name, it's likely that it will be less of a mouthful.

Imagine for a moment that your soul really did plan out your life before you came here, and that you still have free will and choices. And imagine that there really is a map which is hidden in your name. The journey of life or the path of enlightenment doesn't have to be all wiggly. There really

is a roadmap, and the idea is that if you stay on the right path, your life will be fulfilling (even if it's not always easy). And if you're off the path life feels like a struggle.

I had been way off when I was pushing through as a corporate ladder climber, distancing myself from John and my own emotions. I was way off when I ignored the signals screaming for me to stop. That knock to my head turned my life around and reminded me of who I really was. And who I am. I remembered that as a child I could speak to Jesus, but my spiritual connection had been drummed out of me by nuns at the Catholic church I went to and by my family. Actively working with my name helped me get back on track with my life.

So if life is tough, can we simply change our name and all will be fine?

Well, it's not quite as simple as that. If it's to happen at all, it needs to be done consciously. Many people that do change their names can unwittingly bring even more challenges into their lives. A name can support or hinder your life journey, so you need to choose it with care.

I met a woman who had recently changed her name on her own, and within days her life started falling apart. Her renter caused a ruckus in her small community. She then felt unsafe and needed to ask the renter to leave. This left her temporarily with no rental income. When I looked at the Name Alchemy of her new name, I could see that it was not complimentary to who she was or who she would always be, *and* it added an element of having to "do things the hard way" in the world. Not ideal!

Another woman came to me because she was getting divorced and wanted to communicate better with her soon-

to-be ex-husband during the process. I looked at her Name Alchemy and could see that the energies of the relationship had been quite good before she got married, but once she changed her name to her husband's, conflicts and roadblocks ensued. Before getting married, her relationship had in fact been "amazing," but almost immediately after the wedding (the day she took on the new name) things started going downhill. Fast! Thankfully, I was able to help her connect the dots, and we have since found a name that is settling things beautifully in her life.

I love to help people decode the patterns that happen in their lives. It's so empowering. For me, it's had a huge impact on the way I relate to people in life and in business. A great example is my new business partnership.

I knew a lovely, kind-hearted man who was a whiz at all things related to marketing as well as an expert transformer. But we just didn't click. I felt irritated around him in a "nails on chalkboard" sort of way, and I did not understand why.

When he approached me with the joint venture opportunity of a lifetime, I felt conflicted. For all his big lists and expertise, and the amazing gift that he was offering, I just couldn't bring myself to say yes. I didn't completely trust him. More to the point – I didn't trust myself to hold my own power in the partnership.

And then I did what any self-respecting Master Soul Contract Reader would do – I looked at the soul contracts held in our names. Of course, it was staring me in the face. It showed enormous clashes in the realms of disempowerment and distrust.

Within an hour of seeing that, all the charge I had around him dispersed. The next day I called him and we

had an extraordinary conversation that opened the doors to what has turned out to be a beautifully symbiotic and prosperous relationship.

If, however, I had entered into that relationship with that initial "off" feeling, it would have poisoned our relationship, and who knows where we would both be now?

Here's something else: As I write this, a massive forest fire is raging less than half a mile from our house. My husband, John, has a deep fear of forest fires and has huge issues around death. Oh, and by the way, his father died yesterday.

How the hell is it that I've been able to remain calm in the middle of the storm? It's because I understand our soul contracts. I understand what I need and what he needs right now. What he needs is safety and what he needs is consistency, and he needs someone to be calm no matter how up and down he is. And I know this deeply because of knowing deeply what our souls came here to experience. Could I have handled that eight years ago? No, I would have been caught up in trying to manage and work around each one of his emotions.

Here's the moral of the story: if you are getting married, or considering changing your name, know what you are getting into at the deepest level. Be open to the best way forward, whether it means changing your name or not. The only reason I could handle John's pain so well is that I'm conscious of what's going on at the core. At the end of the day, it's not about changing things, it's about consciousness within whatever is happening.

Life can be intense, and you don't have to experience it as so hard. I did it the hard way, going through more than eight years of miserable health problems, marriage troubles, burn out and disconnection. You don't have to do that. I had to die

and experience all these health issues to learn this. So now I'm here to help you learn an easier way.

Thank goodness I learned these tools and I've used them for myself, and now I use them with other people so I can speed up their healing process. It's worked for me, it's worked for my clients. I love this work! I love seeing people living their full potential with ease and grace instead of scrambling around in the dark.

What are the recurring patterns in your life? If you've had name changes, what changed for you? Notice that, be curious about it. There are clues and bread crumbs to follow. As I look back at my life, I was dealing with lack of trust, disempowerment, not being able to be authentic. When I could see those clearly in my name, it made complete sense, and part of my healing process was to consciously work with those energies on a daily basis.

If you have recurring patterns, you may want to have a look at what's going on in your name. It's not as simple as choosing a new name on your own, because unless this is one of your gifts, you could choose a really bad one!

In the Name Alchemy process I begin with your birth name, interpreting the Map of Your Soul Wisdom to put your life experiences into perspective. I show you where you are going and provide you with recommendations to help you achieve your maximum potential in this lifetime.

We next take a look at any name changes and significant relationships. We can take it to the next level and optimize your name for the most successful experiences in this lifetime.

If you in any way feel fractured or scattered and yearn to come to a place of clarity and wholeness, then I encourage you to uncover the secrets hidden in your name. If you are

successful in many ways and yet feel a lack of connection or confidence, if you doubt yourself in any way and wonder what you're doing here on the planet, if you've had a head trauma or a health crisis and can't seem to get it together, if you wonder why you married your spouse or why you haven't yet attracted your soul mate, or if you're at a crossroads in life and are about to make a major decision, take a look at your name.

It is my joy and passion to serve you, to support you in living the fullest life possible. And to that end, I have free educational materials, resources and special bonuses to get you started on your Name Alchemy journey.

I don't want you to have to have the entire planet hit you on the head to wake you up. There's a far quicker way, and the map is hidden in your name!

 **Barbera Ammahlia Schaefer Berdner** is a Soul's Wisdom Muse and champion sled dog musher. She is the co-author of the number one Women's Leadership Book: *Be the Lead Dog, 7- Life Changing Lessons Taught by Sled Dogs.* She teaches women leaders how to live a life of ease and grace by using the skills of serendipity through reconnection and clarity. And she got here in a most...well...serendipitous way.

Barbera was on the fast track in corporate management. She loved her job, but her marriage and health were suffering greatly. She tried changing jobs, but she was getting the message that it wasn't the job that needed changing. *She* needed to change. She took up sled-dog racing and suffered a traumatic brain injury that took her out of her body for seven minutes. It was a classic and life-changing near-death experience that set her on a brand new path.

During Barbera's journey to her own source consciousness, she received information that she offers to others as Soul Wisdom Sessions. In these sessions, Barbera connects women to their soul wisdom codes—hidden inner knowledge deep in the heart of each woman that unlocks her own empowered confidence. As a woman understands her own wisdom codes, she can eliminate self-doubt, rebuild self-trust, and have a lot more fun and adventure in life.

If you are ready to reveal your own gifts, integrating and grounding your Light, so that you can reconnect with your authenticity without hardship, contact her.

Visit: **NameAlchemy.net/ContactBarbera** or
Call: **415-797-7749**

The Unique Financial Challenges Women Face

By Patti Fagan

AS A YOUNG GIRL, I watched my single mother struggle to raise three young children. At that time, she was a high school dropout, was on welfare and she didn't know how to drive a car. She eventually got a part-time job as an elementary school teacher's assistant. She absolutely loved the teacher she was assigned to assist. That woman inspired her to get her GED and go to college to get her degree in teaching. I thank God every day that she did, because now as a retiree, my mother is able to have a secure retirement living off of her pension.

However, that is not the case for most women today. Pensions are practically nonexistent, becoming more and more a thing of the past. And, quite frankly, women born in the boomer generation, and after, are simply not savers. In fact, most aren't familiar with the basics of personal money management, which poses a big problem for these women down the road.

As I see it, there are three distinct issues threatening women's financial security.

1. For women, money is an emotional topic. They don't want to feel uncomfortable or vulnerable, and they don't want to look ignorant or naïve about money. So if the topic of finances brings up those uncomfortable feelings, they will avoid it altogether.

2. Women are being underserved by financial institutions because those institutions typically cater to men. Traditionally speaking, the topics of money, investments and retirement are the domain of men. As such, the financial services industry has let women down. According to a study entitled, *Women, Money & Power*, commissioned by Allianz, a financial conglomerate, "fifty-four percent of women believe the financial industry is geared to men." Additionally, financial advisors are not trained on the emotional aspects of money and the unique emotional challenges women face around it. So most advisors will not know how to help women recognize and overcome these challenges, which leaves women feeling undervalued and misunderstood by most financial representatives they encounter. Only recently has the financial industry begun to take notice of the emotional issues women face financially. But that's only because financial forecasts now indicate that women will be the beneficiaries of unprecedented levels of wealth in the coming decades. Consequently, we are finally starting to see financial companies taking notice and commissioning studies about women and money in hopes of understanding and capitalizing on this forthcoming shift in wealth ownership for fear that they will miss out on the

opportunity to manage these sizable assets.

3. A number of social and economic factors threaten the financial security of women, especially in their retirement years. By far, the biggest threat comes from the fact that women outlive men, not only because men tend to marry women who are younger than them, but because women live longer. For example, for those born in 1950, the life expectancy for women was five and a half years more than the life expectancy for men. (National Vital Statistics Reports, United State Life Tables, 2006) What this means is that if a husband requires extensive (and expensive) medical care before he passes, the wife will be left with depleted savings to live on. Also, the average age a woman becomes widowed is now age fifty-nine and a half. So, if she lives into her nineties (or to age 100!), she will need at least thirty years of retirement income saved up. Add to this the fact that forty-nine percent of women over the age of seventy-five live alone, according to a profile on older Americans by the U.S. Department of Health and Human Services' Administration on Aging, and it is not difficult to see that women are in danger of outliving their financial resources if they don't strategically plan for their own financial security.

When sitting with clients in a retirement planning meeting, it was not unusual for me to observe behavior in women that I did not observe in men. It was obvious that women felt disempowered around the topic of finances. In fact, many confessed to me that they simply did not understand money. In her book, *The Soul of Money*, inspirational financial visionary, Lynne Twist says that women are adorably

clueless on that topic. In my own experience, it was not uncommon for a woman to show up for our meeting with her retirement account statements in hand and tell me that she was confused because she had no idea how her money was invested. Other times, women confided in me that they had no idea where their paycheck went each month. When it came to income and expenses, I found it typical for women to not know how much they made or how much they spent each month. A common thing I saw was that they'd be surprised by how much they actually made because they had never tracked their income. This was especially true when working with self-employed women.

In fact, I worked with a client who was so overwhelmed at the idea of tracking her expenses that I actually had to sit with her as we went through her checkbook register, line by line, in order to help determine her monthly expenses. At the end of our meeting, she was overjoyed that we had gone through her finances and that she felt she finally had a handle on what she was spending. She was one of my single female clients. I found this type of behavior to be more prevalent among this group of women. According to an ING study, independent women often struggle with handling daily living expenses and finding the funds to set aside for retirement.

Another frequent occurrence with single women was in the area of debt. For example, a client who had $30,000 of credit card debt told me she stopped opening her credit card statements because she felt so much guilt and overwhelm about having the debt.

Of course, feeling a lack of confidence with money was not the case with all women. There were indeed those who seemed to have a firm grasp on their finances. They had a

plan for their retirement income and they were on track with how much they needed to retire. Everything was in order, financially speaking.

Yet, for the most part, the majority of women felt overwhelmed about the topic of money.

For me, these retirement planning meetings were a frustrating experience, because as a financial advisor, I was not professionally trained to help these women overcome their inner emotional blocks around finances.

Clearly they were experiencing inner barrier and limiting beliefs around money that needed to be transformed, perhaps through coaching. Yet I constantly had to remind myself that the purpose of these meetings was not to provide extensive coaching because I was not getting paid to coach people. I was getting paid to sell financial products. I eventually came to realize that I was feeling out of alignment with my passion for helping women, because I was not truly serving them by selling them financial products when what they really needed was a personal breakthrough around the emotional side of money, as well as a basic level of financial literacy.

As a result, I decided to follow my heart and become a life and money coach so that I could truly empower women in their confidence with money. I have found that a woman's net worth is impacted by her self-worth and vice versa. By combining coaching with financial planning, my work is now truly aligned with my higher purpose of empowering women. When women feel more confident about the topic of money, they can have the inner trust they need to then go on and work with a financial advisor, because they will be coming from an empowered, healed and more wholesome place with money.

If you're a woman who wants a money breakthrough, I think the best place to begin is to stop beating yourself up, which so many women do. Instead, do the contrary and ease up on yourself. Give yourself a pat on the back. The goal is to get to a place where you feel compassion towards yourself. Even if you've made some bad money mistakes in the past, find something for which you can acknowledge yourself. Remember, you were, and are, doing the best you can with what you know.

Women sometimes need permission to be kinder to themselves. Many times women don't even realize how harsh they are with themselves, especially around money. When women realize they don't need to be so hard on themselves and that they can be more compassionate instead, it can be enough to take them out of their financial story. I have found that women have a tendency to create a lot of drama around money, perhaps because they get addicted to the adrenaline rush. They become self-critical and tell themselves stories about being a bad person because they have debt or because they over-spend or because they feel clueless about money. This is what keeps them feeling stuck.

Instead, women can get to a place of forgiveness for the past money mistakes they have made. This forgiveness leads to feeling more empowered with money. When women feel empowered, they become aware of choices that they were not aware of before. They actually begin to create these choices for themselves out of the new, empowered space because they become more creative and resourceful.

From that point, they become more aware of their money behaviors so that the next time they feel compelled to spend money mindlessly, they can be at choice, which in turn breaks the negative cycle of their money story. The story

usually goes something like this: They spend unconsciously, then feel guilty and berate themselves, so they feel badly about themselves, which then leads to feeling hopeless and overwhelmed. It's becomes a habitual pattern of self-abuse.

The good news is that, amazingly, the simple process of becoming aware of unconscious patterns with money, and forgiving oneself for unwanted financial behavior, is enough to begin to break and transform the negative cycle.

The next step is then to deal with the inner emotional blocks around money.

The four most common negative emotions around money are guilt, shame, resentment and fear.

Guilt around money comes from judgement of oneself. The question I like to ask women is, "What if judging yourself were no longer acceptable to you?" When the client replaces self-condemnation with self-acceptance, she becomes open to self-forgiveness, which in turn, increases her self-esteem. This is an essential step to financial empowerment. Guilt can keep women from receiving more money and more income because they believe they don't deserve abundance.

Shame commonly shows up when debt is present. Shame is an emotion that causes a woman to really question her self-worth. It is usually accompanied by berating and self-condemnation. There is usually some type of story the client is telling herself and perhaps reliving over and over in her mind, reminding herself of her short-comings and unworthiness.

Resentment is common for women who have nurturing personalities. Feelings of resentment surface when they take care of other people in their life financially but neglect their own financial wellbeing. Women may find themselves paying for things for other people out of a feeling of obligation or in

an attempt to please. There is usually an issue with a lack of boundaries, especially around money and self-care. These women tend to put other people's needs ahead of their own. For them, creating healthy boundaries around money is particularly important, as is the deeper exploration of why they feel compelled to take care of others by giving them money or paying for things when really they should be taking care of themselves financially. It would also behoove these women to explore areas in their lives where they might need to implement more self-care.

Fear and worrying about money is quite common for women when they avoid dealing with their money. Fear of the unknown tends to cause excessive anxiety. They worry about not being able to take care of themselves financially, and since financial security is important for women, this is a big deal.

One irrational fear that women face is referred to as the Bag Lady Syndrome. According the Allianz *Women, Money & Power* study, forty-nine percent of women fear ending up broke and homeless regardless of their current income level. Among the women surveyed, a third of the highest income earners (those earning $200,000 and more) couldn't shake this fear. The study states that "the pervasiveness of this worry may point to a deep-set financial insecurity that seems to be particular to women."

We have to remember that our emotional blueprint around money is deeply rooted in our childhood experiences. The behaviors and patterns we observed in our primary caregivers, usually our parents and grandparents, form our beliefs about money, wealth and, ironically, self-worth.

Without realizing it, many of us tend to unconsciously play out the negative money habits we observed in our parents and grandparents. These negative habits are

not transformed until the unconscious beliefs, fears and expectations we hold around money and financial security become conscious.

Also, it's interesting to note that much of our emotional blueprint around money tends to be generational. We are literally carrying generations of emotions around money such as shame, guilt and fear that were handed down to us by our ancestors. This inner emotional blueprint creates our current external financial reality. Your financial reality is really a reflection of your inner relationship with money, or your money blueprint. The good news is that you can change this relationship.

Money is involved in so many aspects of our lives. We need to realize that how we do money is how we do everything. So, if you're avoiding dealing with money, you might want to ask yourself where else in your life you are not taking care of your needs? I like to remind women that it is crucial to take a stand for themselves and their financial wellbeing. It doesn't matter whether women are single, married, divorced or widowed. They cannot afford to depend on anyone else to take care of their financial security. It is their responsibility to do so. This may sound harsh, but you can thank me later when you're in retirement and have plenty of assets to afford a comfortable lifestyle.

Since money can be an uncomfortable topic for women, they need a safe space to explore their emotions, beliefs and experiences with it. They need to feel that they are not being judged for their irrational money behavior. The feeling of security and safety will create an environment and an opportunity for a breakthrough.

Many times after working with a woman in a coaching session where her unnecessary spending was brought to

light, I found that at the very next session, she would happily report that she had not spent nearly as much since our prior session simply because she was now aware of her habits.

For instance, I had a client who was able to lower her food bill by fifty percent simply because she became aware of how much she was spending on food. She realized that she was eating out all the time. And sometimes when she went to eat with friends, she would pick up their tab, too. She also wasted a lot of money on food that she didn't eat and would end up throwing it out.

By just being aware of what she was spending, she cut her food bill from a range of $1,500 to $1,800 a month down to only $800.

One of the most effective ways of creating a sense of safety around money is with pen and paper. I have found journaling to be a great tool for personal transformation. It is one of the most elegant ways I know for transforming your inner blocks, especially around money. The power of journaling is quite often underestimated because it seems too simple. But let me tell you, the biggest shifts I observe in myself and my clients come from consistent journaling, which is why I require my clients to journal every day for at least fifteen minutes.

In my own life, I've found journaling to produce profound insights that would not have become evident otherwise.

The method of writing without filtering your thoughts helps to clarify your thinking, bring to the surface unresolved emotions and connect you with what's in your heart. It's an intuitive process that somehow allows your innate wisdom to manifest in various ways.

Since money is an emotionally charged topic for a lot of women, journaling is an excellent way to explore and dig

deeper into these issues, creating huge opportunities for personal breakthroughs. What I suggest is that you make a commitment to journal for at least fifteen minutes a day, or write three pages—whichever feels right for you. Next, select a time of day that you will commit to journaling and make it a new habit of self-care.

I like to journal as part of my morning ritual. Since one of my values is beauty, I like to write in a pretty journal, which also makes my journal time feel special. To me, journaling is sacred, and using a pretty journal that inspires me signals to my subconscious mind that this time is a priority and that I, also, am a priority.

What should you journal about? Here are some questions to kick-start your writing:

- What would it mean to finally take charge of my finances?
- What is not working in my current relationship with money?
- As a child, what did I learn from my parents about money?
- In what ways do I feel disempowered with money?
- What is my story about money?
- What would having enough money do for me?
- What would it take for me to feel empowered with my money?
- If money had a voice, what message would it have for me?

One last thing I would like to point out is that there can be a tendency to use journal writing as an opportunity to complain, whine or vent, which is fine. However, I suggest

that you make it a point to end your journal writing on a positive note. Do this by intentionally looking for a positive perspective from which to view your current situation. This way your journal time feels empowering to you. And that's the whole idea—to empower yourself.

One way to do this is to finish by writing down at least five things for which you are grateful. It is commonly believed that appreciation and gratitude is the doorway to prosperity and creating a wealthy mindset. I believe women need a huge dose of prosperity thinking each and every day in order to create financial security for themselves.

I have found that the women who are most motivated to transform their relationship with money are single women who are in business for themselves or are independent contractors who essentially are responsible for creating their own income. In other words, they don't automatically get a regular paycheck. And they don't have a husband to support them. These are the women who are most aware of their money blocks. It isn't until women find themselves in charge of their own finances—via divorce or widowhood— that they realize they should have gotten involved in their financial wellbeing earlier in life. According to the Allianz study, sixty-two percent of women wished they had saved more, and fifty-five percent of women wished they had begun saving earlier. Additionally, the study found that fifty-three percent of baby boomer women were concerned about outliving their sources of retirement income, and twenty-eight percent of baby boomer women didn't think they could afford to retire.

Perhaps we should heed the advice of the wise women of the boomer generation and learn from their mistakes, rather than making our own.

My best advice is to start where you are. Don't fall into the trap of thinking you need to wait until you make more money or that you have to wait because you can't afford to save right now. I've had many clients who have managed to save plenty of money on annual salaries as low as $40,000. And I've had six-figure income earning clients who didn't have a savings plan before they met me. Your level of income doesn't matter. Start where you are right now. Decide that you will become financially savvy with what you have right now. Decide that you will connect with your money, which means you know what you have coming in each month, you know what your expenses are, and you know how much you need to be saving for retirement.

Make becoming financially literate a priority this year. Sign up for financial classes, read books on women and money and subscribe to financial newsletters.

To find additional financial information, including articles, tips and resources on women and money, visit my website at **www.pattifagan.com**.

 **Patti Fagan,** a retired financial advisor, is considered an expert on Women, Money and Retirement. She owned and operated her independent insurance and financial services agency for nine years, helping women achieve financial security for their retirement years.

Audiences of professional women from various backgrounds, ranging from school teachers, dentists, and small business owners to financial advisors and school administrators, rave about Patti's seminars on topics such as:

- Understanding Your Cal-STRS (CA State Teachers Retirement System)
- Growing Your Circle of Wealth
- Tax-Free Retirement
- The Unique Financial Challenges Women Face in Retirement
- Women, Money & Power

Patti holds dual certifications as a money coach. She's certified with the International Association of Women in Business Coaching and is a member of the National Association of Insurance & Financial Advisors.

Additionally, Patti mentor's other financial professionals and is one of a select group of advisors in the country who are certified and authorized to provide retirement planning in public school districts.

As a blogger, coach and writer, Patti is passionate about empowering women with their money mindset because she wants every woman to be financially secure, both now and in their retirement years. Her vision is for every woman to heal her relationship with money and own her economic power so that she can learn to be financially literate and confident. Ultimately, Patti believes that knowledge is power and that every woman has the capacity, intelligence and strength to rule her own financial affairs.

Three Secrets to Aging with Vibrance and Pizazz

By Ariel Lexina Adams

Age cannot wither her,
nor custom stale
her infinite variety.
—*Shakespeare, Anthony and Cleopatra*

IMAGINE YOU'RE DRIVING north on Highway 101. It's a gray day and the sky is darkly overcast. The highway is wet. The fields and trees are wet. You're in your late fifties, feeling despondent about your life, and you're hoping this day will be a turning point. You're driving up to see your wise friend Joan, who's an energy worker in the small Northern California town of Sebastopol.

As you drive, the clouds part a tiny bit, a ray of sun breaks through, and then a rainbow forms, making a perfect arc over the highway ahead. You keep driving. The rainbow stays there. You're getting closer, and it's still there. Now it's right ahead, right over where you're driving. You pass under the still-vivid rainbow. This has got to be a good omen!

And it was; I was the driver. I drove under the rainbow and up to Joan's beautiful home, where I spent the weekend with her, and she skillfully helped me retrieve my good spirits and begin to turn my life around. Now, at the time of writing this book, I'm seventy-five. I met my husband and love of my life when I was sixty-eight; we got married when I was seventy-two, and things keep getting better. I can truthfully say this is the best time in my life—and it can be for you, too.

I was fifty-eight at the time of the rainbow story and for the past few years had been at the mercy of the aging experience. All my inherited beliefs, all the expectations imprinted on me by my elders and my society were coming to pass. I felt pallid and powerless. Unattractive, with all my sexual magnetism gone.

My Story

When I was a girl in the 1940s I used to listen to a soap opera called *The Romance of Helen Trent*—"the story that asks the question, 'Can a woman find adventure and romance after the age of thirty-five?'" (Maybe you remember it too.) And right around then I read a story in one of my mother's magazines. It opened with an unmarried woman looking into the mirror on her thirtieth birthday and feeling like she'd lost her chance at life.

These cultural attitudes about what I had to look forward to as a woman were deeply etched into my mind. Thirty-five loomed ahead ominously.

But somehow my life unfolded in a different way. When I hit thirty-five I was, after a brief marriage, living in a house with other creative people. I didn't have a life partner but I usually had a boyfriend. I felt very attractive.

I had always looked and felt young for my age. When

I was in my early forties my students (I was teaching English as a second language in adult schools) said I looked twenty-five. I usually had boyfriends who were younger than I was. I felt like I wasn't aging, like it wasn't going to happen.

At forty-seven I went back to school to do what I'd always wanted: become a psychotherapist. Then one day when I was about fifty I looked in the mirror and saw that my upper eyelids were all swollen. They were puffy and droopy and weighted down my eyelashes. "It must be a cat allergy," I thought, and I stopped letting Attila, our sweet orange cat, come into my room.

So I ruined my relationship with my favorite cat ever—and the eyelids stayed puffy and droopy. It was my first clear sign of aging and I felt betrayed. I realized I had felt entitled to keep looking young—that was who I was, after all. But I had started aging, and would keep on doing so.

People started calling me "ma'am." Oh, how I hated that! Guys' eyes stopped lighting up when they saw me, or they'd look right through me. I'd enviously look at a young, attractive woman walking toward me on the sidewalk and think, "Just wait, honey, it'll happen to you too!" And when some old lecherous guy would eye me, I'd actually be grateful! I had a boyfriend who was younger than I, and on a trip to Mexico, more than once some young person asked him, "Es su madre?" (Is she your mother?) In pictures taken of me during that period I look droopy and apologetic.

My self-esteem plummeted. The worst part was realizing how much it was based on my good looks—or should I say on what our culture regards as good looks, meaning young looks. I'd thought my self-worth was based on intelligence, creativity, compassion. But no. When I'd started looking older and stopped receiving that reflection back that attractive

younger people constantly get from the world, I wanted to dig a hole and crawl into it.

This went on for a year or two. They were very bad years in my life. Finally I woke up one morning with those insulting voices going in my head—"Lost your looks," "Not attractive anymore," "Not spiritual either," "What good are you?"—and I rebelled.

"That's enough!" I told myself. "I've had it! I'm going to turn this around."

I had studied some Tibetan Buddhism and always loved what Chogyam Trungpa said about skilled farmers: they collected the dung left by their cattle and turned it into fertilizer. And that, of course, was what I needed to do with my own negativity.

A Turning Point

So I decided to go get help from Joan, my shamanically trained friend up north. In our sessions, she helped me to go deep inside and retrieve something that was much deeper than all the stereotypes and judgments I'd been battling with: my vibrant spirit. I returned to my life regenerated, vowing to free myself from the age stereotype, and to help other women get free of it.

I wanted to find an older woman who had been through this transition to mentor me, but I didn't know any. I certainly couldn't get help from my mother, who was lonely and obese. So I set out to *become* that mentor. I wrote my master's thesis on the subject of women coming to terms with aging, and I've been working with women on this issue ever since.

I've made a deep study of the question, "How can we avoid the trap of the age stereotype and live fulfilling, creative, juicy lives?"

And from what I've learned (and keep learning), I created my Ageless Pizazz!® groups, where we use art and play to transform our pain and fear into the power to be who we want to be and live the lives we want to live.

In the process of this work I discovered nine guiding principles, which are the subject of my book, *Ageless Pizazz: Nine Secrets for Turning Up Your Oomph, Having More Fun, and Being More Powerful as You Get Older.* The first three follow here:

Secret Number One: Be Here Now

Come new to this day. Remove the
rigid overcoat of experience...
—*Rebecca del Rio*

Secret Number One is something most of you have heard many times. Many of you already have practices for quieting the chatter in your mind and being more present to your sensory experience in the moment... and the next moment... and now this one....

One day during rush hour at the supermarket I was able to transform my experience, and that of some other people, by just getting more present. I was standing in a long, slow-moving line. Every person ahead of me seemed to have some extra quibble or demand. People were impatient and irritated, and I was stuck there behind them. I felt myself sinking into heavy, frustrated resentment. My jaws started clenching, my shoulders contracting, my face falling into that droopy, blank stare of someone helplessly trapped.

Then I caught myself. "Wait a minute!" I thought. "Is this how I want to be? Am I maybe just making it worse with this attitude? Yes, I think so."

So I took a deep breath. Right away I started noticing the tension in my jaws and shoulders, so as I exhaled I let them relax as much as I could, and I made the choice to just be present.

I kept breathing deeply and started noticing things. I felt the soles of my feet, pressing down into the floor. I listened: I heard some music playing over the loudspeakers, the murmur of voices, the occasional wail of a child. I looked around, starting to actually see the people. Who were they? Ahead of me, a little girl in line with her mother had arranged all their items in a neat, clever pattern on the belt. I exchanged glowing smiles with the child and her mother, and everything around seemed to brighten.

"She always does that," said the mother.

"Looks like she's growing up to be an artist," I said.

The little girl grinned.

Then I saw that the pretty cashier was smiling and making a brief, warm contact with each person in line, doing everything she could to make our experience more pleasant. A man checking out was laboriously, interminably writing a check; the cashier turned back to the next customers with a smile and a greeting, letting them know she was on top of things. A man in a wheelchair was next in line. When he dropped something, she came lightly out from behind her counter and picked it up for him.

I let myself be lit up by her good will. Magic was in the air. I talked with people, made quips. They responded with pleasure. My tedious wait in line had become a festive celebration, and the energy I slipped into there carried me through the whole day.

But I could only slip into that beautiful energy by first coming into the here and now and being willing to

experience what was already there: my irritation, my body tensing, the people around me, the items on the conveyer belt—the ordinary, day-to-day things that I don't usually pay much attention to. By doing that, I removed my "rigid overcoat of experience" and was able to experience life in a deeper, richer way.

Presence and Pizazz

When I talk about pizazz, I'm referring to a sort of effervescent joy, a deep pleasure in living that, I believe, is our natural heritage. We can tap into it when we allow ourselves to be fully here in the present moment.

If you are fully present, you can begin to touch into your own pizazz—that alert, unprogrammed, spontaneous spirit at your core. One of the first things I teach in my programs is a simple practice of sensing your body, looking, and listening, to be done every day. We use it to stay present throughout the evening, go more deeply into ourselves, feel our own presence, power, and connection to the world around us, and express our power in new ways that may surprise us. Part of being fully present is being willing to be surprised, as expressed by Rebecca del Rio in the poem that I quoted at the beginning of this section:

Come new to this day.
Remove the rigid overcoat of experience,
the notion of knowing,
the beliefs that cloud your vision.
Leave behind the stories of your life.
Spit out the sour taste of unmet expectation.
Let the old,
almost forgotten scent of what-if
drift back into the swamp

of your useless fears.
Arrive curious,
without the armor of certainty,
without the planned results for the life
you've imagined.
Live the life that chooses you,
New with every breath,
New with every blink of
your astonished eyes.

© *Rebecca del Rio. Printed with permission from the author.*

Yes! When we are present we are open to experience whatever is happening. And part of what gets in the way of that is expecting something in particular and being stuck in a particular outlook. So secret number two is about managing our expectations.

Secret Number Two: Expectations

I know for sure that what we
dwell on is who we become.
—Oprah Winfrey

By expectations, I mean the ideas or beliefs you have acquired about aging over your lifetime—conscious and, more importantly, unconscious.

These expectations are key because they affect our memory, our hearing, our overall health, our enjoyment of life, our sense of ourselves, and our life expectancy.

Dr. Becca Levy of Yale University has done a number of studies on what she named "stereotype embodiment." All around us—on TV and radio, in ads we receive in the mail, in the assumptions people make when they talk—

are stereotypes of aging, and when we're young we don't question them; we just let them in, as I let in the "over-thirty-five" stereotype communicated in the Helen Trent soap opera.

These stereotypes live inside us as unconscious expectations, and then as we get older we start to automatically embody them. That's what I was doing when I was feeling so unattractive. Maybe we start to slump a bit. Or our voices get more apologetic, or sharp, or gravelly. We talk about our "symptoms" more. They even become a viable topic of conversation!

Dr. Levy found that our conscious and unconscious attitudes about aging affect every aspect of our lives. In one study, for example, elderly Chinese subjects performed better on a memory test than elderly Americans—because, she hypothesized, the Chinese tend to have a more positive view about aging than the Americans.

As we unconsciously start to embody the stereotype, our identity starts to change, like that of a Hunter College librarian I knew in the late 1960s. I was in my twenties then, teaching English. One day I was wearing a fashionably short skirt to work and stopped by the library on the way to class. The librarian, who was about forty and still attractive, remarked cattily, "Hmmph! The instructors are getting snappy! Not in my day!" I just smiled, but I wanted to say, "You mean it's not your day anymore?" And in my mind I vowed not to follow in her footsteps.

Then, when I reached my fifties, I got sucked into the aging stereotype in spite of myself. But now, in my seventies, I still do consider it "my day"—even though I'm not wild about twitter and cell-phone apps.

By Ariel Lexina Adams

Turning Back the Clock

Another psychologist who has done amazing work to show that it's our expectations that fuel our aging symptoms is Ellen Langer, who in the fall of 1981 created a total immersion experience for eight men in their seventies. She had come to see that a psychological "prime" could trigger the body to heal itself. The prime in this case was a five-day stay in a converted monastery in New Hampshire, where the environment was set up to reproduce the era when the men were twenty-two years younger: 1959. (Grierson, 2014)

At the beginning of their stay, a few of the men were arthritically stooped, and others walked with canes. They were assessed for dexterity, grip strength, flexibility, hearing and vision, and memory and cognition. From the outset the men were treated as if they were younger. They had to carry their belongings upstairs themselves. They wore the clothing styles from 1959, listened to Perry Como and other popular singers of the day, and watched Ed Sullivan on black-and-white TV and Jimmy Stewart in *Anatomy of a Murder*. On tables and bookshelves were magazines and books from that year. The participants discussed, always in the present tense, "current events" such as the first U.S. satellite launch. Everything was set up to create the illusion that they were back twenty-two years earlier. There were no mirrors, no recent photos or publications to spoil it.

At the end of their stay they were assessed again. They were found to be more supple, with greater manual dexterity and better vision; they walked taller and, according to independent observers, looked younger.

In another study, in 2010, the BBC sponsored a re-creation of Langer's project, called "The Young Ones." Six aging former celebrities were driven via period cars

88

to a country house retrofitted to 1975 and lived as their earlier selves for a week. When they emerged they showed a marked improvement on the test measures.

One, who had rolled up in a wheelchair, walked out with a cane. Another, who couldn't even put his socks on unassisted at the start, hosted the final evening's dinner party, gliding around with purpose and vim. The others walked taller and indeed seemed to look younger (Grierson, 2014).

Freeing Ourselves from the Stereotype

Now we have a name for the phenomenon that's driving our aging: "stereotype embodiment." So what do we do with it? How do we un-embody the stereotype, and is that even possible? How do we divest ourselves of a stereotype?

The first thing is to identify it as a belief, or set of beliefs, and not as ourselves.

A client of mine, Carol, succeeded in doing this. Carol was a successful therapist, wife, and mother who was participating in one of my Ageless Pizazz groups. She came in with the belief that life got boring as you got older, and guess what? She was feeling bored with her life. In the group she was able to turn that belief around. She told us stories of her wild adventures as a young woman and realized that that wild young woman was still alive in her. She began to really relish who she was, and near the end of the group she took off on an adventure, a trip she had been wanting to take for a long time, and came back and told us about it with sparkling eyes.

So after identifying the belief and acknowledging it, we find ways of changing it, or replacing it, as Carol did by calling up her youthful self and going off on a trip. We look

for models—and, now that the health-conscious Boomers are into their sixties, there are a lot of good models out there. We imagine different ways of behaving, dressing, and expressing ourselves and try them out. We hang out with other people who will validate our new, chosen belief. And perhaps the most important thing we can do is play with it. Read on.

Secret Number Three: Laughter and Play

We don't stop playing because we grow old;
we grow old because we stop playing.
—George Bernard Shaw

Because play, which is activity that we do purely for enjoyment, has no goals outside of the activity itself, we may tend to relegate it to a lower rank of importance than money-earning, career-enhancing, or household-maintaining pursuits. But most of us, except for the most hardened puritans and workaholics, know deep in ourselves that play is of core importance in life. It makes us come alive. It connects us to each other. It gives color to our lives.

Just for fun, here are some things people have said about play:

▸ *Lucia Capacchione, art therapist and family therapist:* "Play keeps us vital and alive. It gives us an enthusiasm for life that is irreplaceable. Without it, life just doesn't taste good."

▸ *Tom Robbins, author:* "Humanity has advanced, when it has advanced, not because it has been sober, responsible, and cautious, but because it has been playful, rebellious, and immature."

- *Albert Einstein:* "Play is the highest form of research."

- *Plato:* "Life must be lived as play."

- *Joan Almon, educator:* "Creative play is like a spring that bubbles up from deep within . . ."

The Benefits of Play and Laughter

As I go deeper into my study of play, I identify more and more benefits and a greater variety of ways to play. Here are just some of the benefits that play research has revealed:

- Play triggers the release of endorphins, the body's natural feel-good chemicals.

- It promotes a sense of well-being and relieves stress.

- It stimulates the brain.

- It helps prevent memory problems and improves brain function.

- It boosts creativity and problem solving.

- It stimulates your imagination.

- It improves your relationships and your connection to others.

- It can help you adapt to whatever is going on.

- It can even relieve pain.

Laughter

Try something right now as you read this. Just laugh. Not because of anything funny, but just to laugh. Say out loud, "Hee hee hee! Hoo hoo hoo hoo!" and let that turn into real laughter as you feel how ridiculous you're being. Doesn't it feel good to laugh? Can you feel the benefits to your body and your attitude? I make a point of laughing early in the

day. Sometimes I go to a You Tube page with a baby laughing, and that calls up my own chortles and giggles.

What Is Your Play Personality?

Stuart Brown, a doctor who worked with Patch Adams and author of the book *Play* (2009), tells us play is anything but trivial—it is a biological drive as integral to health as sleep or nutrition. Brown, who has extensively studied play among both humans and animals, describes its essential role in fueling intelligence and happiness, not just during childhood but throughout life. He compares play to oxygen: We need it in order to live, and "it's all around us, yet goes mostly unnoticed or unappreciated until it is missing."

Brown identifies eight modes of play and the "play personality" that prefers each type (pp. 65–70). Of course, we all enjoy more than one mode; we're all combinations of the various types. Which types fit you best?

The Joker

Jokers are often, as children, the class clown at school. They like to do silly things, say funny things to make people laugh. They want to get a response from people. Their delight is when people appreciate their quips and witticisms. Their humor can be broad and uproarious, but might also be witty and more subtle—the point is to get a response.

The Kinesthete

Kinesthetes are people whose bodies thrive on movement. They love to walk, dance, bounce on trampolines, and play active games for the joy of moving rather than the success of winning. As kids they risk being classified as ADD, but when their parents and teachers allow them to move around

instead of sitting still all day, they thrive.

The Explorer

Explorers are attracted by whatever is new or novel. They revel in searching out and experiencing new environments, getting to know new people, feeling new or deeper feelings, exploring new ideas, and researching new subjects. Following their ever-active curiosity is their idea of play. My husband, Michael, is like that. He is always finding different routes to get to work, or to a favorite restaurant or store. The routes are not always more efficient, but take us into new neighborhoods we otherwise wouldn't know about.

The Competitor

Competitors love playing to win, love focusing on getting good at the pursuit and racking up those points—whether it's tennis, video games, or the stock market. What's fun for these people is the thrill of competition and the joy of winning. And if they lose? Good competitor types will make use of every experience to improve their game, and consider the time well spent; losing is something to learn from and joke about.

The Director

Directors enjoy making things happen. They like organizing events, working out the logistics, delegating roles—starting out with a vision and orchestrating it in real life. When collaborating with others they can be much appreciated, but if they're not careful, and just assume their friends or associates will be eager to carry out their ideas, they may find people avoiding them. My friend Clarinda, when she was a girl, found out her friends were avoiding her because she was so "bossy," always assigning them roles in little projects.

She had just thought she was enthusiastic. She learned from the incident, and now as an adult she constantly finds people turning to her when a creative leader is needed.

The Collector

Collectors focus on a particular kind of object or experience and collect them enthusiastically. One friend of mine traveled to various locations in Europe to see Black Madonnas, and brought back wonderful pictures, which she gave to friends. Another has figures and pictures of all kinds of frogs. Collectors are great to give presents to, because you know just what they'll like—if they don't already have it.

The Artist/Creator

These people love to make things—beautiful, artistic things, works of art; or practical things, new inventions; or even silly things, like those oversize, strangely shaped sunglasses. I find that all of us have some artist/creator in ourselves, and this comes out with enthusiasm in groups where we make collages, provided there are enough magazines and scissors to go around.

One More Type: The Performer

I think that Brown left out a play personality type that rings true for a lot of us: the Performer. Performers love to tell stories and dramatize, for large or small audiences, or for just one person, or even alone for themselves. When my sister and I were kids we used to get together with friends, create little shows, and perform them for our parents, or just for each other (I was particularly good at doing witches). And even when alone, the performer might dance around, make up a line of song about some task she's doing, or talk to herself dramatically.

How to Bring More Play into Your Life

To stay healthy and vibrant, it's good to sprinkle play throughout your day, every day. If you've identified a couple of your play personalities from the list above, you can start from there. If you're a kinesthete (and most of us are, to some degree), begin the day by moving your body, dancing, moving to music. And throughout the day, punctuate your activities with movement and dance. If you're a performer or a joker, add some silly or dramatic attitudes to your movement. Or let your explorer self find ways to move that are different from your habitual ones. If you're motivated by competition, you can compete with yourself by getting a jump rope, and continuing to increase the number of jumps you can do without missing a step. Or you can play competitive games with others, such as tennis, basketball, or bridge.

A wonderful website you can use to punctuate your day is Mindfulness Bell (fungie.info/bell). You can set the gong sound to ring at any interval you choose: every 30 minutes, every 60 minutes, or whatever you prefer. Then when it rings, take a deep breath, smile, stand up and move, sing, shout, say a line of poetry, or whatever lights you up.

Here are some more ways to bring play into your daily life:

▸ Cultivate a playful attitude. Wake up in the morning and say to yourself, "What mischief can I get into today?"

▸ Imagine you're wearing a pair of Goofy Glasses and looking out at the world through them.

▸ Make faces at yourself in the mirror.

▸ Sing loud and off key in the shower.

- Hang out with young children and play games with them. Let them show you the way and leave your grownup mind behind.

- Take a walk or day trip without any plans or route.

- To make it extra playful, toss a coin to decide on the direction you'll start out in. Then just go wherever you are drawn. Let your playfulness lead the way.

- Spend more time with the most playful person you know.

- Join meetup groups dedicated to doing fun things.

And if you've enjoyed this article, you can come to my Ageless Pizazz!® group in the San Francisco East Bay, where we are devoted to having fun as we transform our pain and resistance into power and creativity. Or you can take my online class and be part of a larger community of women who are dedicated to becoming not only more powerful, vibrant, and fulfilled in their lives, but more influential as wise women elders in steering the course of our beautiful planet, which is so threatened by the dominator culture.

If you resonate with what I have been saying, please visit my website at **www.AgelessPizazz.net**, where you can subscribe to my email newsletter or sign up for a complimentary "Powerful You" discovery session by telephone. I send you my love and blessings and wishes for joyful well-being and never-ending openness to new discoveries and adventures.

References

Brown, Stuart. (2009). *Play: How It Shapes the Brain, Opens the Imagination, and Invigorates the Soul.* New York: Penguin.

del Rio, Rebecca. (Date unknown). Accessed July 9, 2015, at: http://www.wisdombridge.net/the-generous-heart.html

Grierson, Bruce. (2014, October 22). "What if Age Is Nothing but a Mind-Set?" *New York Times Magazine.* Accessed at: http://www.nytimes.com/2014/10/26/magazine/what-if-age-is-nothing-but-a-mind-set.html?_r=0

Ariel Lexina Adams is a marriage and family therapist, teacher, and speaker who was born with a question: "What am I? Why am I here?" This question led her to study literature at Reed College, where topics like "What is it to be human?" were batted about in seminars. Then she got her master's degree in English literature at Cornell.

Ariel's life-question led her to Berkeley, Paris, Madrid, New York, and back to Berkeley, where she studied with Dr. Claudio Naranjo. His group explored her question big time, with Zen meditation, Sufi stories, Gestalt therapy, the Enneagram, and the Gurdjieff movements, among other modalities. Ariel became a group leader and led groups in Berkeley, New York, Pittsburgh, and Boston.

She loved Gestalt, which lets people express the many characters within—carping critic, dumb blob, brilliant leader, seductress—and this interest led her to study improv in Boston and San Francisco, and later to become a drama therapist.

Ariel fell in love with theater games as a way to tap into creativity and developed Assertiveness Through Drama groups, for people who wanted to express themselves but were too shy, and The Fifth Act workshop, in which participants used drama, costumes, and masks to step into the self they wanted to become. She now offers Ageless Pizazz!® empowerment groups for women forty-seven and up. She's the author of *Ageless Pizazz: Nine Secrets for Turning Up Your Oomph, Having More Fun, and Being More Powerful as You Get Older.*

Ariel's website is **www.AgelessPizazz.net**

No More
Mr. Nice Guy

By Sharon Lee

I DISCOVERED THAT there is a path to success, and when you understand it, you can **Master Success**. You can do and have anything you desire. I am passionate about sharing my story of success and helping people like you to have the same kind of success I am experiencing. I discovered the hard way that pleasing others before yourself doesn't get you the results you desire. They say being selfish is a bad thing, but it's not true.

My mother intimidated the entire family. It was toxic when she was angry. She was rarely happy, and never happy with me. Mom was just twenty-one and Daddy was twenty-ning when I was born. The love I received from my father felt wholesome and natural but with my mom, I felt more like a doll or a possession than a child with feelings who was loved and cherished. My father was joyful and good humored while my mom was critical, moody and ill tempered. I was afraid of her. I could never complain or talk back. If I did, it was always my fault when things went bad. She was rarely happy, and never happy with me. I stayed out of trouble by being a good girl. She trained me to be a people pleaser. She controlled everything, including me. She criticized how

I walked, talked, dressed, looked, ate — everything, even how I breathed. I had to do it her way, which was the only right way. I did whatever she told me to do, and I was praised for being pretty and good. But I never really felt "all that." I felt like a fake, pretending what I was programmed to be. I second-guessed my instincts because her opinions overruled my thoughts. I was good at making other people happy. I learned that other people were more important than myself. It was wrong to be selfish.

When I was thirteen, I was devastated when my father died of a heart attack within a year after my parents divorce. My mother had already remarried, taking us with her out of state with my step-dad by then. When my dad died, I felt lost, abandoned, alone. I really don't know how I got through those years. I had no one I could count on. Still, I finished school, completed my cosmetology license and went on to get a bachelor of arts in psychology at Berkeley.

By thirty, I was married with two boys. I was doing all the "right" things — working hard, honoring and respecting my elders and husband. I found the pressure of pleasing my clients, husband, mother and children overwhelming. Eventually, the pain and isolation of being married to a man I didn't love was heavier than the guilt of being a home wrecker. I was in a no-win situation. I wasn't good if I stayed or left. I asked for a divorce and my husband kidnapped our son for six weeks until I agreed to stay and make it work. I felt I was being punished for being selfish. I wanted to die.

We finally split up and after a traumatic divorce. My next suitor wanted me more than I wanted him. I wanted to be rescued from my controlling mother. I thought this relationship was better because I had begun my spiritual healing. I was learning how to manifest things I'd been asking

for. I should have been grateful for having great clients, making good money, and having a beautiful new home, with healthy kids. I didn't understand that I was feeling "off" until much later. I was waking up depressed and I didn't know it. I noticed I designed my life to please everyone else, and I struggled to accept joy in myself.

I was praying for freedom, peace, and security. I won $17,000 betting on the winning teams during a football season in 1999 as a practice with a small psychic development circle. That was my miracle to start my own business. I launched my product, The Handy Caddy, in 2000, but by 2008 I was separated, broke and maxing out my credit. I was behind six years on my taxes. The business was growing, but my expenses and debts were my demise. I had lost control of my stable life, and I developed Graves' disease, high blood pressure, and high cholesterol.

Things began to change after I met someone who showed me a particular *unconscious* pattern that I had been creating and recreating all of my life. My years of spiritual studies were tied together with this last piece. He helped me to identify the *unconscious core story* in which I had always played a particular character. When I began to see my own pattern and how I played out my role, I learned what I had to do to change that role and create something better.

It took a year, but I healed my diseases naturally. I no longer take the medications that the doctors said I would be on for life. I was blessed to learn how to identify those old patterns and change them. I discovered some valuable methods that would reveal the things we believe and think that make us sick.

Being too nice can sabotage success. There is a way to be nice *and* get what you desire. Maybe you'd like to start

a business, find new love, begin a new career, get a raise in your current career, lose weight, have more vitality, get your children to behave better...or something else.Being selfish is the only thing you can be in life. We're programmed to believe being selfish is bad, but in reality, who knows better than yourself what is right for you? You are experiencing through your body, but through constant programming from outside influences, you forget how to navigate with your own feelings. What business do you have making decisions for someone other than yourself? When I began to tune into what my body was telling me, being true to myself, miracles began to happen. It helps to have a GPS system, aka a mentor, to help you navigate your destiny.

Suppose you already know you are very ready for change. What does that change really mean? Do you have a clear vision of what you desire? Who do you turn to for the right advice? Who would you trust to give you some clear perspective on what your next step is? Who will give you the attention you need to support you through a challenging stage in life? Are you afraid to be a burden to others? These are questions that will keep you stuck. How do you find the right kind of help?

Your complimentary Master Success Breakthrough Session is thirty minutes of my personal one-on-one time where I can give you some insight on the challenges you are facing and how can I assist you in changing them for the better. This could be the lifeline that you have been praying for.

Text Sharon at 650-483-2866 for your Master Success Breakthrough Session

Why is mentorship valuable? Life is short. If it's possible to learn from others, get clarification on your goals, and shave years off of your learning curve, imagine how much

more you can accomplish. Wealthy and successful people use advisors to get expert advice in all endeavors to move them quickly through a project. King Solomon, the richest man in the world, through wisdom to grow his empire with cooperation with his people.

I have witnessed a consistent correlation between being too nice and a person's ability to create success. My program addresses how success happens when you master your presence in the world. Being nice, or being sensitive to others' needs is a wonderful skill to master. But giving too much means giving up your personal power at your own expense. Giving away your power isn't beneficial when it's your place to shine and be the gift you were intended to be. You will feel empowered when you can master the art of service with your gift and thrive mentally, emotionally and physically as a result. I am attracting a flood of clients whose success is being challenged by being too nice, too caring and too compassionate. There is an art to giving and receiving. Like breathing, it must be done in equal measure.

A desire to be good, or nice, drives many of us to be people pleasers. It's a common belief that if you are nice, you will be rewarded. You want to believe that God rewards you for being nice. You think that good things are supposed to happen to good people. Is it confusing that your efforts at being nice and caring are going unrewarded? Is it difficult to accept that you might be taken for granted, and even taken advantage of? Is your giving paying off? Are you putting in way more effort into your work and family than you get in return? Are you uncomfortable asking for help?

Have you ever noticed that the critical wife gets a husband who is very attentive? Do you think that a nice person doesn't say no or have confrontations with people? Is it hard saying

"no" to friends and family? Do you avoid confrontations at all costs? Do you complain that you take care of everyone else, but the one time you really need someone, they're not there for you? Do you find yourself getting the short end of the stick too often?

What's going on? It's time to change all this! Avoidance and distraction are common ways to get around having to say "no" or have a confrontation with someone. You can only use the tactic of avoidance or distraction for so long, until you find yourself frustrated and angry.

Would you like to learn how to get your needs met and still be a nice person? Nice people often don't feel nurtured in their lives. Here are three common beliefs about being nice that just aren't true!

1. It's nice to go along with what others want.
2. It's nicer to keep the peace than to risk an argument.
3. Nice people should try to please everyone.

I'd like to share with you some examples of my clients who habitually gave away their power in daily situations and how their lives improved after they went through my program. I've changed their names, but the stories have the essence of their transformation. The energy they were projecting caused them to miss out on opportunities or to be taken advantage of. They allowed something or someone else dictate their direction in life, leaving them feeling unfulfilled, frustrated, inferior, and powerless. They lacked confidence in being able to stand in their power.

When upleveling your power, it's not necessary to stop being nice, but there is an art to knowing how and when being nice is appropriate, and when it's self-sabotaging.

Arturo, was a very talented musician, healer,

artist, and sign painter. He was kind and generous with his time and energy. He never said no when asked for a favor. At sixty-five, Arturo was still struggling with money and being taken advantage of by "friends" for his kindness. And even though he had a car, he lost it to a friend's negligence, and now he was back depending on others to drive him around for work. Arturo was a people pleaser. He allowed his "friends" to borrow his car, and the friends racked up so many parking tickets and failed to pay them that his car was ultimately impounded and he never got it back.

Within a week after we discovered his patterns and worked on a new paradigm, his long time wealthy client gifted him his well-loved old car and computer. Arturo then found a long-term job assisting an elderly man who enjoyed his music, cooking, and companionship. His life definitely changed for the better, and two years later he's still doing very well and feeling appreciated by his new employer.

Sara, twenty-seven, was inconsolable if someone rejected her on a first date. She knew it didn't make sense, but the feelings where obvious and unshakable. She was attractive and smart. Even though she made herself available in relationships, men didn't call for a second date, and it crushed her emotionally. The kind of relationships that she had were abusive. She was choosing to stay in a bad relationship rather than be alone. Within six months of coaching, she was enjoying a healthy relationship with a man who appreciated her and shared her interests, and she learned to close the door on the more toxic relationships in her past.

Tracy, fifty, was a social worker for twenty-five years and had trouble seeing herself as a success. She was quick to admit her mistakes and failures and had relatives and co-workers who were critical of her.

Her shoulders were rounded over. She suffered from constant neck and back pain and was often apologetic before she had done anything wrong. There was a skittishness about her, and she was quick to apologize for her faults and mistakes without being asked. It made me uncomfortable seeing her behave so submissively. She was a hard worker, often working late, until her boss forbade her to work overtime. She was anxious about not getting her work complete. She was choosing to work unpaid to complete tasks. Her verbally manipulating older husband had been threatening to leave her anytime she wouldn't give in to his demands. She admitted that she wouldn't really mind much if he left because he was not very nice to her most of the time. When I was able to show Tracy the core habits that were shaping her relationships, she was ready to make some new decisions. She gave herself permission to say "no" more often. When she accepted that her husband was leaving, he changed his tune. Now he's being nicer to her. I admire how quickly she caught on to her patterns and her willingness to be more assertive with family and peers. She is grateful for the change.

Martin, forty-seven, had been a strong athlete all of his life. He had never sick for a day. He was the head of a physical therapy office and during a most intense, demanding schedule, he developed a rare kidney disorder that left him feeling drained and weak.

Martin has deep compassion for his clients and was extending himself beyond natural expectations. He was known to give more than expected. He became manager of the physical therapy practice. His motivation to create a successful practice meant he was doing all the hard work to manage cases that he felt his co-workers couldn't or wouldn't

do. He needed them and he didn't want them to quit from too much pressure of time commitments and deadlines. He had no time left for his family, and that was stressful to him. He couldn't see a way out of his dilemma.

To complicate matters, his mother in law was dying from cancer and his wife accused him of not being supportive during that difficult time. He fit in time to sit with his mother-in-law and was willing to jump in at her request, so he was blindsided when his wife didn't acknowledge his support. His health began to decline rapidly. He didn't have the stamina he was used to having and was finally diagnosed with a rare cancer in the kidneys. His illness meant he had to quit his job and commit himself to healing. This was when I met him. We were able to reveal some core stories that he believed were causing a dis-ease in his body. Since reprogramming these thoughts and beliefs, by clearing the energetic blockage in his body, he has seen significant changes in his energy and in his blood tests. In fact, he is on his way to a full recovery. He is practicing and learning what the conflicts were in his thinking, beliefs and emotions and is taking appropriate action to empower himself and live a more balanced life.

I am calling out to those of you who are really kind, nice and generous souls who seek more balance and joy in life. You are a hard working person and you should be able to have a good life, and yet you are feeling misunderstood, underserved, and unrewarded for all that you have done. You might feel alone, because you can't be sure there will be someone to rescue you, if you need help.

Don't you owe it to yourself to make the changes you must have to live the rest of your life with more joy and peace?

Being a slave to someone else's vision or path means that you may not be on your own path. It is possible to co-create with others. It is possible to live your path in service to others for a greater cause with which you are in alignment. So you have to be honest with yourself. You might have to give up a life that isn't working for you. You are not a bad person if you have to say "no" sometimes. You must get yourself back on track to your own soul's purpose to be truly at peace with yourself.

Are you ready to begin a life of your own brand of success? Would you benefit from having a coach who will give you skills and tools to empower yourself and stand up for yourself? Would it benefit you to know that there is a process that will identify core beliefs, feelings and thoughts that are running your life, and not just identify them, but help you reprogram them to something much better?

When you are serving others and there is no sense of appreciation for your efforts, then you have become a slave. Instead of being in service to others, you enter servitude. I lived that life, and I found myself at a dead end. Today, I love to help people that are ready to receive it. I feel appreciation from those I get to serve with respect and gratitude. And when it's not appreciated, I know what to do.

I am passionate about being supportive of those of you who suffer from that same state of mind. We all deserve to live heaven on Earth. We don't need to be punished for not being perfect.

Life is very short, and you have probably already lived half of your life as it is. Wouldn't you like to enjoy the rest of your life living out your dreams?

Now is the time to take advantage of a complimentary Master Success Breakthrough Session. You are worthy! You

deserve to be happy! You owe it to yourself to live your best life and for be a role model to your peers, co-workers and family. Don't hesitate, procrastinate, or convince yourself that you don't need this. Don't waste precious time.

If you don't make the changes in your life you know you want, when will the next opportunity show up for you? How many years of life do you have? Are you living your highest potential? Why shouldn't you?

The fastest way to connect with me is to text me right now at 650-483-2866 and text in the subject box: Breakthrough Session. Message me your name, email and phone number, and I'll contact you by email with the intention of within forty-eight hours.

I don't know how many books will be sold, and I don't know how many people I'll reach. If this book becomes a bestseller, then I will happily cross that bridge when I reach it! I like to say, I work for God. I am committed to contributing to "heaven on Earth," and I am offering my services to help my soul sisters and brothers to have the kind of success I have had in my life. I am grateful for this opportunity to share my story with you. In divine alignment with Source of All Creation... I hope to meet you, if it's meant to be!

Blessings, Sharon Lee

**No More Mr. Nice Guy.
It's time to take back your power.
Unleash your super powers and
master success.**

My name is Sharon Lee. I'm an entrepreneur, mother, spiritual seeker, intuitive counselor, product designer, business coach, artist, writer, event producer, and world traveler. I've had a very colorful life. I've practiced success and miracles in this life and I feel it in my body that I understand the mechanics of success, and I hope that I can show you how you can master success in your life.

If you are drawn to my story, I am inviting you to have a Master Success Breakthrough Session with me, as a gift. I am not sure how many I will reach, but it's my intention to be able to help you with Divine Guidance and Timing.

Blessings, Sharon Lee
SharonLee@me.com
650-483-2866

Living the
Second Half

By Sally Domingo

THE CAB OF THE Dodge truck was dusty, and as always, the smell of dirt and sweat hung in the air. Sunflower seeds filled the console, along with a pile of old receipts, some pocket change and a ballpoint pen. The old orange hardhat and a notepad sat on the passenger seat, ready for the next job — echoes of a life suddenly cut short. All that was left of the man who was my husband. And there it was again, the terrible aching in my chest. Remember to breathe, just breathe, this will pass. And then the silence, heavy silence. No more jangling of keys, slamming of doors, no more work boots caked with mud sliding over the pedals. What to do with the old truck, still sitting in the driveway, waiting like an abandoned dog for its owner's return. Silence, just silence, and more tears.

As I write this, four years have vanished since the day we buried Mike. Our beautiful kids, Holly and Kurtis, are four years older on the outside, many years older on the inside. It hasn't been easy — the medical bills and funeral bills have all been paid, the house and the old truck and the motorcycle have all been sold. And all that remains are the tools, the old magazines, and odds and ends I could never part with. I've

closed that chapter and opened a new one, and the second half of my life has finally begun. It's been a long and painful road filled with anxiety, hard work, financial strain, and spiritual upheaval. I've seen my kids go through depression, fear, isolation and defiance, and emerge as thoughtful and compassionate young adults. I've walked through the worst that life can bring, and have come out of it wiser and more open to the joys of living. I've grown to become a teacher and a mentor, a leader and a healer of women. There is no suffering that does not lead to growth.

How do I know this? Because I've lived it; and this is how it unfolded for me. I started out at the age of twenty-one with a bachelor's degree in Plant Science from UC Davis. My plan was to become a landscape architect, and I had even begun some post-graduate work at UCLA towards a landscape architecture license, however I ended up accepting a job offer instead, working in the landscape industry in production and purchasing for a large corporate tree grower. This led me to sales and a twenty-year career as an entrepreneur representing wholesale lumber manufacturers to the wholesale landscape industry across the Western United States. I quickly found myself traveling to new cities on a regular basis, opening new territories and setting up distributorships, working trade shows and conventions and navigating my way through the world of marketing and advertising. And I gradually became a trusted advisor to growers, farmers and distributors, big and small.

The path that has taken me to what I'm doing now has been a winding, twisting one. Along the way, I've been many things. I've earned a consistent six-figure income working from home while raising my two children. And I've explored a lot of ways to give back to my community at the same

time. When Holly was in elementary school, I became a Girl Scout leader, and I joined the PTA and served for the next seven years as a committee chair, renovating the school's nature area into an arboretum. When Kurtis was six years old, I became a Cub Scout den leader, and when he bridged to Boy Scouts I trained to be an Assistant Scoutmaster. When Holly's track team needed new leadership, I took up running and became a CYO track coach. I worked alongside my husband for the next nine years, building the team from thirty kids up to one hundred and twenty-five. Somewhere in the process I had become "Superwoman." I did it all, an American woman's dream, and time went by fast. Eventually, working full time in my career and also volunteering full time took its toll. I found that I had no time left for myself, let alone for my husband. Self-care? Unheard of. Sex? Who had time? Travel? I didn't think I could afford it...

Have you ever realized that a whole year has gone by, or maybe five, and you've been working so hard to build your business that you've forgotten to live your life in the meantime? All your friends talk about all the places they've been, like France and Peru and Hawaii, and you wonder why you can't remember the last time you went anywhere? The trouble is, you can always make more money, but you can't get back lost years! So how do they do it? How do other people find the time and money to travel? Do you have to be wealthy to see the world? No! Anyone can do it if they want to! But how? With intention, that's how! And with purpose and vision, that's how! And these don't cost a thing.

So why is it that so many Americans work hard and take so little time off, and yet have so little savings? The average American family had just $5,900 in savings accounts in 2011, according to a report by Pitney Bowes. So if they

don't go anywhere, where does their money go? Health care, for one. There is an epidemic of workers now suffering from chronic-fatigue syndrome, back injuries, anxiety, depression and joint disease, to name a few. We are taking more sick days than vacation days, all because of the stress from overworking.

One of my clients, I'll call her "Mary", is an attorney and a single mom who was battling anxiety, chronic fatigue and psoriatic arthritis after suffering a financial loss from a failed business, followed by a few years of limited employment. When we started working together, she had been avoiding charges by the IRS that she owed $400,000 in unpaid taxes, and although she knew it was in error, she simply didn't have the energy to fight it. I helped her to get her finances in order, and to get her tax advisor to expedite the challenge to IRS charges. Six months later, the majority of the taxes were dropped as paperwork errors from the sale of a previous home, and Mary was able to accept a small inheritance from which she was able to pay off her bills. Miraculously, once the cause of her stress was gone, her health improved! Her migraines were less frequent, and her energy returned. She began planning a cruise to the Caribbean with her daughter, and soon after that she got a full-time at-home position with a law firm. I helped her to invest her remaining inheritance by diversifying in a variety of risk-free, moderate and higher growth portfolios through a trusted investment expert, and now she is living a more relaxed, happy and confident future.

My grandfather used to say, "The key to a good life is moderation in all things." I'd like to go a little further and say that the key to a happy life is BALANCE in all things.

We need to take as much time for self-care and personal pleasure as we do for work. If we do this, then we have

fewer sick days and more vacation days. Less money spent on prescriptions and doctor visits and procedures leaves more money for travel and fun. Sounds easy, but how do we do this?

I ask my clients to take out a calendar and intentionally plan for four or five three-day weekends scattered through the year. Then I ask them to make a list of places they want to go within one to four hours from home, and to start plugging them in. Then I ask that they set aside seven to ten days of solid vacation time with the intention of travelling farther away or even abroad. If you do this, you will find that your life will start revolving around these times instead of revolving around work. The next step is to begin setting aside daily and weekly time for self-care. This can be walking, meditation, exercise, or whatever grounds you and clears your mind. Put YOU first on every day of your calendar. We all have twenty-four hours in a day, so try setting aside at least one to two hours for yourself.

In 2008, the stock market crashed and forever changed the lives of a majority of Americans. Since the beginning of the Great Recession, billions of dollars have been lost from portfolios and savings accounts all across the country. In 2010, I made a bold decision. I'd worked for twenty years as an entrepreneur, and I'd made a lot of money and I'd risen to the top of my profession. But I was tired of doing what I had done for so long, and I felt that somehow I had a bigger purpose to serve. The landscape and lumber industries had been hit hard by the recession, and this was as good a time as any to make a change. When I was approached by New York Life Insurance Company with an offer to train for a new career in the financial industry, I was interested. This opportunity would allow me to help families to plan better

for life events, and since I had recently witnessed my parents go through the emotional, physical and financial challenges of old age, I thought it might be fulfilling. And so, I accepted their offer and began training for my new calling in the financial industry. I passed my first of many licensing exams and accepted a contract working as an independent agent. And that's when life took an unexpected turn.

One month later, my husband Mike was diagnosed with Stage IV esophageal cancer. He had a grapefruit-sized tumor located directly on his heart. He was only fifty-two, and to all appearances he seemed to be in good health. It was a shock to all of us. How was I going to tell our kids that their dad probably wouldn't live through this?

And thus began the relentless and painful journey through cancer treatment. The first step was surgery, to prepare him for chemotherapy and possible future procedures. Poor Mike, he didn't even know what hit him. The fear, the denial, the intense pain and heartache at the thought of losing his kids and his life was overwhelming. I remember sitting out on the patio with him one beautiful sunny day, underneath the large and spectacular pergola that he had recently built, which looked just like the one we'd seen once while visiting a wild animal park. He had built it just for me. I looked at him and said, "Mike, you don't have to do this. There's a choice, you don't have to go through the chemo and radiation. Let me take you fishing in Canada. Or we could go to Paris. Anywhere you like. I'll take you there. It'll be you and me and the kids, anywhere in the world." But his answer was, "No, I think I can fight this." The doctors had held out the irresistible possibility that if he went through all of the treatments, he could live. And that's how oncologists make their money. They hold out the promise of life, at any cost,

and it's hard to refuse. And they aren't always up front and honest with their patients, perhaps because they don't want to limit their beliefs in even the smallest hope of recovery. In fact, our family doctor was the only one who was honest with me. She held my hand one day and told me that in all probability he wouldn't live more than three or four months. In fact, he lived for five painful months while our kids looked helplessly on.

Then came the day we'd all dreaded. The tumor hemorrhaged. As I held Mike's hand that night, I realized that not only was I losing my husband and best friend of twenty-five years, and our kids were losing their father. But that most of all, Mike was about to lose everything he ever had, everyone he had ever loved, and everything he had yet to do. Life was too short.

And time just stopped. After the funeral, and for weeks thereafter, we all sat around the living room staring into space. Shock and grief gradually turned to numbness and a total lack of motion or thought. And then one day I got up off the couch, and I forced myself to get dressed and go to work. I felt that if I didn't move, my kids might just stay in that lost, empty space with me indefinitely. If I could summon the strength to go out in the world again, then they would follow my example. Numbness turned to tears as I drove away, but at least the tears and the pain were better than the emptiness I left behind. And so I moved forward, making my way through each ensuing long day, training, working, making a pretense of living, and adopting new routines to fill the days so I didn't have time to think. And there was plenty to be done. Losing my husband meant also losing all of the things that he embodied. I lost my handyman, the plumber, the gardener, and the guy who stopped for groceries and who

took our son to soccer practice. On the weekends, I found myself raking leaves for hours and hours, since I didn't know how to use the blower. And when I wasn't doing that, I was mowing the lawns or taking out the trash. The kids retreated to their rooms, while their closest friends came and went, taking turns keeping them company. They seldom left the house that summer, staying within the dark and sorrowful cocoon of our old life.

I had become a widow. What a creepy depressing word for a lonely single woman. I had also become a single mom. That meant that I soon had to learn new survival techniques, such as "Pizza Mondays." Mondays were my longest days, when I worked all day and then went in for training all evening. I would leave the kids a twenty dollar bill and a pizza menu, and they got to order their own dinners and greet the pizza man at the door. They, in turn, learned some new life skills and enjoyed some newfound independence! I began filling the refrigerator on Sundays with easy-to-eat foods the kids liked, such as rice, beans, cheese and tortillas. It was a nutritional disaster called survival. I got through the long days with energy boosts from cookies and coffee. It wasn't ideal, but neither was anything else about our lives during that period. All I really wanted was time: time to heal, and time to work through my sorrow and let go of my grief. I desperately wanted to take a year off and spend it with the kids, but my fears and anxieties around providing a secure future for them kept me forging ahead in my new career.

After a year had come and gone, I decided to sell the house and downsize. I lacked the time, the money and the energy to clean and maintain a 3,000 square-foot house. So, I loaded up my credit cards in order to fund a remodeling of a bedroom and bathroom, and I began the monstrous

job of getting the house ready to put on the market. And so I spent the ensuing six months selling my house twice and going through probate court at an expense totaling $10,000 in attorney fees. Little had I known that a small error on the deed to our house would cause such a horrendous complication upon Mike's death. But it finally resolved itself all at once at the end of that year.

And so it was that the second half of my life began. I took out a lease on a small cottage located across town in a cute old neighborhood that was filled with granny houses with white picket fences and geraniums. In the process of downsizing, I spent months selling, storing and giving away a lot of my material possessions, and that helped me to clear space in my life for new love, passion and adventures yet to come.

It was while I was trying to get my old house ready to sell that some mutual friends introduced me to a man they knew and loved who had recently suffered the tragic breakup of his own twenty year marriage. And so they dragged Pete over one day to help me fix my broken stove. A cocky repairman had quoted me over $1,000 just to open it up to look at it. I found that it is one of the downsides to being a single woman — so many contractors and repairmen try to take advantage of you. And so it happened that my friends hoped that not only would Pete fix my stove, but that the two of us would find we had something in common. They had absolutely no idea how well we would hit it off. He came in like a knight in shining armor, a very tall, very kind and handsome man who instantly reminded me of a great big teddy bear. He fixed my stove for the cost of a $60 part, and I thanked him by offering him a glass of wine. We talked for hours, comparing stories and enjoying each other's company.

After that, he started coming around often to help me with everything from painting doors to fixing everything that was wrong with my life. We've supported each other ever since, in so many ways, with gentleness, deep compassion, and the knowledge that life is a precious thing not to be wasted. And together over time, we have moved forward into a happy and loving relationship. We've made room in our small house for a new puppy, Annie, a vegetable garden, loads of geraniums, and even a chicken coop! Pete surprised me on my birthday one year with a box of baby chickens. Soon after, he built me a chicken coop worthy of a magazine spread, complete with an antique chandelier, a staircase and shuttered windows. These days, whenever I need to take a break and meditate or relax, I just walk out in our backyard and spend time with my chickens. They always make me smile and I walk away feeling calm and happy.

Downsizing has changed my life in many ways. Having less space to maintain has freed up more of my time for relaxation and fun. And now that I no longer have a mortgage, I am free of the responsibilities and expenses that I once had to deal with. I can take all the money that I used to spend on property taxes, utility bills and home maintenance and put it into savings. And a part of that savings can be used for travel and fun that I haven't had in years. I once spent my weekends cleaning four bathrooms and raking endless piles of leaves. Now my weekends are spent traveling to visit friends in other cities and having adventures in beautiful places. And I love to plan future vacations in distant locations. I've made a nice long list of all the countries I want to see. And now I fulfill my calling by helping other women to do the same.

I'll never know how I survived those first few years, but at some point I became more determined than ever to

build a stronger foundation for my new life. When Mike died, I began to realize what it meant for other women to be widows and single parents. And I found myself advising other professional women like myself with their finances, beginning with the fundamentals of life insurance and how to save and organize their money. At one point, I had a client who died suddenly, and I learned what it was like to deliver a life insurance check to his widow. I was able to look her in the eye and tell her it would be okay, that at least she would have some financial security after losing her husband, thanks to the smart planning they had done. I discovered that I had a new purpose in life and that I wanted to use my experience and knowledge to help other women. I wanted to help them to prevent all of the physical and financial hardships that I had had to endure. There is a great need for women to educate themselves about finances in order to prepare for the day when they might find themselves divorced or widowed and perhaps with children who depend on them for security and education.

Many of my clients are divorced women with teenage or college-aged children. Throughout their marriages they had relied on their spouses to plan for their financial security, never dreaming that someday they would find themselves divorced and on their own. Suddenly, they were faced with starting over with little savings and even less knowledge about financial strategies. Their lives had become a whirlwind of working long hours and supporting their children, with no real plan to get ahead or to find balance. And divorce often results in a general distrust of advisors and attorneys, especially if the women don't understand the jargon or concepts.

One of my clients, I'll call her "Anne," is a good example. After her divorce, she threw herself into her business as an aesthetician, commuting an hour each way to work in order to keep her condominium. When I met her, her business was taking off, but although she was keeping track of her business income, her personal accounts were mixed in with her business accounts, and she had no idea what her profit was or how to track her expenses. She was trying hard to save, but she was putting everything into her IRA account and had no short term savings for emergencies or for fun. She was leading a life that she thought was "successful," but she was working herself into a state of perpetual muscle pain and self-deprivation. She had even stopped buying herself small things, like weekly coffees or lunches out. Once I taught her how to separate her personal accounts from her business and to plan for a variety of things, both short-term and long-term, she became more confident in herself and in her business. She began spending more time with friends and began to see herself as a priority. Now her business continues to thrive, but she sees how valuable her time is, and she has found a way to have balance in both.

Today, I am a financial educator, and a wealth empowerment expert and mentor to women who work hard and want more from life. My mission, which I live through my company, Women Wealth Mastery, is to raise women's awareness all around the world and give them the tools they need to become financially confident, educated and organized. And I help them learn the keys to systematic savings and investing, with the purpose of living life fully and with intention. To transform your life requires a mentor, someone who is willing to take your hand and walk that path with you as you begin to live the second half of your life. I am passionate about helping

successful women who find themselves working too hard and not having time. I love to help them prioritize, putting their needs for fun, self-care, and travel before their work. And I help them to save and organize their money around their short-term and long-term needs. If this resonates with you and you would like to speak with me about how I can help you, just go to my website, where you can sign up for a complimentary Money Breakthrough Consultation. There are free gifts and tips available on my site as well, at **www. womenwealthmastery.com.**

Sally Domingo is a wealth empowerment expert, speaker, writer and coach, and is the founder of Women Wealth Mastery.

As a six-figure entrepreneur for over twenty-five years, working in advising and sales in three industries, she is familiar with the challenges of balancing work with a happy personal life. She has worked as a financial advisor for many professional men and women, focusing on retirement planning, life insurance and financial strategies. Having experienced what it's like to be a widow and a single mom, she has real stories to tell that have a lasting impact on her audiences.

Sally brings a joyful and positive element to her writings, workshops and speaking events. Her power lies in engaging her audience in envisioning and embracing the future and drawing on that as a source for change in their personal and financial lives.

She lives in Walnut Creek, Calif., with her husband, her son, two dogs, two cats and her beloved chickens.

For more information, go to
www.womenwealthmastery.com or email her at
sdomingo1800@gmail.com.

Create a Life That Will Skyrocket Your Success

By Lisa Meisels

AT THE VERY BASIS of success is a spark—the intention or idea coupled with momentum in thinking and doing. Debbie Ford in her book *The Best Year of Your Life* writes, "An intent is a commitment to yourself to bring into existence a particular result." That intent or initial spark is ignited from deep within your core, arising from your passion, your purpose and the essence of who you are. Without the intention and momentum coming from deep within you, success does not occur.

What is success? Success is a word that can be defined differently by everyone. Yet instead of defining the word success as a statement, let's examine success by the feeling it gives you.

When you understand how success feels in your body, you can then relate that feeling to the definition. Try now to go within to that feeling. Close your eyes and think of a time when you remember having success or when you felt successful. What feelings do you have? It may be a feeling of peace, empowerment, compassion, love, vitality, excitement

or another emotion. To me, success feels light and bouncy. You may not land on the feeling right away and it may be more of a sensation. There is no right or wrong feeling or sensation. The more you can recall that feeling, the more you will attract similar situations that make you feel that way into your life.

Motivation and direction for success come from a driving force within you. What happens in your outside world is a reflection of what is going on in your inner world. When you start to work from the inside out, you will have more energy, think more clearly, set higher intentions and see them manifested from thought to reality.

There are four crucial elements that must be included in your life in order to skyrocket your success. These are a healthy body, a healthy mind, going within, and deep connections. The exploration of these elements will lead you to a better understanding of who you are in the depth of your being. This is a place I call your core. Getting in touch with your core, that place in your heart and soul that is the essence of who you are, requires you to reach deep inside.

You may have the faint feeling of knowing who you are. You might even dream of what you want. You might think you want success, however what most people really want is freedom. Often, the day to day routine of life clouds your dream and obstructs your goals. You start to live unconsciously, comfortable in your routines and habits but unwilling to make the changes needed to allow you to grow into that vision.

"The most important kind of freedom is to be what you really are. You trade in your reality for a role. You give up your ability to feel, and in exchange, put on a mask." — Jim Morrison, The Doors

This quest to get in touch with your core is a wonderful self-discovery process. In order to jump-start the process, it's important to start with clear mind and a healthy body.

Healthy Body

Long-lasting success is strongest when built on a foundation of health. How do you achieve ultimate health? Let's start with body health first. There are five pillars to the foundation of a healthy body. These include diet, physical activity, sleep and rejuvenation. You've heard these topics discussed before, probably many times. However, there is new information emerging all the time and it is my hope that you will learn something new here. Integrating these five pillars into your life will help you achieve a healthy body, clarity and energy to be successful.

I remember a time when I used to think, "Yeah, yeah, our body is our temple," but I really believed that my body was there to work for me. I knew I needed to do certain things to have a healthy lifestyle and eat right, but I thought that after that it was up to my body to figure things out and simply function properly.

What I have come to understand is that your body houses your soul, the true essence of who you are, at your core. If your body doesn't function, it is because you haven't given it the sustenance it needs. It may need food. It may need oxygen. Perhaps it needs fun, or it may need rest.

When I started to realize this, my perception of the saying, "Our body is our temple," changed. I discovered a new appreciation for the body that housed my core. This body is the vessel that carries me through my life experiences. The more I protect my body, the more I get to choose which life experiences I get to have.

If you don't protect your body, you can't function properly and this affects the quality of your life as well as your ability to attract success. If you don't have a mindset that supports treating your body as the beautiful shell for your soul that it is, you aren't going to reach your full potential. Remember, though, it's a process, a journey and not a destination. Enjoy all of what life offers!

Diet

What you put into your mouth is important. You've heard the saying, "You are what you eat," and it has much truth. Eating to provide your body with fuel is different than eating for taste or comfort. That's not to say that what provides fuel and necessary nutrients doesn't taste good or comfort you. On the contrary, a real, "whole foods" experience is both delicious and comforting. Food should be pleasurable.

Let's be practical. It is common knowledge in developed countries that fruits and vegetables are good for you. They provide nutrients, antioxidants, phytochemicals, and other properties that your body needs to function optimally. A large majority of your diet should include fresh, colorful fruits and vegetables. We know that our bodies need protein. Lean proteins are the best type of protein. Lean proteins include eggs, dairy, lean cuts of beef, chicken and pork as well as nuts, seeds and legumes. There are more and more studies being published about the benefits of eating a vegetarian diet. However, there are also many studies that show the benefits of including the nutrients offered from consuming non-vegetarian proteins. Often a vegetarian diet is simply a matter of personal choice.

We've become so accustomed to instant gratification in all areas of our life, including the area of food. As a nation,

we've demanded convenient foods—conveniently packaged, conveniently located, and time-convenient.

The problem is that these foods that we have created a demand for are packed with chemicals. These preservatives and additives are necessary for creating longer lasting, more colorful foods that last for months on the shelves in the grocery store. These chemicals may seem harmless, but they can have a big impact on how you feel. These types of foods can cause immediate reactions, and they can also contribute to chronic inflammation.

What is inflammation and why is it dangerous?

Inflammation is what happens when your body tries to defend itself. There are two kinds of inflammation: acute and chronic. The acute type of inflammation is what happens when you bump your head and there is swelling or when you have an infection. In the body, the immune system tells the (white blood) cells to come to the rescue. This type of inflammation is considered good. Chronic inflammation, on the other hand, is what happens when there is slow but steady injury to your body. For example, chronic inflammation may result from toxic cellular immune reactions that go on for a prolonged period of time. This starts to damage tissue and organs.

Chronic inflammation is called a silent disease and contributes to the development of chronic illness. Your diet can play a major role in either increasing or decreasing inflammation in your body. If your diet is high in processed foods, lacking in nutrients or a whole food group, chronic inflammation may develop. When you eat a healthy diet made up of fresh, whole foods, it can actually help decrease inflammation.

The effects of diet-induced inflammation can be seen in a myriad of conditions such as hay-fever, food allergies, diabetes, obesity, migraines, autism, depression, multiple sclerosis, irritable bowel syndrome, colitis, fibromyalgia, rheumatoid arthritis, chronic fatigue syndrome, thyroid conditions and dermatitis, to name a few. There are three categories of diet-induced inflammation: food allergies which affect four to six percent of the population, auto-immune diseases, which affect three to five percent of the population, and food sensitivities, which affect thirty to forty percent of the population. The numbers for diet-induced inflammation are rising at alarming rates.

The majority of our immune system is in our gut. The wall of the intestines is an important barrier keeping in what should stay within the walls and keeping out indigestible fragments of food. When this lining is compromised, it becomes permeable. The particles that leak out of the intestinal wall can trigger an immune reaction. This is what is commonly known as "leaky gut."

The foods and chemicals you consume also have certain side effects, such as gut permeability. Side effects of eating foods that are not in alignment with your body include the development of food intolerances, food sensitivities and food allergies. What is important for you to know is that there is a difference between a food allergy, an intolerance and a sensitivity because they are all treated differently.

I'm going to talk a little about food sensitivities since this is my specialty and because there are so many people who have them and don't know it. I'll discuss what the symptoms are and then what the treatment is.

Food sensitivities can be challenging. A small amount of food may trigger only a minor reaction that mimics a seasonal allergy, a cold or the flu. Food sensitivities have a delayed onset, which means that if you eat something to which you have a sensitivity on Monday, your symptoms may not occur until Wednesday. You will usually brush your symptoms off as you just not feeling well.

Symptoms may show up as an actual illness or they can include less severe symptoms. Some people feel like they are in a fog. You may get the after-lunch slump where you feel extremely tired and can't think straight. Some people get a stuffy or runny nose. You may get abdominal cramps, gas and bloating, diarrhea or constipation, sore joints, a stiff neck, flushing, water retention or irritability to name a few. These symptoms may seem minor, but over time they can lead to a real illness.

To avoid symptoms and illnesses brought on by your diet, eat fresh produce and whole foods closest to their natural state, and eat organic. Avoid convenience foods, processed foods with additives and preservatives, and avoid pesticides. Consume meat and dairy that come from small, local farms where they treat animals with love and compassion. I know a woman who travels miles to get her goat milk from a certain farm where they raise happy, healthy goats. She swears the milk tastes better.

Part of eating healthy is allowing yourself to enjoy the goodness of the foods you eat and the beverages you drink. Historically in nearly all cultures, food is part of social traditions. People have gathered around food for centuries. In addition to providing fuel for our brains and bodies, food is meant to be enjoyed. From planting the seed to the end of using the fork, the entire process should be one of joy.

Physical Activity

Exercise doesn't have to be a bad word! The key to good health is including physical activity in your daily life. This has been shown to be beneficial to your quality of life and longevity. Exercise doesn't have to be boring. Who said you had to go to the gym to work out? Do something fun! Do what you love to do and move!

People laugh when I tell them part of my personal exercise program is caring for my horses. It takes work. I lift hay, sweep, rake and wheelbarrow daily. Are there any daily chores you do that could be considered exercise? It's important to include both aerobic and resistance type exercises. Each has its own unique benefits. Be creative and have fun. When you have fun, you will want to continue to move. Play! Exercise doesn't have to suck!

The good news is that research is showing that it's as beneficial to exercise for ten minutes three times daily as it is to exercise for a full thirty minutes a day. I learned this from a dietitian who specialized in exercise physiology at the Certificate of Training in Adult Weight Management conference in 2014.

Sleep and Rejuvenation

With the demands of our work and home lives, it seems like we don't have enough time in the day. Sleep is easily the last priority. Many people have gotten accustomed to living on only four or five hours of sleep. The general consensus is that we need seven to nine hours of sleep every single night. Sleep influences the hormones that influence our metabolism. Those hormones also contribute to our moods and level of irritability from lack of sleep.

As you age and as hormonal changes occur, you may find around the middle of your life that sleeping becomes more

difficult. This is also the time of life when a career may be ramping up, teens are in the house or daily routines are demanding and stress levels are at their highest. This is the time when good quality sleep is necessary.

To get the best quality sleep, try to develop a sleep ritual—one that you can follow every night that will calm you and prepare you for relaxation. This ritual will help relax you and will make a difference in the type and quality of your sleep.

Sleep is not the only thing that is important in the healing and repair of the body. Simply relaxing is good for you. Having down time where you relax, let go of stress and have fun can put the quality back into your life.

A Healthy Mind

We all have a past. We all have different upbringings. People from around the world are brought up with a different set of beliefs stemming from their culture and traditions. We have been brought up with parents, teachers, friends and family around us. Each person that you have encountered has brought their experiences and beliefs to you. As you grew up, you heard what you should do and what you shouldn't do from those people you looked up to. You developed a belief system of your own. You learned right from wrong and good from bad.

As you got older, you had different experiences. You developed friendships, went to school and maybe even got a job and had a family. Your experiences make up your past history. Your beliefs about your past history make up your story. The difference is that you attach opinions and judgements to circumstances that have occurred in your life. These opinions and judgements come from your beliefs.

If you think back to your childhood, I'm sure you can remember being told "don't do that" or "you're wrong." Those were someone's opinions of how you should think or act. Those opinions came from your parents, teachers, friends and family and were projected onto you.

Becoming aware of your thoughts and habits or actions is the first and very important step in your personal evolution. Do you take full responsibility for the choices you've made in life or do you tend to blame others? You're human, you have made some mistakes in your life. We all have.

Mindset is not simply attitude. It includes the way you think and your beliefs, while attitude is an opinion or your habits that are carried out as a result of your beliefs.

"Expose yourself to your deepest fear; after that, fear has no power, and the fear of freedom shrinks and vanishes. You are free." — Jim Morrison

Your thoughts create the emotions you have. You can change your thoughts if you are aware of them. So much of the time we go about our day with this chatter constantly going on in our heads. Chatter is the ego. It's not who you are. There is such a big difference.

Your mindset must be explored if you want to succeed in any area of your life. Are you aware of your emotional and mental triggers from the past? So many of your past beliefs will show up as barriers to your success.

Remember, your beliefs, although firmly set in your mind, are simply the opinions and judgements others have given you. You can change your beliefs any time you want. It takes work, but it can be done. And often, this needs to be done in order for you to become successful.

I remember when I was in a relationship that was definitely unhealthy. In my mind, it was wrong to get

divorced. When you said the marriage vows, you made a promise, and I was taught by my family and church that you kept that promise. If you didn't keep the promise and got a divorce, you were wrong, bad or insufficient in some way. That was what I believed. That belief kept me in a marriage that was unfulfilling and destructive.

I'm sure you can think of a time when you made a choice based on your beliefs of that time. Chances are, you look back on that choice as a mistake.

I believe that all those stories are necessary in our life. I believe those experiences in our past, and the experiences we'll have in our future, are there to move us to the next level in life.

If you are dissatisfied or unhappy with your life, it has less to do with your circumstances than it has to do with your beliefs. You may be wondering how this can be true if you are in an unhealthy relationship, your business is failing or you have health problems. And this is the problem. You are looking outside yourself for the answers, and the answers lie within.

You Are the Answer

You may be able to state your strengths, weaknesses, skills and talents. These are not what we will be discussing in this section. This section is about turning inward to your heart. I'll discuss how thoughts and emotions play a role in your ability to turn to yourself for the answer.

Do you ever wonder why you may feel uncomfortable when you have to confront someone with a concern you have? Or maybe you have a fear or some guilt that you carry around with you and you don't know where it came from. In order to create the most success in your lie, it's important to

explore your beliefs and the stories you tell yourself about your life. It's important to understand yourself, forgive your past and move on to what's ahead. You deserve to have success! You are worthy of love and it starts with loving yourself for who you are in this moment. Connect with who you are at the core. Start living from that place inside yourself and you will attract to you what you want to show up in your external world.

We were taught by society from an early age that our life as it is, is not enough. Happiness, peace, and all that we want are always just out of reach. The reason is there is always something more we feel that we need, like more money, more clothes, a bigger, better house, a nicer car and more success.

And that's why many of us run ourselves into the ground trying to reach for something "out there" because we aren't happy with what we have. We think we need to work long hours at a stressful job to make more money, or we overextend ourselves by scheduling commitment after commitment, taking care of everyone else – because we think, "Only then will my life be perfect."

Knowing yourself and learning to turn inward for the answers are keys to peace and success.

Deeply Connecting

You are connected to all there is. Remember that we are all energy. There is never more or less energy, just a difference in where the energy is place. That's why you'll hear healers tell you that there is no bad or good energy—it all just is.

It's important to feel this deep connection. Feeling the connection to all there is—some would call it going into the stillness or emptiness—helps you focus, and it gives you peace and a sense of calm throughout the day. Every day,

spend time by yourself in the stillness and quiet to just be. It's easiest to get a feel for this if you go outside in nature, close your eyes and listen. Then you can begin to feel the connection and the surrounding energy. As your mind starts to calm and the chatter subsides, you can begin to focus on your breathing. As you focus on your breathing, everything outside of you will fall away. Do this exercise for five minutes or more every day, and I guarantee you'll experience greater focus and a more positive attitude.

Use this daily stillness technique as a starting point for being one with Universal energy. This helps you tap into your own intuition. Only from this place will you have the brilliant clarity to create goals for the future of your successful life.

This chapter has only skimmed the surface of living life from your core. We talked about the importance of having a healthy body. You learned how diet, mindful eating, physical activity and sleep and rejuvenation are the foundation of health. We talked about mindset and perceptions. You now know the importance of being open, non-judgmental, curious and aware of what is in front of you. We talked about thoughts and emotions and how you get to choose how to respond to everything in your life. You learned about your story and your history and how neither is the essence of who you are. You learned that the answers lie within you. And finally, we looked at connecting to all there is, how to do it and why it's important.

I hope this has given you a fresh perspective on life. If you enjoyed my philosophies and would like to go deeper to learn and experience more, I encourage you to head over to my website, www.Femanna.com, where you can access a special gift from me called "5 Secrets to More Energy" by joining my free membership site.

Lisa Meisels, RDN, CLT, CHLC

Lisa loves to help people feel better and get excited about life. She is Founder and CEO of Femanna, a company that helps women have the energy, the courage and mindset necessary to experience the life they were born to live.

Lisa helps women live from their core by getting physical relief, having fun and feeling supported so they can stand in their personal power. In her programs, Lisa helps women get results and reclaim their life!

She is a Registered Dietitian Nutritionist, holds certifications in Holistic Life Coaching, LEAP Therapy and she's an expert in food and weight management. She is also certified in the Law of Attraction and is a Reiki practitioner.

Lisa belongs to the Academies of Nutrition and Dietetics and Integrative and Functional Nutritionists. She is a member of Dietitians in Integrative and Functional Medicine, Dietitians in Women's Health and Certified LEAP Therapists.

Lisa's developed and taught weight loss programs for companies and taught at the college level. She's been spotlighted in cookbooks, newspapers, newsletters and on Blog-Talk Radio. She was recognized as Women of the Year by the National Association of Professional Women in 2012/2013 and is named in the Women of Distinction Magazine in 2015. Lisa's clients get results. They say they feel lighter, healthier and beautiful inside and out.

When she's not coaching, teaching and mentoring, you can find her riding her horses, hiking, creating new recipes, gardening or learning new skills.

Learn more about having more energy and fun, feeling beautiful and living from your core at **www.Femanna.com.**

The Passion Practitioner

By Fariha Jafri

WHAT WOULD IT be like to live the life of your dreams, creating and designing every aspect of it exactly as you want and experiencing the delicious ecstasy of heart-felt, self-gratifying contentment and "in-loveness?" It would be great wouldn't it!! Here's how to start:

Ekhart Tolle says: "Always say 'yes' to the present moment.... Surrender to what is. Say 'yes' to life — and see how life suddenly starts working for you rather than against you." When we say "yes" to all that comes our way, when we learn from it and then consciously determine how we want the next moment to be, and then the next, and the next, and so on, we start to consciously create our life. Before we know it, EVERY moment becomes a welcomed one as we astonish ourselves at how things seemingly effortlessly, consistently and continuously keep working out for us. It's as simple as that....

I follow my own advice—most of the time. Not 24/7, but hey, I'm human and very much in touch with my constraints. I've learned to be compassionate about them now. I no longer beat myself up about "mistakes" I've made, whether they be "bad choices" from complying with others, wanting to people

please, not knowing any better, or wanting to experiment with different experiences, people, ideologies, and belief systems. I now consider them "learning lessons," regardless of how things may have turned out. Taking on this approach and learning from all the experiences life sent my way, I am now clear about all that I want. And thanks to all I have lived (I am truly grateful for it all), which provided me with clarity about how I want my life to be, I now proactively create it, moment by moment. I lay the foundation for every moment before it arrives (or at least try to!), expecting all aspects of my life to work, whether they relate to relationships, finances, travel, or career.

How many of us live this way, consciously designing and choosing our best life? How many of us can honestly say, "I create, design, and am responsible for all I am living"?

Probably not many. However, whether we're aware of it or not, that is exactly what is going on. We ARE creating all aspects of our life through our thoughts, actions, behavior, conversations, and even, or perhaps most powerfully, through internal dialogue. We live what we are constantly creating by default and then think that life is happening to us, instead of taking responsibility for all we have created. I know because that is how I lived my life for the longest time—by default—doing what was demanded and expected of me, regardless of whether I wanted to or not.

I recall a life of unconsciously drifting like a log in a river, day in, day out, and from situation to situation. Until I awoke one day and realized that the only reason I was happy to see the new day was because I knew it was bringing me one day closer to my grave. To my astonishment, it hit me that all I was doing was waiting to die. Wow! What a revelation! Or

more fittingly, what a "dawning," as it was the morning when this happened.

As I further thought about it, it became apparent to me that I couldn't recall when I had been living for the sake of joyfully being alive, as opposed to looking forward to it all being over. That was a big "thinking day" for me, until my thoughts led me to think how I would feel if somebody else approached me and said she, too, was solely waiting to die. I knew I would tell her it was not acceptable for her to live that way. If I didn't think it was acceptable for anyone else on Earth to live that way, why, then, was it acceptable for me?

This realization shook me to the core, and it was at that point that I decided to make some major changes in my life, the biggest I had ever made. I left my husband of twenty years; it was better to be single and happy than married and miserable. I did it even though it meant moving in with my parents and taking my children with me. It didn't happen overnight! Initially I pondered over the prospect, thinking it would be difficult. Our finances were tied. Our eldest daughter had special needs. She was (and is) wheelchair bound and non-verbal, and at the time she was dependent upon me for all care in daily life. How would I manage her and the rest of the kids on my own? How would the children be impacted? Where would I go?

One thing I wasn't concerned about was what people would think. I was so beyond that! As per Dr. Seuss: "Be who you are and say what you feel, because those who mind don't matter and those who matter don't mind." I did have people approach me, mostly my former spouse's friends and family, attempting to convince me not to leave. I heard things like, "Stay for the sake of your kids," and "Your life is over, think of

the kids." The rebuttals were primarily focused on the kids. Many people also stated what a shock it was for them to hear that I was leaving, as I had never verbalized any sadness nor complained during the course of the marriage.

I heard comments like, "You seemed happy," and "Everything seemed fine whenever we visited." I realized what a "farce" I had been living. People had seen our life as I had wanted them to: idealistic. Some were deeply offended that I hadn't said anything sooner. I responded in my defense that I had been working on the marriage, wanting it to succeed, so why would I say anything contrary to that? I was most astonished by people congratulating me, saying it was the best thing I'd ever done and asking why I hadn't done it sooner! My son and younger daughters felt guilty as they didn't want to hurt their father, but like their elder sisters, they remained adamant that they wanted to stay with me and keep all the siblings together. My ex-husband had wanted to split them up.

I researched facilities where my eldest daughter could reside. I did not want her in an "institution" or a hospital-type environment. In perfect timing, a placement became available at a special needs home in a residential area. Our daughter now lives there with four other ladies with special needs and the most loving, devoted staff I could have asked for. Her father had been insisting that I keep taking care of her. However, I knew I wouldn't be able to take care of her as she deserved and made the first executive decision ever in the marriage (ironically as I was getting out of it!) Our daughter moved to this residence where she now enjoys a better quality of life and receives more attention than I could have given her. She regularly participates in hot yoga and is taken swimming. She frequents live shows such as

"Wicked," "Jersey Boys," and all the local parades and is fully integrated into community activities. I feel so blessed and appreciative of the social services offered. The home is a fifteen-minute drive away, making it convenient to visit her any time we wish.

It is a blessing to have the love, support, understanding, and shelter my parents kindly and generously provided. I left a full time job I loved, as a Client Account Manager for a large financial services corporation. While working there I used to call it "my shelter/respite" from home life. I was grateful for the respect, appreciation, kindness, and compassion I received. I enjoyed the responsibility, too. I spent as much time as I could there, just so that I wouldn't have to go home. My clients were my best friends and it was sad leaving them. I felt as if I was letting them down, but I knew I had to leave as I would not be able to work and pick up and drop off the kids at school on time.

I also wanted to be there for the kids during this time of transition from the life they had known to one without their father and the acclimation to living with grandparents. It was challenging adjusting to life with my elderly parents and for them to habituate to young kids they were not accustomed to having around. Working outside the home was no longer an option for me due to being the sole driver in the house, the person responsible for grocery shopping, banking, and car maintenance, as well as everyone's pickups, drop offs, doctor's, dental, school or any other appointments. In my spare time I did a lot of reading and frequented the library. I enjoyed reading philosophical books—books about quantum physics, and some fiction, like Paolo Coehlo's "The Alchemist." After about a year of living this way, I missed peer interaction, and as I had spent so much time self-studying

subjects, I wanted to experience an intellectual exchange of ideas that were formulating in my mind.

"The Alchemist" had had a profound impact on my outlook of life and inspired me to want to create and live a "personal legacy" (a concept the author talks about in the book) of my own. Therefore I decided to apply to a local university. Having married as a teenager, I hadn't had the opportunity nor the inclination to go before. I am a strong believer that there is a time for everything. I wanted to go, and it fit well with my daily driving schedule as I could attend classes in between the pickups and drop offs, make appointments when I didn't have class, and go to evening classes when everyone was at home.

I discovered that I loved university life. I finally had a chance to blossom as a person, and my love of learning flourished. The wide array of courses offered were like a huge buffet of delicious entrees I could feed my mind on, and I indulged in all that caught my interest, from physics and astronomy and cellular biology, to human rights and equities, and power and persuasion in dialogue.

I remember walking the halls feeling content, fulfilled and happy, as if I was exactly where I should be at that particular time. I felt elated and alive. I had given myself five years to complete a BA Honours degree in one major. As it happened, due to my hunger and excitement about the acquisition of academic knowledge, I completed two Honours degrees, majoring in three subjects in three years. My mom and kids were so proud of me. Apart from the courses I took at university, I participated in a number of personal growth, training, development and leadership courses with Dynamind and Landmark Worldwide. I continued to read books by authors such as Dr. Wayne Dyer, Deepak Chopra,

Paulo Coehlo, Abraham Hicks, and Doreen Virtue, to name a few. Each one opened my mind a little more and contributed to my life's quest and the development of my personal legacy.

The first course I took was with Dynamind. It was introduced to me by my elder daughter's teacher, who had shared with her class that her mom had taken a course about "mind development" and the "alpha-state of mind," which puts your brain in a relaxed, yet awake and most productive state. As I was studying psychology and the neurological and biological basis of behavior at university, this intrigued me and I wanted to find out more. I spoke with my daughter's teacher, who then asked her mom to call and give me the details of how to take the course. I attended the complimentary introduction and then took three out of the many courses they offered.

The next course I was introduced to was The Landmark Forum. A close friend of mine told me that her cousin in Las Vegas had taken a course which had caused her life to "take off." I wanted my life to take off! I researched the location where it was offered in Toronto, as Landmark Worldwide is an international growth, training, and development company which offers over fifty programs in at least 100 locations around the world. I then proceeded to take a ten-week seminar, The Advanced Course, The Self-Expression and Leadership Program, (which I coached upon completion), both of The Communication Courses, and The Introduction Leader's Program (which I also coached upon completion and assistant head-coached).

As a participant in the Introduction Leader's Program, I was approached by peers requesting coaching to assist them in the program as well as various aspects of their own lives, and I was constantly told about the difference my

coaching had made, which is why I proceeded to become an actual coach of the program. Yet despite all the positive feedback, I wanted to give it up, because I doubted and second-guessed myself and my capabilities. Perhaps it was because in my life the emphasis had been on what I couldn't, or wasn't "allowed" to do, for religious or cultural reasons, or because I was a female and the mother of six kids.

I tried to let go of it, however, time and time again people kept approaching me and asking for my coaching services. While others struggled with their coaching practices, there was actually a demand for what I did. And when I heard feedback such as, "I never knew what was missing in my coaching until I received it from you!" or "I couldn't have gotten to where I am without you," and "I was blind until you helped me discover this issue," it melted my heart, and despite my misgivings and lack of confidence, I thought, how could I not offer my services when there were so many sincere requests for them?

I began to realize from my own studies and work with various people how much we give away our power to situations, circumstances, and people without even realizing it, simply because we begin with a life premise that we are powerless. That's what I was suffering from: powerlessness. Fortunately I pulled myself out of that self-sabotaging nosedive and decided to continue sharing my gifts with the world.

The divorce was finalized in September 2009, and my children and I are overjoyed at how things have turned out for us. We are closer than ever, happy, settled, and financially more secure and abundant than we ever were within the marriage. And we're living life as we want: freely, supporting and encouraging each other, and immensely grateful for the incredible life we have.

Who else wants to live a life they love? From where you stand now, it may seem as difficult as breaking out of the Earth's orbit, but it is actually much easier than you think. It's like any regimen you have to follow in order to be successful. For example, you need a proper diet and exercise to achieve a healthy and fit body, or you need to develop gardening skills if you want to create a beautiful backyard. Whatever it is that you desire to achieve, it requires dedication and action on your part, as well as a plan, structures to follow and specific steps to take to get started and well on your way. Momentum does the rest!

It's an art that can be learned, with skills and talents that can be acquired that give you power and control over your life. After all, it is yours to live as YOU want. You may agree that yes, indeed it is, but when it comes to following through, this sounds too simple or too good to be true. Countless people have proved it to themselves and are living creative lives by their own design right now, and so can you.

I have developed a unique methodology combining my academic background, the living of my own life, all I learned and discovered for myself and within myself through participating in the above mentioned courses, as well as the hands-on experience of coaching people and leading introductions to programs. The latter provided me with exposure to several people dealing with diverse and individualistic concerns based on their own life experiences. Which is why I know for a fact that we can all make any "living by default" a thing of the past in our lives right NOW. We can start by viewing whatever type of life we may have lived until now with an "It's okay, all I've been through has served me in some way" attitude along with a firm determination

that how things go from now on will be as you say. Don't beat yourself up for whatever happened in the past when you were unconscious to creating all you've been living. Tell yourself, "Now I know better. Now I am aware. Now I am empowered. Now I'm going to create and design the life I want. Now I will do it!"

And then do it!

Often clients of mine have had ideas of what they would like to do, be, or have related to how they were living their life, what they wanted their financial situation to be, or their dream job or dream relationship, but they were unaware of the steps that would get them there. That is where The Passion Practitioner comes in. Many coaching practices solely provide verbal coaching, and it is up to the individual to do whatever else may be required of them. Oftentimes what holds people back is insufficient time to do all that, a lack of the right knowledge and a feeling of overwhelm. What makes The Passion Practitioner unique is that we provide our clients with step-by-step initial instructions and hand-holding to get them off to a successful start from the first action they take. A team is created for the client and her/his particular needs. Just as it takes a village to raise a child, a community is created to actualize the client's aspirations. Instant results automatically motivate. Ideas and opportunities seem to effortlessly start rolling in. The next step, and the ones following, get easier as confidence, experience, and successes accumulate.

One of my client's passions had him wanting to assist a region he had visited in Africa that was particularly impoverished. His goal was to start with $500,000 through sponsors. He set a time frame of four months to begin his initiatives, which originally started off as "charitable." My

political science background was beneficial in this case; I had studied "participatory budgeting" plans a few Latin American countries had implemented and learned how the communities that took on this approach had flourished.

Through the consultative services provided by The Passion Practitioner, the context changed from "charitable" to "empowerment." The goal became to have conversations with the locals and have them collaborate on projects to be headed up for them. After all, they were the ones who would be living the outcome of the projects. It is very easy for people in the West to want to decide what is required within a community they are saddened to observe and wish to assist. But the community itself may have very different ideas of what they themselves want and need.

Another client was constantly belittled and demeaned by her sister whom she loved dearly. Any attempt she made to "fix" the relationship was rebuked, which created distance and bad feelings on both parts. This client was at her wits end and highly emotional when she approached The Passion Practitioner. She wanted to give up as she didn't know what more she could humanly do. Within a couple of consultations, she was able to see all that was occurring from her sister's perspective. As soon as this realization happened, she experienced a great sense of relief and gratitude and was able to interact with her sister in an entirely different manner. Their relationship has now transformed.

The pain and hurt was written all over another client's face when he approached The Passion Practitioner for assistance after the heartbreak of betrayal within a romantic relationship. Despite his being a young, successful, career-oriented individual, with the love and support of family and friends, this pain of the heart was not easy for him to handle.

The Passion Practitioner assigned him specific "homework," focused on himself, his ideals, his happiness, and the life he always dreamed of. His feedback was that he finally felt hopeful after feeling hopeless for the longest time. In the most recent communication he said the bitterness he was feeling is now in the past, he is at peace and has started meeting new women.

The best advice anyone can give during the process of overcoming past adversities is to be gentle with yourself. Be compassionate and loving towards yourself for all you have lived, as it's exactly those experiences that have brought you to where you are today. They contributed to your advancement by providing the clarity you now have around all you want and all you desire to be.

Realize that everything is a choice. And when you understand how to make empowering choices, you can be and do and have all that you want. This is what all the courses I have taken, all the books I have read and the messages of inspirational speakers I have researched advocate. Even though I had been drawn to motivational books and people since my early twenties, it wasn't until my early thirties that I began to apply any principles or practices. If a single mother of six can do it, anyone can! I took the actions for myself and have now developed the methodology to assist others

No more mere existing or drifting through life by default for any of us! We should all be living life—I mean truly, fully, completely, and passionately living life—and not just any life, but the one we love to live. The one we've created by our own design, not through whatever circumstances and situations that brought us here, but despite them.

The Sufi saint and poet Rumi stated, "What you seek is seeking you." What a beautiful thought! The Passion

Practitioner elaborates on this by illustrating step by step how our personal passions have developed and are a perfect fit for us individually as the unique and special beings we are.

Once we pay attention to them and not dismiss them as wishful thinking, we start to see how our passions have been calling us towards them in different ways, only we did not respond, or even notice. At least not until now. Your personal champion at The Passion Practitioner will be alongside you on this adventure and journey of discovery towards the acquisition of the most enlivening and passionate life of your dreams. We offer the flexibility of in-person, phone or Skype/Facetime services on a weekly or bi-weekly basis, along with weekly email follow-ups.

John Lennon said, "A dream dreamt alone is only a dream, but a dream dreamt together is reality." I encourage anyone desiring to create a life they love to bring their dreams to The Passion Practitioner, where they can be dreamt, designed, and realized together with your personal champion right before your eyes. Another favorite by Rumi: "Set your life on fire. Seek those who fan your flames." The Passion Practitioner is here to fan your flames of anything and all you wish to ignite in your life.

To get started, create your own "life by design" and begin living your passion, you may reach me at fariha@thepassionpractitioner.com

Fariha Jafri is the owner and executive consultant of The Passion Practitioner, which provides creative consulting to individuals and organizations wanting to take charge of all aspects their lives and/or work environments and design them with all that ignites them with passion within them. Her background in personal development, philosophy, psychology, and political science with an emphasis on the cognitive neurological and biological basis of behavior helped lay the foundation for her unique method of helping clients live a fabulous life they create by their own design.

In addition to her two BA Honours degrees, she has completed a number of personal growth, training, development, and leadership courses, which she subsequently she proceeded to coach, head-coach, and lead introductions to.

She currently also co-hosts a twice-weekly online radio talk show, "The Mani and Fariha Show," where callers can benefit from her knowledge, expertise, and academic background. The guests of the show are specifically selected people who are living their passions and/or contributing to society in some manner, having overcome past adversities first hand.

Make Friends with the F Word

By Holly Verbeck

A Positive Attitude Won't Ensure Your Success

ONE OF THE MOST widespread beliefs of our modern society is this: the power of positive thinking makes everything possible. Being "positive" is a highly valued temperament, regarded as an essential characteristic in the entrepreneurial world. We're taught that being cheerful, optimistic, and upbeat is the key to success and prosperity. But these false promises and our refusal to consider negative outcomes contribute to our failure. I'm not saying you shouldn't be positive. That's important, but it's only part of the equation.

▸ Failure is real, inevitable and useful.

If you picked up this book to absorb rosy promises of entrepreneurial independence, unlimited wealth and freedom, don't read on — you might not be willing to see the way in which you are holding yourself back from achieving your ideal business.

▸ Talented entrepreneurs and valued companies go belly-up every day because they do not master time, decision-making, fear and failure, and the day-to-day operations of business.

Who Do You Think You Are?

People often misidentify as business owners, when in fact they fall somewhere on this scale of entrepreneurship:

Stage One: Wantrepreneur = You have business dreams, ideas, a catchy business name and clever logo. You talk, but don't take action. You fantasize over the lifestyle you'll enjoy when the money pours in. So why aren't you rich yet? You've got to move to stage two.

Stage Two: Solopreneur = You're your own boss. Maybe you work for yourself because you were frustrated with your last employer and screamed "Enough! Why am I working for you?" (This is called an "entrepreneurial seizure!")

When talented chefs, plumbers and architects decide to work for themselves, they must add to their expertise of cooking, fixing pipes, and drafting plans a whole new set of skills — those required to start, run, grow and manage a business. Most entrepreneurs get stuck here. Move forward fast, because this is the most difficult, costly and time consuming place to stay!

Stage Three: Business Owner = Your company makes money even when you're not working.

Sounds great, right? But to transform your J-O-B into a business you can't be the only one who can do the work. Until you put down on paper what's in your head for others to access and execute your business will run you. Mastering this stage you run a business!

> ▸ Three core difficulties plague every stage of entrepreneurship — time, managing fear and failure, and the fundamentals of daily business.

The Dream Education You Need Is Out There

So you can achieve your dreams if you just skill up on business, right? Maybe, but first you'll have to make a choice that feels more like a nightmare:

You enter the prestigious University of Entrepreneurship to get your textbook and see two lines, each touting the path to freedom and prosperity. You must choose one. The first line overflows with motivated business owners like you waiting for a chance to enroll. The second line has only a few people standing in its queue. Which line will you get in?

Decide before you read on.

The difference in the two lines is the textbooks they offer. The glossy book sold in the overflowing line is entitled *Follow Your Dreams and Success Is Yours!* while the less crowded line offers the workbook, *Your Ideas and Talent Aren't Enough To Make You Rich*.

You can either make your check out to "The Company of Comforting Lies" or "Disturbing Truths Inc." What will it be?

The school of business ownership is tough and fraught with risk. Those most likely to succeed hold a unifying belief:

> ‣ I'm willing to do everything it takes (even difficult stuff that isn't fun or glamorous) to grow my business so it prospers me, my clients and those who work alongside me.

Wantrapreneurs buy the hope and promise of a successful business, while entrepreneurs invest in the fundamental skills needed to make it so. True entrepreneurs know the stakes and improve their odds by directly addressing reality and risk.

> ‣ Great ideas won't make up for a lack of the fundamental skills you need to run a business.

Look In The Mirror.
Do You Have What It Takes?

Now wake up. The world already has enough good ideas. It's filled with talented chefs and their failed restaurants, skilled retailers with excess inventories and broken leases, and professionals who work on a sliding scale and give away their services for trade. That's because the market rewards successful business execution, not ideas or talent. Whether you're the best butcher, most creative baker, or innovative candlestick maker, you'd better know how to run the business side of your business or you'll surely fail.

The good news is this: the same characteristics which bring you success in your personal life will transfer over to your business.

But here's another disturbing truth:

▸ Personal systems and business systems are inseparably connected.

Examine the way you manage time, belongings, responsibilities and people. Look at the organization of your garage or closet. Evaluate the chaos and pace of your weekday morning routine. Be honest about the habits within your primary relationship and the manner in which you handle finances. The way we do one thing is the way we do everything.

The disciplines in which you currently fall short are sign-posts for trouble spots in your business. Change them and fast-track your business. Keep them and you'd better maintain a positive attitude and pray for luck.

That could take a while.

The Not-So-Successful KFC Success Story

No doubt you've heard the xfabled story of Colonel Sanders and his Kentucky Fried Chicken. He was reportedly rejected 1,009 times before finding a buyer for his secret recipe. Holy cow! That proves tenacity, if nothing else. His story is the embodiment of the motto "With the right attitude you can achieve anything" (taken from the Comforting Lies textbook).

▸ Hard work matters a lot. But you only have time for smart work.

The Colonel deserves credit for determination, but I think he was crazy lucky, because he persisted long after a wiser man would have given up or changed his approach.

> *Insanity is doing the same thing over and over and expecting different results.*
> —*Albert Einstein*

I imagine KFC would be different today if Harland had coupled his knowledge of secret herbs and spices with a market research system. Maybe not be the way he originally conceived it, but it's highly likely he'd have sold his concept a lot sooner and suffered less rejection. (After all, chicken isn't rocket science!)

It's worth noting that this businessman became overwhelmed, sold the business, and died penniless as its goodwill ambassador while the flagging company remained stubbornly "original" despite consumers' growing demands for "healthier" fast food. (Looking at it this way kind of strips the crispy coating off the meat of this success story, doesn't it?)

As an entrepreneur you can ill afford to adopt the Colonel's inflexible and time-consuming approach to sales.

▸ A bad system will beat a good person every time.

What Makes Me A Know It All

It's more important to show you what I've done in business than to spend time trying to impress you with the string of letters I earned the right to put below my name on my business card. My background is in teaching and includes years in corporate training, human resources and risk management across all sectors of business (read the bio section of this chapter). Also, in 1995 I took a kayak trip to Alaska and met a chef who became my husband.

Together we founded HeyChef! in 1997 and built a multiple six-figure business with fifty-plus employees. For almost twenty years I've trained and helped hundreds of chefs start and run their own businesses with my *Make Your Business Cook!* program. And I don't even cook.

Our success was rooted in the discovery that chefs know more about cooking than they do about business. This holds true for every other business owner I've worked with over the years:

1. You are all experts at what you do.

2. And you are all frustrated about the same things:
   ▸ Trying to keep pace with the changing world of business
   ▸ Feeling overwhelmed by day-to-day office tasks
   ▸ Exhausting yourselves from doing too much on your own

Talented professionals want to spend time doing what they do best, whether it's cooking, landscaping or dentistry. They want to run their business instead of feeling like it's running them. But they lack basic fundamentals and systems required to succeed, and it's upon these failures of every-day entrepreneurs that our HeyChef! business thrives. I built the *Make Your Business Cook!* program to provide chefs and entrepreneurs what they need most — back office solutions, systems and support that frees them up to do the business they love — making customers happy.

The reality is that the HeyChef! business model is successful because it was built on a foundation of what entrepreneurs lack.

> ▸ The good news is you don't have to be a chef to learn my business fundamentals and build a solid foundation for your business.

My Business Hero — The Master of Fear

Robert Craig signed a sponsorship agreement with PepsiCo, and customers poured in. Over a twenty-year period, he negotiated seventy-five similar arrangements, some wildly sensational successes, others bone crushing failures. In his business he always went big, often paying dearly for it with his body — literally. One such example occurred on May 10, 1971, in Yakima, Washington.

The problem was that Mr. Craig, known world-wide as Evel Knievel, entered a contract with PepsiCo and had to keep his word even though he knew he didn't have enough room to gain the speed required to hit the jump ramp and clear thirteen Pepsi-Cola trucks. He knew his success hinged on his ability to make a decision and keep his word, no matter

what. After all, how many times would audiences buy tickets for his stunts if he bailed out every time he was afraid?

One reason I love Evel Knievel and regard him as a legend in business was his mastery over fear. That's because one of an entrepreneur's toughest jobs is to make a decision — and keep it. In business, our finances and livelihoods are on the line every day. But for Evel, business got real!

▸ Fear of making decisions can sideline solid
   business plans.

Many people simply see an insane, Liberace-style stuntman and dismiss the endorsements, marketing, engineering, event logistics, and products that were his empire. To me, his story illustrates the mastery of fear needed to seriously pursue a business upon which his life literally depended. He was a decision maker to the core.

Evel's spectacular jumps and launches provided entertainment, but he left behind a greater story of sheer nerve in the face of fear and inevitable failures. Given that some of his fans (customers) were excited by the possibility of seeing him fail, this iconic stuntman's life exemplifies entrepreneurial performance under pressure.

Evel Knievel's Biggest Business Mistake

Here's how Evel's work day went that May 10th: He mounted his thousand-pound, 750cc American Eagle motorcycle, waved to the crowds and crashed. Big time.

The motorcycle came down front wheel first at 70 mph. He broke his collarbone, suffered a compound fracture of his right arm and broke both legs. I don't think he failed because of a lack of talent. He simply came up short in a small area of day-to-day business operations.

Think about it. Before attempting the jump, Evel knew the approach runway was insufficient. He was the best in the business and did his homework. So why did he fail? Checklists are a fundamental system of business. And Evel's checklist was in the wrong order! The order should have been 1) Inspect Venue, and 2) Negotiate Contract, not the other way around. His failure, and his injuries, resulted from poor business practices, not a lack of talent. Ironically, his commitment to keep his word and pay for it with his bones resulted in loyal, raving fans for the rest of his career.

What Evel Knievel Can Teach You About Business

In fewer than ten months Evel jumped again, for more money and bigger crowds. Failure paid big dividends in his line of work and earned him a place in the Guinness World Records as survivor of the "most bones broken in a lifetime" (433).

You might be asking what this has to do with you since death isn't on the line in your day-to-day operations. But you often act as if it is.

Do you avoid big decisions because you fear failure? Or worse, lead without systems in hopes that foolish bravery and a helmet are good business strategies?

> ▸ We are meant to learn from our failures, not endure them.

In business you can't afford to throw caution to the wind or avoid big jumps. Each day real bad-ass entrepreneurs don their red, white and blue capes while others sit in the grandstands.

Evel's business never killed him. Yours probably won't either. Still, plenty of talented people fail because they lack

the necessary systems and skill to handle the daily demands and decisions required to run a business. The world already has enough chefs with failed restaurants. Statistics show that the typical restaurateur can pair excellent food with poor business acumen for only about six to twelve months. The crash stats are similar for virtually every other business.

The solution is to work with experts so you can intelligently stare risk in the face. Even then you'll have fear aplenty to overcome, but you'll enjoy the ride more with an experienced coach helping you design a great take-off ramp.

Next time a business decision like hiring, leasing or investing feels life-threatening, remember this: you're engaged in the art and skill of doing business and you're (probably) not going to die.

Then, ask yourself: What would Evel Knievel do?

Failures Build the Foundation of Solid Systems and Successful Practices

The trick is to benefit from failures as quickly as possible. As a risk manager I'm fascinated by certain examples that illustrate this:

1. When children died in a famous 1883 fire because the doors of an auditorium opened inward, push bars (commonly called panic hardware) were invented and the building code has since required all doors to open outward.

2. In 1943, no one had survived as long adrift at sea as Olympic athlete Louis Zamperini. His forty-seven day experience helped the military redesign and better supply life rafts. Survival rates have since increased four-fold.

3. In 1993, a charter aircraft carrying family members and three executives of the legendary fast-food empire In-N-Out Burger followed a Boeing 757 in for landing but became caught in its wake turbulence and crashed, killing all on board. Air travel is safer because the crash led to FAA requirements for adequate distance between heavy and light aircraft.

The dark side can be terribly instructive but it remains largely ignored by proponents of positive thinking. And yes, I have my own "Evel Knievel story" which left me bruised and wiser for my experience. That's why I'm eager to share ways you can benefit from failure.

▸ What doesn't kill you makes you stronger.

The Root of Organization and Systems

Once you see the benefit of using failure to build your business, you can spot opportunities in your daily operations. Look for phrases like these as the starting point to streamline activities, control outcomes, and save money, time and resources:

"I always forget/never remember to ..."

"I never have enough time to..."

"Every time we do this, [   ] happens."

"I want to scream when I spend my time doing [   ]."

"I can't believe [   ] turned out so badly."

"My employees/customers think/do [   ], instead of [what you want]."

Determine Where the System Is Truly Needed

Next, ask the question "Why?" And ask it five times. Here's an example:

<u>Your Problem</u>: Your last potential customer went to a competing bakery for their wedding cake.

<u>Why? (#1)</u> They read a review about someone who had a bad experience with us.

<u>Why? (#2)</u> The review said we failed to deliver their cake in time for sunset photos.

<u>Why? (#3)</u> The driver got lost and ran late on his deliveries.

<u>Why? (#4)</u> The office girl didn't give him the daily delivery report and map.

<u>Why? (#5)</u> The office girl is new.

It's too easy for business owners to spend time and money fixing things that aren't real problems. In this example, if you fixed "the problem," you'd mistakenly think your sales team was to blame. Likewise, applying a fix at the first "why" would waste valuable resources trying to boost reviews on social media. At the third "why," you'd unduly discipline the driver, and at the fourth, you'd blame the new office girl. But she isn't the problem, either. You are.

You failed to give the new employee appropriate training and supply her with quality daily checklists. It takes experience to identify where to point your attention in business.

Almost Every Action Is Part of a Fundamental Business System

Here is a partial list of tasks all businesses do to some degree or another on a daily, weekly, monthly, quarterly and/or yearly basis. Without organization and systems, these tasks will run your day and cause chaos. As you read the list, pay particular attention to items that elicit an emotional response. (These need your attention the most).

▸ Managing Email (A spam filter is not a system, it's a tool)

▸ Paying Bills (Do you spend more time procrastinating than actually doing it?)

▸ Blocking Out Time for Specific Tasks

▸ Filing, Information Handling, Storage and Retrieval (Can you find what you need?)

▸ Recordkeeping (Do you know the figures that are the backbone of decisions?)

▸ Taxes (Do you procrastinate or file extensions?)

▸ Execution of Products/Services (Do you consistently exceed customers' expectations?)

▸ Handling Voice Mail (Do you return calls promptly?)

▸ Conducting Projects as a Group (Do you meet team goals and deadlines?)

▸ To-Do Lists (Do you prioritize daily tasks and long-term projects?)

▸ Hiring, Training and Developing Employees (This includes discipline and dismissal, too.)

▸ Essential Scripting (Do you constantly repeat information about your products/services to customers by phone or email?)

▸ Meetings (Are they planned, short and productive?)

▸ Job Duties (Does each person have specific tasks and goals to reach?)

▸ Problem Solving, Decision Making, Brainstorming (Do you have a method to address challenges, evaluate purchase and identify opportunities?)

▸ Outsourcing (Do you properly screen and evaluate professionals working on your behalf?)

"Watch the little things; a small
leak will sink a great ship."
—Benjamin Franklin

Every business owner I work with says they want more time to do what they do best; no one wants more time behind their desk.

I'm Ready to Help, If You're Ready to Decide and Act

▸ These core difficulties plague every entrepreneur — the mastery of time, decision-making, fear and failure, and the day-to-day operations of business.

Business really suffers when the owner lacks an understanding of these fundamentals. I'm not talking about your talent or skills — you're an expert at what you do. I'm talking about running your business so it doesn't run you.

When I conduct strategy sessions with business owners just like you, we dive into the specific struggles of the company and of the entrepreneur who runs it. I work directly with each business owner and give customized support to help them conquer chaos, reclaim their time, and create systems and teams that are the foundation of a dream business.

The core difficulties plaguing every business are, at their source, a function of the entrepreneur. So, it's quite likely YOU (i.e., your habits and skills) are getting in the way of the time you need for your life and business. Embrace this and you're headed toward great change!

The challenge is that most people need ongoing support

to eliminate years of poor work and personal habits and to implement new ones.

> ▸ Remember, it takes twenty-one days to form a wanted habit and ten times longer to unlearn an unwanted one.

If you're truly committed to leading and operating an efficient and profitable business but find yourself up to your eyeballs in chaos, I want to do something special for you. Normally, I charge hundreds of dollars an hour for private coaching, and more than a thousand dollars a day for group events on site at your company.

But since you've read this far, I'd like to offer you a complimentary one-on-one strategy session. In this phone session we'll take a look at where you are now, where you'd like to be and what's keeping you from getting there. I offer you my time, because I want you to regain yours.

Each week I dedicate a few time slots to people like you who crave the successful business practices I help them create. This is my gift to you because I remember what it's like to be where you are. I want you to succeed, so reach out to me and I'll happily share an opening in my calendar to get to know you and your business.

The information you've just read is merely paper, until you take action. I'm devoted to helping you make friends with the F word and making your mark in the world with your talents and entrepreneurial dreams. All you have to do is get resourceful and look me up!

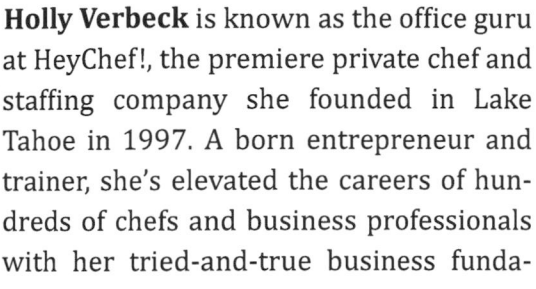

Holly Verbeck is known as the office guru at HeyChef!, the premiere private chef and staffing company she founded in Lake Tahoe in 1997. A born entrepreneur and trainer, she's elevated the careers of hundreds of chefs and business professionals with her tried-and-true business fundamentals training programs.

Holly's credentials as a trainer, coach and business leader include experience as a school teacher (so she can handle most business teams!), and certifications and administrative licenses as a California Insurance Administrator, OSHA trainer, Workers' Compensation Claims Administrator, and Insurance Institute of America degree in risk management. Her first firm in Los Angeles, Employers Comp Management, created employee programs and audited insurance policies for businesses like Mission Foods, Orowheat, and Prime Time Shuttle.

Her human resources, risk management and training career includes nearly a decade of leadership in the fascinating ski resort industry, which provided the opportunity to train managers working in food and beverage, mechanical, retail, fire and public transportation, hotel, lodging, sanitation, health spas, patrol, and search and rescue operations. Seeing common pitfalls of managers in every industry fuels her passion for transforming small and mid-size businesses by teaching fundamentals.

She's an expert at creating the systems and organization needed to operate a business, ensuring talented professionals get to focus on what they do best. Holly is direct and passionate about helping entrepreneurs make money by mastering business fundamentals, conquering chaos and increasing their time to work on their business rather than *in* it.

Overcoming Obstacles

By Rose Scott

I RECEIVED ENCOURAGEMENT from Ralph Waldo Emerson's words, "Challenges are what make life interesting; overcoming them is what makes life meaningful."

One such challenge commenced for me at the age of ten. I began to binge eat. By the age of sixteen, I weighed 195 pounds. Even for my 5'6" frame, that was a lot of weight to carry. My doctor suggested a diet and outlined a plan to follow. In my attempt to comply, I felt restricted and imagined it impossible.

Growing up with my mom and sister, I felt further restricted by our limited income and environment. For several years, our home was a one-bedroom apartment; then, when I was seven, my mom moved us to government housing. Our new apartment building wasn't in the greatest of neighborhoods. The staircase often reeked of urine, we had to step around empty beer bottles, and the elevators were filled with graffiti. This new environment also opened my eyes to the world of bullying. As the older kids bullied me, I rebelled and bullied in return, using my extra weight to push others around.

As my weight crept up, I became slower and slower and was unable to participate in sports. I enjoyed basketball, but when playing, the boys would make fun of me, calling me "double dribble" because of my fully endowed breasts. I had inherited some of my grandmother's physical traits. Still, one of my biggest regrets in high school was that I didn't join the girls' basketball team.

Because of my obesity, I became the brunt of many of the neighborhood kids' jokes. The girls called me "thunder thighs" and "bolted breast"; the boys, the "Goodyear Blimp" and the "Rose Bowl." This constant barrage of negative comments caused me to isolate myself at home. At school, I was ostracized and never invited to pool parties or social functions.

My mom came to the rescue. She enrolled me in a private co-ed Catholic high school. Uniforms were required. My tuition was partially funded by the government until Grade 10, when parents had to become totally responsible for payment. But somehow there must have been a generous donor or guardian angel in attendance on my behalf. I was able to attend and graduate without having to pay or work to earn that monthly fee. However it occurred, this new environment provided me an opportunity to meet and make new friends. Most of the students came from middle- to upper- class families, with both parents in the picture. As I was invited to visit their homes, I gained a vision of how I desired my future to look. I began unconsciously reinforcing the philosophy that "you become most like the people with whom you surround yourself."

One day after school, after meeting with my Grade 10 math teacher, I overheard a boy in the hallway say out loud to a group of teenagers, "Look at the shape of her." That comment struck my heart like a sour chord on a violin.

I cried myself to sleep that night for the first time, vowing I would lose my excess weight. For several ensuing nights, I found myself praying, crying, and asking God to give me the necessary wisdom to overcome my unattractive appearance. Someone suggested to me that the Book of Proverbs was written by a wise man, Solomon, and that I might find my answers in that book. But even though I had studied and was able to comprehend Shakespeare in school, I found the Bible beyond my comprehension. I felt like a blind person reading braille for the first time.

After a few months of the tortuous stresses of schoolwork, teasing and crying, I reached my breaking point one night. Upon waking the next morning, I found myself unable to swallow any solid food. My throat actually felt like it was closing up on me. I was frightened, to say the least. I knew I had to eat something and tried vanilla pudding, but I felt sick to my stomach after only a couple of teaspoons. For the remainder of that day, I very slowly swallowed boiled and mashed potatoes swimming in butter. I realized baby food might be the answer and asked my mom for the necessary money. At the store, I stood, attempting to discern which baby food might provide the necessary protein while also appealing to me flavor-wise. I ended up buying Gerber beef and vegetables, chicken, fruit, and other enticing flavors.

After existing like this for four months, I finally made an appointment with my doctor to seek a referral to a specialist. The resulting barium x-ray the specialist ordered of my esophagus and stomach revealed that my esophagus was functioning normally. Despite this confirmation, I still wasn't able to swallow anything solid and began to feel weakened by the lack of necessary nutrients. But it was time for our annual summer vacation to visit my grandmother in New

York City, and that routine provided the startling solution.

My appearance surprised my grandmother. My weight had plummeted to 135 pounds over my five-month subsistence on baby and pureed foods. But the miracle wasn't her excellent cooking or the favorite foods she usually made for me, it was her unconditional love. That commodity, given in extremely powerful doses, actually relaxed my throat and soothed my digestive tract and shattered heart. Soon after our arrival, I was able to consume solid food once again. The attention I garnered from the remainder of my New York City family and the new clothes I was able to purchase added to my healthier mental and physical conditions. I felt alive once again!

An unforeseen problem next reared its unpleasantly wrinkled self: a myriad of stretch marks and loose skin resulting from my rapid weight loss. I looked like a skinny elephant. One day when I was relaxing on the beach with my cousin, she kindly suggested I needed to tone up.

Returning home, I immediately joined a gym and started an exercise program. However, I also often sabotaged the results of the workouts by eating the wrong foods as a reward for having exercised. I could not resist my tendency to indulge in my favorite comfort foods. My dietary habits were therefore all over the map, and so was my workout success.

The new school year at last began, and I entered Grade 11. The families of the boy who had made the negative comment and the other kids who had unmercifully teased me could no longer afford the monthly tuition. My additional refusal to respond to the knocks of neighborhood kids at our front door—because I said I was concentrating on homework—had further isolated me from my environment. I felt like a stranger in my own school and neighborhood. I had studied

and lived there, but didn't feel a part of anything. That all began to change when a girl who recognized me from the Grade 10 said she nearly fainted when she saw me in my new smaller uniform. I began to gain a new sense of confidence as I received more and more positive comments regarding my weight loss from others who'd previously been aware of my presence. They eagerly approached, wanting to know how I'd lost the weight so quickly, but found my story almost impossible to believe. With each step, I began to feel a part of something good, something to look forward to.

Something inside me also changed; my demeanor became calmer. My teachers began to take notice. I even earned an award for becoming the most improved student in my music class. I began to understand that when we put things out there, we are heard and our desires are drawn back to us. I'd determined I was not going to put up with the school or neighborhood kids after our New York trip, and it was as if my thoughts made that torment disappear.

Throughout my early adult years, I continued the combination of gym membership and unhealthy eating habits. This caused me to constantly remain within the cycle of yo-yo dieting. Eventually, I settled down, married and had children.

After the birth of my second child, I made the conscious decision to lose the weight permanently and attain the body I'd always longed for. I recalled a statement I'd made to others in high school—that I wanted my body to be solid muscle. Some had listened, and some had scoffed because of my then obesity. But what I had learned since then was that when we set an objective and maintain our focus with determination, imagination, and belief in ourselves, we can and will achieve our goals.

I made changes to my exercise routine and continued

to challenge myself. The vegetarian diet I'd maintained for almost twenty years, eating primarily high density carbohydrate foods, had resulted in weight concentrating on my buttocks and thighs. I supplemented that diet with fish.

A key to successful weight loss, I'd realized, was that I had to make permanent changes to my lifestyle. I was ready to fight this battle like a Spartan warrior. My love for sweet pies, crackers, bagels and croissants had to be replaced with healthier choices.

Watching the movie *The Secret* had a significant impact on my continual growth and development. I began to deliberately change both internally and externally. Looking at the world through different eyes, I began my quest to identify my soul's purpose. My inner belief that everyone is placed upon this Earth for a reason became real to me. I began my inner search to identify in my case the unique gifts and talents with which we are all created in order to help others.

I began to write down the things I loved to do, the things that came easily to me and the things I did that drew requests from others for my opinion. I was able to identify that I loved health, oral and written communication, and that I had a genuine desire to help others. It became clear to me that certifications in personal training and health and wellness coaching would provide a pathway to my purpose. That training became a natural fit for me after years of a diversified career. I also became actively involved at this time with my local Toastmasters club and went on to win first place in an area-wide speaking contest.

However, it also became clear to me that the contribution our mind plays in our inner and external successes cannot be underestimated. As I became fascinated with that concept, I opened my mind and body to Bob Proctor's webinars and

his book, *You Were Born Rich*. Internalizing his theories, I was able to fully understand our two states of mind: conscious and subconscious. The conscious mind deals with intellect, reason, logic, and analysis; the subconscious, our emotions, habits, beliefs and connection to a Higher Source. Through Bob's theories, I developed the skillset necessary to directly enter into my subconscious mind to change the beliefs and habits stored therein.

Other strong, influential teachers emerged as I opened up and became more receptive to this mind/body connection. They included Dr. Wayne Dyer, who became another extremely strong influence in my development, because of his belief in "excuses be gone." He remains today, despite his successes, a humble and inspiring example of living a life without excuses. I was able to understand, through his role modeling with eight children of his own, that I could do anything I yearned to do despite the fact I was responsible for the well-being of my two young children. Although nearing tenure as a university professor, he'd left that job, and all the responsibilities he'd assumed, to follow his passion and to live the life he was created to live. His quote, "If you change the way you look at things, the things you look at change," inspired me to change my attitude about my higher possibilities, despite my assumed responsibilities.

Dr. Joe Dispenza, a neuroscientist exploring the many facets of the brain, was featured in the movie *What the Bleep Do We Know!?* Once paralyzed, he was able to successfully recover and regain full use of his limbs through thought, focus and meditation. Embracing his scientific explanation for the "woo woo" others suspect might overrule the law of attraction, he was able to tune out the outer circumstances and connect to his inner self. He changed his own state of

mind and body. As he autographed his book *Evolve Your Brain* for me, I could actually sense his connection to his own internal source of power.

Dr. Bruce Lipton, another scientist whose theories fascinated me, explained the process of epigenetics (how our genes are primarily affected by our internal and external environment as opposed to hereditary conditions alone). It is his belief that if we allow stress to assume control, it creates negative thoughts, eventually creating some form of genetic breakdown/disease. Focusing on positive emotions such as love and unlimited possibilities, we create a more positive internal environment in which our genes can thrive and grow, despite any genetic predisposition to disease or disability.

Tony Robbins, a motivational speaker/teacher, believes we should "change our story and raise our standards." If we can overcome our past and the excuses we make for not moving forward,

he teaches, there will be nothing that can stop us from becoming more productive and reaching our highest potential. It's all a state of mind with Tony, and this, in fact, is one of the reasons why people can successfully walk on fire at his seminars. His philosophy that if we change our physiology through exercise, remaining active and simply moving our bodies, we will "change our story," is one that I utilize in my own work with clients. Tony knows how to move an audience.

Oprah is on every worldwide list of important and motivational individuals that I've seen, including mine. She is an amazing, charismatic and inspirational woman. She made a wise decision, in my opinion, to change the focus of her decades-long, extremely popular television show to her

own inspirational, motivational, teaching and entertainment network. She boldly reaches out to all inspirational teachers within our universe, learning from every available source, then generously passes those pearls of wisdom on to the public through her interviews. I concur with the belief she passed on to students at Stanford that "when we connect our personality with our purpose, we become almost invincible and successful in our endeavors." One of my goals is to meet Oprah, and so I will!

Many other transformational teachers became powerful influences in my life at this time, including Christy Whitman, host of the weekly online show "Magnetic Monday," Lisa Nichols, author of *No Matter What* and a teacher in the previously referred to, *The Secret*, John Assaraf, an author focusing on "winning the inner game of money and fear in order to overcome the obstacles holding us back from achieving our goals," also a teacher in *The Secret*, and others.

However, the most significant influence in my life has been my relationship with my Source, being my God. I found God at the lowest point in my life during early adulthood after the breakup of a long-term relationship. God has always been guiding me even when I did not know where my life was going. I have a daily spiritual practice and highly encourage everyone to have one, too.

I was able to shift many of my disruptive thought processes utilizing the theories of the leaders I mentioned. The fact that they were able to overcome overwhelming odds through indomitable willpower and connecting to a Higher Power strengthened my desire to persistently continue my whole body well-being despite all obstacles.

I next researched the effects of the Emotional Freedom Technique (EFT), or tapping, as some refer to the process.

Gary Craig developed this tool during the 1990s. It has been described as emotional acupuncture, since it involves tapping on the identical meridians of the body where acupuncturists insert needles. The primary difference is that we may access similar relief through our fingers and simultaneous verbalization of negative emotions associated with memory, enabling a cognitive shift. EFT goes directly to our subconscious mind, allowing this shift to occur. It is like talk therapy combined with acupressure, allowing individuals to release stored emotions from memories trapped within their bodies. Trapped emotions can create disruptions within our bodies, resulting in pain and/or troubling emotions. I personally utilized the tapping tool during my divorce and preparatory to public speaking and bodybuilding shows. My resulting clarity, immediately following tapping, enabled me to relax and perform to my highest ability at that time. I am in the process of becoming clinically certified as an EFT practitioner.

Internalizing all of the theories of these powerful teachers, I was prepared and open to continue my own self-actualization process while assisting others. Together, we will become magnificent works in progress.

Remember the comment I'd made when in high school about that muscular body I'd envisioned? It happened! Eventually in 2014, I entered competition in two natural bodybuilding shows. I won second place in women's masters natural bodybuilding and third place in women's open natural bodybuilding. A "master" indicates that one is over forty, proving that age is nothing but a number and that anyone can achieve anything at any age. The polygraph test required of all contestants indicated I had, indeed, obtained my physical body through healthy eating and exercise.

Winning my awards in bodybuilding and public speaking came about shortly after my divorce. I had refused to allow circumstances to prevent me from achieving my goals. Some might look at certain points in their lives and give up, coming to a halt when the going gets tough. But that is exactly when bold moves forward must continue or you will never realize what it is you can accomplish.

It has been said that eighty percent of weight loss is diet, and twenty percent is correct exercise. I would like to make clear that I agree with this; however, I also strongly believe in the mind/body connection. I had to get past the mental blocks preventing my loss of weight and the accomplishment of my goals. The tools I used to get past those blocks served me well. ("Stay out of the fridge," being one.) I utilize that knowledge and experience to assist my clients in identifying the blocks holding them back.

As for the nutrition component to weight loss, my belief is that each individual has a unique body type that metabolizes food differently. Some can consume lots of bread and never notice a difference on the scale, whereas others can eat a few slices and instantly show the results. This goes for protein-rich foods like meat, beans, or soy, as well. The body is an intelligent, well-operating machine that will also reveal specific responses to particular food categories, such as allergic reactions, blowing up like a puffer fish.

This is why I do not believe in a "one-diet-fits-all" approach. My philosophy has always been that life was created to be enjoyed, and that once there no longer remains stress around food or restrictions, success will be achieved. It is most definitely possible to lose weight and never find it again.

My feelings are the same regarding exercise. Not everyone can do burpee jumps or one-arm pushups. If we could, we would all be supermen and women. Some may need to lose weight; others to gain it. One person may have back problems, whereas another has shoulder, neck or knee issues.

While exercise is medicine for the body and can help with a host of different conditions, from high cholesterol to diabetes and back pain to wrist pain, there is always a different exercise prescription for each individual. It is always advisable to see a primary care physician before starting an exercise program. And if you feel moved to coach with me, I look forward to working along with the consent of your doctor and creating a program designed just for you. I love helping individuals with chronic conditions gain a better, stronger and healthier lifestyle.

With all of that said, if we look deeply into ourselves, we will rise above and conquer false and limiting beliefs such as the following: "I am frightened of gaining unwanted attention," "You will always be big," "It runs in the family," "So maybe what Auntie says is true," "You are too big to ever have muscles," "It won't work on your body," and the many other reasons we give ourselves.

Remember that what you will gain is the feeling of accomplishment and success that accompanies overcoming life's challenges. Having the determination and intestinal fortitude (guts) will allow you to climb the mountains in your life, to reach the top and shout, "HOORAY, I DID IT!"

For more information, Rose can be contacted at **www.riseabovewithrose.com** or (559) 797-1593.

 **Rose Scott**'s certifications as a personal trainer and health and wellness coach enable her to quickly assess the needs of her clients. Although her goal for each individual is whole body wellness, her specialties include conditions such as obesity, back pain, arthritis, diabetes, high blood pressure, high cholesterol, scoliosis, osteoporosis, chronic pain and weakness.

Her passion to inspire clients comes from her personal experiences growing up in Canada. As her childhood weight increased, she suffered the accompanying biases and bullying of schoolmates. The process she endured in overcoming her eventual weight gain to 195 pounds in her teens led to her current wellness program. Her strong belief in the mind-body connection advanced her own success and enabled her to assist clients in identifying blocks and/or limiting beliefs in the accomplishment of their health, longevity, stress reduction and happiness goals. The program Rose developed also led to her award-winning performances in bodybuilding shows.

Rose further developed her speaking and leadership skills as an award-winning Toastmaster and currently serves as Area Director, overseeing four clubs in her Toastmaster District. Her Toastmaster and general public motivational speeches, presentations and seminars on the importance of health and wellness include her research into the contributing functions of the mind.

Rose obtained a bachelor of science degree in business from Western Governors University and is certified as a

trainer through the American College of Sports Medicine and as a coach through Wellcoaches School of Coaching.

Rose can be contacted at **www.riseabovewithrose.com** or (559) 797-1593.

Wealth Without Worry

By Kimberly Sherry

*"If you want to know the secrets of
the Universe, think in terms of energy,
frequency, and vibration."*
—Nicola Tesla

THE SECRET TO making and keeping more money is less about going out and working hard to get it than it is about aligning yourself to a specific frequency and energy that resonates with your intentions. I want to show you how I came into such an alignment so that I'm able to make a six-figure-plus income and how you can, too!

This is not a get rich quick methodology. It requires a consistent, easy-to-do practice that creates deep peace, clarity, and more money with less effort.

Here are the three things you need to know.

- ‣ The simple shift to managing money without stress
- ‣ The number one secret to having more peace of mind and ease with money
- ‣ The money blocks of six figure women

Before I unveil my secret discoveries, I'd like to share a little about myself.

Like many, I was financially crippled by the economic downturn in 2007. At the time, I had a retail flooring store which I had opened with the remainder of my father's inheritance. My partner at the time was a flooring contractor who was ready to get off of his knees after thirty years laying carpets. I contributed my expertise of having owned and operated several businesses with my ex-husband. I was also ready to save my body from more than a dozen years of full-time bodywork as a massage therapist. We had high hopes of turning our eco-friendly flooring store into a model for other stores that were selling toxic products.

However, the Universe had other plans. After pouring every last penny into this black hole, we finally resigned ourselves to failure and filed for bankruptcy in 2009.

It was with great shame and embarrassment that I walked away from a dream that would have been a huge success in any other economic climate. Additionally, it contributed to the end of my relationship.

Even though I was grateful to have a huge thirty-two-foot motorhome in which to retreat, I felt like a total loser and more like trailer trash than the adventurous gypsy I have since become. Because I had no money, I parked the motorhome on the side of the road where I could legally park for seventy-two hours at a time. It was illegal to sleep in it, but I had no choice. I rode my bike or took the bus to work at a local gym where I had a massage studio. I got on food stamps and went back to doing what I loved, which was massage and energy healing.

It was then that I made it my mission to understand the energetic mechanics of why some people were so financially successful while others struggled endlessly. I drew upon more than a fifteen years working as an energy healer. My

previous training had involved going to Aesclepion Intuitive Training, a psychic school where I had learned, practiced, and led clinics every week for twelve years.

The path of a healer requires much healing of one's own. You've no doubt heard the phrase, "Healer, heal thyself!" A healer can only heal others to the extent that they've healed themselves. So every person who came into the clinic and sat in front of me became a mirror for all the things I needed to heal in myself.

The endless amounts I needed to heal started at age two-and-a-half, when I was sexually abused by my alcoholic father. That continued until I went to kindergarten. I have no memories of the abuse, but the body never forgets.

On top of that, my mother raised me and my four siblings in a religious cult. I was a baby when she became a Jehovah's Witnesses. They celebrate no holidays, birthdays or a host of other milestones in a child's life, and it was brutal being the only child to show up at school without a Halloween costume and then have to wait to be picked up at lunchtime before the parade began. Christmas was my least favorite day of the year. Without fail, I had to face the annual question over and over..."And what did you get for Christmas?"

"Nothing" was my answer. Sometimes I would say, "The same as last year."

Every birthday was an annual reminder that I was not worth remembering...actually worth less than remembering, or in other words, "worthless." There were no Valentine's Days, no New Year's celebrations, and no competitive sports, even though every year the gymnastics teacher would ask me to join the team. I was more talented than ninety percent of those in class. But I was not allowed to have friends outside of the cult, and college was forbidden.

I could go on and on about the deprivation, isolation, and general effects of a lifetime of fear, guilt, and shame. It felt criminal to be raised this way, and I was left with much to heal.

I married another cult member who later admitted visiting prostitutes for twenty-three of the twenty-five years we were married. This adultery would have been the only acceptable cause for divorce, if I could have proved it to the elders of the congregation.

Feeling trapped, hopeless and full of despair, my lowest point came when I walked into a sporting goods store to buy a gun to end my life. But at the last minute, I realized I couldn't do that to my two children. So instead I got angry and used that as the fuel to finally leave the cult and get divorced.

The psychic training I received after I left became my new cult only in reverse. Every person who sat before me provided an opportunity for me to release and clear all the ways I'd been programmed to suppress and dim my brilliance and light.

The Simple Shift to
Managing Money without Stress

Most of the people who are attracted to my work love the Law of Attraction, are familiar with chakras, and generally have a meditation or yoga practice.

However, I see people all the time who use positive affirmations, who are in good spirits, who take care of their bodies, and may even be very organized, with good systems in place for their businesses, who still struggle to make enough money. They never seem to get ahead. There's always another bill that blindsides them just as they're making progress. They seem caught between the tsunami of financial success and the desert.

Perhaps like you, many of them have repetitive voices in their heads that are like a slave driver saying, "You have to work hard for a living!" Or that belittle them with things like, "You're not smart enough, like your brother, to make a six-figure income." Or that make them feel selfish with words such as, "You need to share what you make or you're being greedy." Or that pester them with questions like, "Do you think money grows on trees?"

The first secret discovery I'm going to share with you is an energetic one. There is an energetic reason that conscious entrepreneurs cannot make enough money and worry endlessly, even though so many other areas of their lives are working. That reason can be found at the base of your spine.

There are seven energy centers that run along your spine. Each processes different kinds of energy, just as each of your organs has a different function that contributes to a healthy body.

The most important of these energy centers—your root chakra—sits at the base of your spine. This energy vortex sets the tone for all the chakras above it. If it's not healthy and flowing, it will affect the functioning of all other chakras.

Now you might be saying, "I know all about the chakras and I ground every day." You may even be a healer with extensive knowledge of your invisible energy system. However, if you're not making the kind of money you'd like, I can guarantee that you have some serious congestion in your root.

Unlike the other chakras, except for the crown at the top of your head, the root does not have a front and back. It's more like an upside down tornado of energy that starts small where it connects at the base of the spine and widens to about six to eight inches as it feeds into the center of the

Earth. This is called your grounding cord and should be charged daily.

However, the discovery I made with myself and with clients who were struggling with money was this: the energy surrounding the root chakra, where it connects, ripples out 360 degrees around, like when you drop a pebble in a pond. This is the energy that needs to be cleared and which is missed when you're just using your grounding cord.

This root chakra is responsible for processing energy that has to do with survival, and feeling safe, confident, and full of vitality. And it affects those things that can affect feeling secure, like having a place to live or making money. When we worry and feel stressed, wondering how everything is going to work out, that energy is the result of congestion in and around our energy root.

When I lead groups in meditation or in private practice, I show people how to make this simple shift in their energy that ends sleepless nights, body aches and pains as a result of chronic stress, ulcers, over eating comfort foods, worrying, and the general sapping of life's joy.

I'll describe the simple process briefly here. Using your imagination, gather all the congestion as it extends out horizontally from the root chakra out through all the layers of your aura. You don't end at your skin. As you imagine pulling this congestion into your root, you send it down your grounding cord to the center of the Earth. The Earth recycles this energy.

So the simple shift that needs to be made to enjoy more money without stress is to be sure your energetic plumbing at your root chakra is free of worry. If that sounds too easy to be true, you undoubtedly still have the belief that you have to work hard for a living. It's not true, as you will soon see.

The #1 Secret to Having More Peace of Mind and Ease with Money

I keep hearing everywhere that we should raise our vibrations. This raises some important questions, such as, "How do I know if my vibration is low? How do I know if I've raised it, and how high?"

In his book, *Power vs Force,* Dr. David Hawkins lays an important foundation for what I'll share next.

Dr. Hawkins created a scale that measures human consciousness and awareness. This was done after calibrating tens of thousands of people, places and things using kinesiology, or scientific muscle testing. He even calibrated every chapter in his book, the highest of which was 890/1000. Therefore, by his own admission, the book did not contain complete truth. After using his scale over a period of three years, I discovered some things that were not true and will share them here.

First of all, I share my finding not to discredit the work he pioneered, but more importantly to show what expansion has become possible.

Power vs Force was published more than a dozen years ago and has actually gained in popularity more recently. It was definitely written ahead of its time. Dr. Hawkins wrote the book after doing twenty years of research. Since we are evolving so rapidly, some of what may have been true when he first started his research is no longer true.

For instance, one of the things Dr. Hawkins believed was that you could not change your vibrational frequency by more than a few points in a lifetime. This is simply not true.

Another thing Dr. Hawkins did with his calibrations, or the measurement of vibrations, was to give one number to one thing, for instance a person. However, we are complex

and comprised of an endless number of calibrations. I have discovered that every organ and system in the body can be vibrationally measured to ascertain its relative health.

When I work with my clients, I determine five basic calibrations using the Hawkins scale to form a baseline. This is how I know where you are vibrationally at the present moment and where you do or do not need to raise your vibration.

How are these measured? When I first started to get intuition I wanted to confirm, I used a pendulum for dowsing. Then I began to use kinesiology, the same scientific muscle testing Dr. Hawkins used. Today I just count until I get an internal signal. Often I see the number in my head and count to confirm whether the number I'm seeing is correct.

The five basic calibrations I measure are as follows:

The vibration of your **mind** tells me the kinds of thoughts you're thinking. If you're stuck in a low mind vibration, you'll be very negative, critical, and judgmental. The high vibrational mind that sees optimism everywhere can easily give others the benefit of the doubt, and possibilities abound.

The vibration of your **spirit** tells me how you are feeling, like when someone says they are feeling low in spirits. A low spirit vibration could be in indicator of a low-grade depression. If your spirit vibration is high, you'll no doubt be in a good mood. If you have a high spirit vibration and a low mind vibration, you'll be very enthusiastic and passionate about your negative thinking.

The vibration of your **body** tells me how much tension you're holding. We're all becoming increasingly aware of the toxic effect that chronic stress can have on the body. While all kinds of calibrations can be made on the body, this is not meant to replace working with your doctor. If you have a

serious illness or mental health issue, consult a physician or mental health professional.

The vibration of your **wealth** measures your container... how much you can hold. People who win the lottery and then lose it all within three to four years have a container the size of a thimble. You can have a wealth of knowledge, friends, and maybe even shoes, and still not have enough money. This is the last calibration I measure.

The vibration of your **money** tells me the capacity you have to attract and magnetize money. Obviously, the higher the money vibration the more money you can make. Combined with a high wealth vibration, you will be able to keep more of it instead of offering it to the sabotage gods.

There is one last thing I measure in addition to these five calibrations, and that is the degree to which your heart chakra is open. When we pursue our day-to-day life with an open heart, it's easier to have enrollment conversations. Relationships smooth out, and we feel less defensive, suspicious, and guarded as we interact with life.

Once these calibrations are made, the next steps for raising those that are low can be determined.

So the number one secret to having more peace of mind and ease with money is to raise your energetic vibration so you can be a vibrational match to the place in those high vibrations where money loves to live.

Money Blocks of Six Figure Women...
(Even your financial planner doesn't know about these!)
The last thing I'd like to share is how you may be blaming everyone else for not giving to you and appreciating you when *you* are the one not open to receiving.

Let me explain...

Most people believe that "give and take" is the same as "give and receive." While the end result may be the same, the energy behind each is very different.

When your "give and take," you are in control. You control how much, when, where, to whom, etc. On the other hand, when you "give and receive," you need to be open to the receiving. This requires a certain amount of vulnerability. You are not in control. You may not know when you will receive, how much you will receive, or how it will manifest. Then when the amount arrives, appreciation is in order to let the Universe know that this is what you desire more of. Gratitude tells the Universe that you not only desire more, but also that you can be a good steward of what you have been given.

Being open to receive is additionally supported energetically. There is an energetic reason that you may not be receiving. To explain, let me give you another brief energetic anatomy lesson.

Your right arm is your giving, masculine side. This is the hand most people extend with a handshake. This is where receiving starts, with giving.

Your left arm is your receiving, feminine side.

In order to keep your feminine and masculine energies balanced and your giving and receiving flowing, this circle of energy needs to stay clear. Here's how to do it using your free and simple imagination:

I call this the *Circle of Reciprocity*. Start by placing your attention at your heart chakra in the center of your chest. Watch or energetically move the energy out your right arm and then loop the energy up your left hand and up your left arm as it passes through the front and back of your heart center and your upper three chakras in your neck, forehead, and through the top of your head.

As this energy passes through your heart, it can clear all of the judgements you hold against yourself and all the ways you think you can never do or be enough. This lack mindset translates into "not enough" money.

As this energy passes through your throat, it can clear the energies behind not being able to speak your truth or to set appropriate boundaries. It can also clear your fears around having conversations around money and asking for more money as you raise your prices.

As this energy passes through your forehead, it can clear the beliefs that cause you to see the world through skewed filters and truths that are not yours. These beliefs and mindsets that belong to others create confusion if they're not true for you. Clearing the energy here will allow more clarity.

As the energy passes through your crown at the top of your head, this opens your connection to the divine, to source energy, God, or whatever you'd like to call the energy that binds entire universes in complete harmony. This is also where you gain access to your personal permission. Then you do not need to get the approval of anyone else before you do, have or be what you desire in your life.

If you wonder if your left arm is energetically blocking your ability to receive, notice how easily you receive. Most people have an innate sense of whether or not they can easily receive or not. Trust that. Once you know you are the one blocking your receiving, then you can be the one to change it, and you can stop blaming others.

If you're thinking this all sounds too simple to be true or you're wondering if it really works, let me share a few brief stories I've gathered over the past three years from clients who were committed to the practice, considered themselves

awakening or conscious, and were seriously ready to change their relationship with money.

A computer techie who was a big skeptic and was struggling financially decided to do a trade, since I needed some computer work at the time. After our third session, he had his first $10,000 month ever! This was followed by a successive $10,000 month by the time we finished.

A stay-at-home mom in Switzerland came to me with three coaching clients in her business. Today she has over thirty-five clients, conducts $2,500 VIP days with them and is making over six figures. She has been able to travel and buy a home and is currently remodeling it.

A conscious entrepreneur I knew who wanted to start a business so he could leave his job followed my instructions for clearing his money blocks, and the following day he received a phone call that netted him $150,000.

A struggling artist who rarely heard from her mother received a check completely out of the blue for $10,000 after working together for a couple of months.

A woman who was the designer for her family's stationary business increased her revenue from $1.8 million to $3 million and received her highest year-end bonus ever— $400,000—during the time we worked together.

While I could go on about all kinds of success stories, the most common experiences were feeling calmer and less worried about money, being able to sleep at night, being able to get caught up on bills, coming home to a freshly cleaned house, taking a long awaited vacation, and not feeling guilty for buying a dozen roses.

Creating a life of wealth without worry is easier than people think. Based on the universal Law of Attraction, the foundation of this success is rooted in effective grounding,

sustaining a high energy vibration especially with your money, and being open to receive so that you don't blame others.

I hope you find the secrets I've shared here to be helpful as you implement these simple practices. If you are sensitive and conscious enough to use these tools on your own to increase your success, hallelujah!

However, what often happens when people start to clear things on their own is that they will start to bump up against deeper congestion hiding in the shadows. There's a reason it has been hiding from you. Fear is holding it in place, and it can be nearly impossible to move these deeper energies on your own because you start to feel the fear as it begins to release. The fear is meant to protect you, but it will stop you.

Therefore, if you are a six-figure-plus earner or you previously made six figures and you're finding that what used to work is no longer working and you're living in fear, I invite you to sign up for a complimentary one-hour Money Breakthrough Assessment. Let's see what you desire to create for your life and whether I'm the one who can help you get that. This is powerful work and only for those who are seriously ready to invest in themselves and create the life of their dreams. If this sounds like you, I'm eager to explore that possibility together! http://www.hearts-expanding-allow-love.com/schedule-your-appointment/

 **Kimberly Sherry** is an International Energy Healer, Speaker, Author, and Spiritual Mentor.

She has traveled to more than a dozen countries with a primary focus on sacred sites. She has worked directly with many indigenous healers and three times spent eighteen days with the Shipibo shamans deep in the Amazon jungle of Peru, participating in sacred ceremony with their master plant teacher, Ayahausca. It was there that she received sacred information that completely changed how she works with clients.

Kimberly spent fifteen years in the financial planning world. She owned and operated an eco-flooring store for five years, earning three quarters of a million dollars in her third year.

She spent twelve years training at *Aesclepion Intuitive Healing Center*, where she discovered her intuitive abilities, channeled, led healing clinics, and learned how to manage her energy.

Born and raised in a religious cult that created a life of fear, guilt, and shame that later landed her in poverty and on welfare, Kimberly turned a lifetime of despair into the infinite joy she now shares around the world. She has a gift and a passion for connecting world changing women to the power of their money and has helped thousands release hidden blocks and fears.

The #1 Secret to CREATING EPIC EXPERIENCES

–With Your Clients, Tribe, Team and Events

By Tracy Wiseman

HAVE YOU EVER noticed how we constantly use other people to validate who we are? We want to know, "How am I doing? Am I okay? Do you like and trust me?" I am seldom bothered by these doubts. I know my value. I am worth four camels, or so thought an Arab gentleman who wanted to own me and made the offer to my traveling companion.

After graduating from college, I took off on a three-month backpacking trip which turned into a six-year journey! I had few doubts about myself during many years of travel that took me to four continents, not as a tourist with a safety net of cash in my pocket, but as an adventurer with little more than a backpack. My travels included crossing the Nullabor Plain in the Australian outback, sailing an Arab Dhow up the Nile after the skipper passed out, waitressing in a resort in the Sinai desert, criss-crossing India from the burning Ghats of Coromandel to an abandoned monkey shrine in the Himalayan foothills. Journeys that included riding

camels and elephants on safari, to sharing a railway carriage for several days with fifteen Indian travelers. I have lived with friendly strangers in a primitive Mexican village, in a commune of squatters at an abandoned house in a London slum, and more exotically – a night in the Israeli fortress of Masada, hiding from the security guards.

What have I learned from this? To trust myself and divine providence that when the need arises, I shall do what is needed. What is the secret of such confidence? Trust! Something seldom considered as a key to personal and worldly success, but I shall share my secret with you today.

Emma is standing in front of the room, looking out over a sea of eager faces, all waiting for her to speak. You can feel the buzz of excitement, the energy of anticipation. Everything is perfect, the room, the lights, and the beautiful flowers. She looks to the back of the room and smiles. Her team is there running everything smoothly so she can be absolutely present and shine on her big day. She trusts her team implicitly. She draws her attention back to the present, takes a big breath and starts to speak. She is relaxed, confident, radiant and joyful, and everyone can feel it. They love her and trust her on the journey they are about to begin. Emma begins to spin her magic and has an amazing connected experience with her audience.

Why are some people really successful and have a team that loves and supports them while others have a team full of conflict and mistrust? How do you create this deep trust with your clients, team mates and yourself? What is it about creating a deep connection with people that builds trust? Let's dive a little deeper to discover some of these answers.

We must all ask ourselves, am I the kind of leader I would follow? Am I confident, decisive, inspiring, magnetic, and

trustworthy? Am I 100 percent committed to getting results? Am I so passionate about what I am doing that I can lift people up when they experience doubt and fear? Do I confidently know that working with me will provide them with the transformation they are looking for? You see, to have people follow you or trust you, you must first trust yourself.

Let me share a personal story with you:

I was born in Ghana, and one day my mum took me and my brother and sister to the market. We had a really cool convertible, and my brother and sister and I were riding in the back. All of the sudden, I could hear shouting and an angry mob surrounded the car. They started to shake it and shout threats. My mum stood up in the car and shouted, "How dare you?" The crowd went silent instantly. "How dare you scare my children like this? You should be ashamed of yourselves! Do you have children? Would you want this to happen to you? Go away and leave us alone." She looked everyone in the eye, demanding without words that they listen to her. I could see people looking down at the ground. Grown men started to apologize and quickly moved away. She sat back in her seat and started the car, and they opened a path for her to go through safely back to our home

Courage, confidence, conviction: This is what self-trust looks like. She was willing to stand for her values. Was she scared? Of course, but she didn't let that stop her! Take a moment and think of a time when you were unsure or timid. What happened? How did people around you react? Now think of a time you were so sure of yourself that people lined up to follow you. How do you think you can create that same feeling when you are in doubt? To create trust for ourselves and create a situation for others to be confident in with us,

we must stand with courage and conviction. That doesn't mean that you don't have fear. It means you must feel the fear and do it anyway!! You don't always need a plan. Sometimes you just need to breathe, trust, and let go.

What exactly is being trustworthy and how do you convey that to people? Interestingly enough, as we look at how to build your tribe and expand your business or referrals, we must look at how we are being. It is not the words we say, it is our way of being that matters. It all begins with the relationship you have with yourself. When you sit down to write a speech, a presentation, or a chapter in a book, do you look externally or internally for the answer? As I was writing this chapter, I thought of several different topics I could share from thirty years of research, experience, and studying, but I needed to choose one. I had to trust that the choice I was making was the right choice. How did I know that? I have learned to trust that there is a bigger plan for my life that has been lain out for me by my higher power, and I trust my heart and my core when ideas percolate up from the inside.

Before I learned how to completely trust myself and my journey, I had a reccurring dream for over thirty years. In this dream, I am a child in a beautiful forest that is lush. It reminds me of the forest in the story of Hansel and Gretel. I start walking through the meadow, with daisies brushing against my legs, the sun kissing my face, the butterflies flittering through the field, and I can feel a gentle breeze gently streaming past me. I feel happy. I look ahead to the little wooden bridge in front of me that leads to the forest, and suddenly I see a little elf. I blink a few times and see that he is waving me to cross the bridge. *How fun!* I run over to meet him, and as I get closer, he laughs and starts

to run. And so the chase begins. We run through the forest, giggling. Just ahead is a large cave and I see him run into it. (Of course I follow him; this is a dream.) As soon as I enter the cave I start looking for him. Then, to my horror, I hear a loud rumbling. I look behind me to an avalanche. As if in slow motion, the rocks fall down and block the entrance to the cave. I stand there in amazement for a moment. *Oh no, I am trapped. There is not a way out. What am I going to do?* Gradually my eyes adjust to the dim light and I look ahead, my heart pounding in my chest. Five tunnels open up in front of me. *Which tunnel do I go down? Where do they lead? What is at the end of the tunnel? What if I go down the wrong tunnel?* I stand, paralyzed. My mind is racing with possibilities and choices. Fear of making the wrong decision grips me. *What if I make a decision, can I go back?* I look at each tunnel, trying to use my brain logically and pick what looks like the safest path. And then I start walking. I play it safe. I go down the tunnel in the middle. As I continue to walk, it splits again. Now there are three more tunnels. I take the one on the right. I can feel myself going deeper and deeper into the tunnel. It splits again and again and again. I look over my shoulder, and my anxiety increases with each step. *I can't go back!* I don't even remember what tunnels I took, and then I wake up!

Quite the nightmare, huh? Does it feel similar to what you feel about your real world on some days?

I have had this dream many times in my life when I had big choices to make. I finally realized the lesson from the dream. It doesn't matter which tunnel I go down. It's about trusting myself and trusting that the tunnel I take will be the correct one at the time and that I will be taken care of.

When have you had times in your life when you had to make a decision? Do you spend hours second guessing yourself, beating yourself up, or feeling trapped? How is that helping you? I have come to realize that when an opportunity arises, it is best for me to listen with my heart. If I really feel it is the best decision at the time, I should trust myself and trust that it is as it should be. One of my favorite quotes goes like this, "Make a decision and then make it right." In other words, STOP IT! Stop agonizing over decisions, stop second guessing yourself, stop being afraid of making the wrong decision, causing yourself to not make a decision at all. It is in action that we gain clarity, and so just by moving forward, things will become clearer.

There's a famous story about a wealthy Chinese man who owned a lot of horses. One day his prized horse ran away. "How terrible!" everyone in his town said. One man said, "You had a beautiful horse and now you have nothing. That is really bad." The wise old man looked at him and said, "It's not good or bad, it just is." The very next day, the horse came back with five other wild stallions. "Oh, how wonderful," his neighbor said. "You must be so happy." The wise old man just said, "It is what it is." The very next day, his son tried to break the horse and fell off and broke his leg. Yes, you guessed it, everyone said how terrible that was, and the wise old man said, "It is what it is." To everyone's surprise, the Chinese army came through the town two days later and took all the young men away that could fight, never to be seen again. Since his son was injured, he was not taken.

It is only us who assign meanings to things, and there is no good or bad. Things happen sometimes for reasons we don't understand. Maybe it's a lesson, and maybe it's just so we can learn to trust. I can think of many occasions when

something didn't happen the way I wanted it to, and it turned out to be a blessing in disguise.

Another very integral part of learning to trust yourself is keeping your commitments to yourself. Just like we can create mistrust in people around us when we do not keep our word, we create mistrust in ourselves when we habitually cheat ourselves out of our promises. I could talk a lot about how to build your team and tribe and what you could do differently, but for this chapter, I want you to really get that YOU are the first place to start. When you keep commitments to yourself and respect and value yourself by living with your values daily and not compromising them, and by speaking out truth, you will turn into beacons of light that will attract people. They won't necessarily know why they want to work with you, only that you have something that they want and that they feel a connection with you. To start trusting yourself so that others can trust you, remember this sequence. BE. DO. HAVE.

Ask yourself, "Am I someone that people (including myself) can trust? Do I keep commitments to myself? Do I hold myself to my word, value and standards, or do I give in to others? These are hard questions to look at. Each day that passes with you not fulfilling your commitments to yourself causes a lack of self-trust and a diminishing of self-confidence.

I remember a funny story I overheard.....Sara and Crystal were talking about their self-care and fitness. Sara asked Crystal, "What do you do for self-care?" Crystal replied, "I get up at 6:00 am, I juice all organic fruit with some wheat grass and vitamins. I meditate for thirty minutes, write in my journal, do a bit of yoga and then hit the gym for an hour of aerobic exercises." "Wow!" said Sara, "That's fantastic.

How long have you been doing that?"

"I start tomorrow," said Crystal.

How many times do you set goals for yourself and then wake up in the morning and think, "I don't feel like it today. I will do it later or tomorrow"? I realized that with myself, every time I did that, I was eroding my self-trust and my belief in myself to be able to set a goal and stick to it. This kind of thing will slowly erode your confidence, which then seeps into your life and business. What would your life look like if you actually did what you said you would do? The best definition of commitment that I know of goes like this: Doing what I said I would do, long after the feeling I said it with is gone.

Sometimes it is a necessity for us to have a hard conversation with ourselves. Are we trying to do too much? Are we scared of missing out or scared of not being everything to everyone? Do we over-commit without any intention of fulfilling the commitment – or even worse – do we think we can fulfill it and then not structure our time with self-discipline so that we can follow through? Have you ever done that?

Self-trust is often the most difficult trust to restore within ourselves. When we violate a promise we've made to ourselves—like a failure to follow through on a goal, or acting in ways that go against our deepest values—we lessen our confidence. With repeated infractions, we often beat ourselves up so thoroughly that we wonder whether we can ever have faith in ourselves again. But the good news is that you can behave your way back to self-trust and regain peace!

I cannot stress the importance of doing what is necessary

to keep the commitments we make to ourselves. So now that we have talked about who we have to BE to be a trusted leader, let's look at things we need to DO for others to create trust within themselves for us.

Take a minute and think of a person with whom you have a high trust relationship. Now describe that relationship. What is it like? How does it feel? How does it make you feel? How well do you communicate? How quickly can you get things done? How much do you enjoy this relationship? Now think of a person with whom you have low trust. What is that like? How does that feel? Do you feel you are walking through land mines and being misunderstood? Does it take a disproportionate amount of time and energy to reach agreements? Do you enjoy them or does it feel cumbersome, tedious, and draining? Can you think of a relationship or project that went well? Who do you trust in your life and why? Are *you* trustworthy? When you say something, do you keep the commitments you have made to yourself or others? Stephen Covey once said, "...trust is the ultimate root and source of our influence."

There is so much we can do to help build trust within our teams. Here are a few things for you to implement.

Be straightforward in your communication and approach. There should be no hidden agendas within a team!

Be respectful of everyone on your team. Always treat people as you would want to be treated.

Be transparent. It's beneficial to be an open book, to be emotional, to be human. People will feel your realness, and you give them permission to do the same.

When you screw up, apologize!

Be loyal. Do not take credit for your team's successes.

Letting them have the glory and praising them will only bring them and you more success.

Be competent. Deliver awesome content that truly helps people transform.

Confront challenges head on. Don't try to cover them up.

Be accountable. Great leaders hold themselves accountable first.

Now I would like to dive deep into what I believe is the main determining factor that determines whether people will trust you or not. YOUR INTEGRITY. It is very important to align your words and actions in a way that your team can see. Keep your promises. It seems simple. But if it is so simple, why is it so rarely seen? No single aspect of manager behavior that has ever been measured has had as large an impact on profits than integrity. Credibility is slow to build and quick to dissipate. It only takes one act of being disloyal to earn the label of hypocrite and one act of deceitfulness to be labeled a liar. Your word is so very powerful, and so many of us use words so frivolously. Do you? Have you ever told a colleague you would meet them for lunch at noon and arrived at 12:05? Have you ever been asked to join a training call on a conference line at a certain time only to have the person doing the training pop on five minutes late? Have you ever been to a meeting or conference that was supposed to start at 8:00 am, only to have it finally begin when the "important people" were good and ready to start at 8:45? How did you feel? Very important? Have you ever told a child that you would be off the phone, computer, TV etc., in five minutes to tuck them in only to find them asleep thirty minutes later when you finally finished what you were doing? Do these things really matter? You tell me. If people cannot trust you with the small things, how can they trust

you with their money, time, or dreams? As we do one thing, we do everything.

If you have not read *The Four Agreements*, by Don Miguel Ruiz, I highly recommend that you do. The first agreement he teaches is about being impeccable with your word. This means speaking with integrity. Don't say things you don't mean. Don't gossip or put yourself down. Again... words are so powerful.

Be a person of integrity when it comes to truly wanting those around you to win. Be willing to say things that may make you or your clients uncomfortable if it is for their benefit. Grow yourself and stretch and expect your clients to do the same. Are you really willing to step out of your comfort zone, to feel, see and know that you can help others to transform their lives? Are you willing to stand in the fire with them and see that life can be different without being attached to the outcome?

This is what inspires people. They see who you are being and what you have, and they want to have more, to be with you, to learn from you. You have to 100 percent believe that you can help people transform. They need to believe that you are there to listen, to understand them, to give them the tools, support, inspiration and encouragement to grow. This needs to be done without judgment, without criticism, without them feeling "less than." When you think about people you like to be around, what is it about them that attracts you? I have thought about this a lot, and what I realized was that they make me feel like I am good enough, that they respect me, that they value me and that they are willing to be strong for me so that I can lean on their belief until I have the belief myself. This is how you create trusting followers. You inspire them, you demonstrate by leading through example.

Trust is an amazing gift you can give someone. Once we learn to trust ourselves, and we gain the trust of our team, we get to pass the torch of trust to each person following us.

If you want to have a successful event, a successful team, a growing tribe, remember the importance of trust. Trust yourself. Know yourself. It takes courage to look at yourself and your patterns. When you act with integrity and are living according to your values, being accountable, keeping your promises and actuating with integrity – you build a belief in yourself which you can then extend to others.

If you take just one thing away with you today, let it be this: your journey to be all you wish for yourself starts from within. Develop trust in yourself and all else will follow.

 **Tracy Wiseman** is a heart centered businesswoman, passionate about empowering women. She is a mother and a world adventurer, enlightened by her journeys abroad. Tracy is an Executive Business Coach. She facilitates leadership, teambuilding, workshops, and webinars and helps entrepreneurs create epic experiences with their clients, team, tribes and events. As a former Bank of America executive with more than fifteen years of experience as a project manager, operations manager and learning and leadership development leader, Tracy draws on her wide range of experience in conceptualizing and implementing leadership training, program development, enrollment sales conversations and events. Trained in process improvement as a certified Green Belt, DFSS and LEAN consultant, as well as being a certified Master of Influence leadership and enrollment consultant, Tracy understands processes as well as people and the role they play in building your business.

Tracy is a speaker, trainer and coach. She has a talent for finding innovative solutions to the challenges entrepreneurs face today. She has trained thousands of people and developed hundreds of programs and events.

Born in Ghana, Tracy has lived, worked, and traveled all over the world. As a lifelong student of the Human Potential Movement, she has great insight into how to motivate and communicate with people to build real, authentic connections. As a twenty-year Toastmaster, she loves to speak and coach people to inspire and empower them to make real changes in their lives.

To find out more and contact Tracy:
email: tracywiseman13@gmail.com,

By Tracy Wiseman

www.linkedin.com/in/tracywiseman1/,
https://www.facebook.com/tracy.wiseman.507,
www.tracywiseman.com

49622447R00116

Made in the USA
Charleston, SC
29 November 2015